Muslim Culture in Indian Cinema

to our composite heritage

Muslim Culture in Indian Cinema

Edited by

Jasbir Jain

RAWAT PUBLICATIONS

Jaipur • New Delhi • Bangalore • Hyderabad • Guwahati

ISBN 978-81-316-0468-7

Published by
Prem Rawat for **Rawat Publications**
Satyam Apts, Sector 3, Jawahar Nagar, Jaipur 302 004 (India)
Phone: 0141 265 1748 / 7006 Fax: 0141 265 1748
E-mail: info@rawatbooks.com
Website: www.rawatbooks.com

New Delhi Office
4858/24, Ansari Road, Daryaganj, New Delhi 110 002
Phone: 011 2326 3290

Also at *Bangalore, Hyderabad* and *Guwahati*

Typeset by Rawat Computers, Jaipur
Printed at Chaman Enterprises, New Delhi

Contents

Acknowledgements

Every volume of this kind is the collaborative effort of a number of people, many of whose names do not appear before the public eye. My warmest gratitude to each one of them.

Our sincere appreciation for the cooperation of all our contributors who unsparingly gave of their learning and scholarship as well as for the lively discussions and debates of the participants of the seminar, which in actuality marked the beginning of this journey. Their keen enthusiasm inspired us to address difficult questions of representation and reception.

A special word of thanks for Saeed Mirza both for being present at the seminar and for generously giving permission to include selected excerpts from his novel *Ammi* in the present volume.

I also need to acknowledge the help and advice which was available to me from Anisur Rahman whenever I faced any difficulties in interpreting the deeper nuances of culture.

Contributors

Saeed Akhtar Mirza is a pioneer of the New Wave, progressive cinema in India. His iconoclastic films, including *Arvind Desai ki Ajeeb Dastaan* (1978), *Albert Pinto ko Gussa Kyun Aata Hai?* (1980), *Mohan Joshi Haazir Ho* (1984), *Salim Langde pe Mat Ro* (1989) and *Naseem* (1995) captured the passions and frustrations of an India emerging uneasily into the 21st century. His films have all won major awards including the national awards for film excellence in India. He is the director of the popular TV serials *Nukkad* (1986) and *Intezaar* (1988), along with various documentary films on social welfare and cultural activism. Mirza trained at the Film and Television Institute of India (FTII), Pune, and has also taught there. He has lectured widely on Indian cinema at universities in India and the US. He contributes regularly to Indian newspapers and magazines on current political debates and through film reviews. He lives in Mumbai and Goa. *Ammi: Letter to a Democratic Mother* is his first novel.

Anisur Rahman, Professor in English at Jamia Millia Islamia, a Central University in New Delhi, has worked and published in the areas of literary translation and postcolonial literature(s) with special reference to the literatures of India, Canada, Australia and

New Zealand. One of his major interest areas is poetry and he has published critiques on Nissim Ezekiel and Kamala Das. Dr Rahman is also a translator of repute, translating from Urdu to English and vice-versa. *Fire and the Rose* (1995) is his anthology of modern Urdu poetry in English translation while *Translation: Poetics and Practice* (2001) is an edited volume of critical studies with reference to the Indian text and context. Amongst his recent publications are *Translation/Representation* (2007) and *Indian English Women Poets* (2009) (co-edited). Dr Rahman has been a Shastri Fellow at the University of Alberta, Canada (2001–2002) and a Visiting Scholar at Purdue University, USA (2007).

Rashmi Attri, Associate Professor in English at Aligarh Muslim University, Aligarh, has worked intensively on Modern British Drama. Her other areas of interest include Indian English Writing, Nigerian Literature in English and African American Writing. Interested in music, Dr Attri has also studied its history and forms. She teaches Modern Drama, ELT and Business Communication.

Madhuri Chatterjee teaches English and is in Rajasthan Education Service. She worked on the theme of homecoming in John Updike for her doctoral thesis and has later moved into exploring Bengali women's autobiographies and the contemporary travelogue. Her areas of interest include Latin American writers.

Gita Viswanath is an independent researcher in film studies and has also made a few short films. Her doctoral work was on literature and film studies. Dr Viswanath has published several articles in reputed academic journals and has participated in seminars and workshops both at home and abroad. She is currently working on a book on film theory and lives in Baroda.

Santosh Gupta, former Professor and Chairperson of the Department of English at the University of Rajasthan, has recently completed a project on Modern Prison Narratives. Her other areas of interest are Modern Fiction—American, British and Indian. Dr Gupta has worked extensively in Critical Theory including psycho-analytical approaches and has participated in conferences both at home and abroad. She has co-edited *Contemporary British Writing* and *Literary Constructs of the Self*.

Jasbir Jain, formerly of the University of Rajasthan, Jaipur is currently Director of the Institute for Research in Interdisciplinary Studies (IRIS). Recipient of the Sala Award (2008) and the IACS Award (2003), she has worked extensively on drama, fiction, critical theory and feminism. Her latest publications include *The Writer as Critic* (ed.) (2011) and *Indigenous Roots of Feminism* (2011). Dr Jain has several monographs on Indian writers including Henry Derozio, Nayantara Sahgal, Anita Desai and Shashi Deshpande. Currently, she is engaged in research on the problems of periodisation in Indian literature.

Charu Mathur teaches English at the University of Rajasthan, Jaipur. She worked for her doctoral degree on *Perspectives on Women in the Selected Plays of Eugene O'Neill and Tennessee Williams*. Besides American drama, her other areas of interest are Indian drama, postcolonial literature and women's writing.

Bandana Chakrabarty is presently Principal, Rajasthan School of Art, Jaipur. She worked for her doctoral dissertation on the short stories of the Canadian author, Alice Munro. Co-editor of *Contemporary Indian Drama: Astride Two Traditions*, she has published articles on Indian and Canadian fiction. Dr Chakrabarty is the President of English Language Teachers' Association of India (Rajasthan Chapter) and an accomplished vocalist.

S. Asha, a member of the Rajasthan Education Service, is presently posted at Government P.G. College, Tonk. She has a teaching experience of over 20 years. Her research interest is in drama and her published work is on Harold Pinter's Screenplays (1993). Currently she is working on Indian writing. Vice-President of English Language Teachers' Association of India (Rajasthan Chapter), she actively participates in its activities.

Mini Nanda is an Associate Professor in English at the University of Rajasthan. Having worked on Graham Greene for her doctoral work, her areas of interest have moved across Europe to Canadian and American literatures. She also has an interest in subcontinental writing with special reference to Pakistan and Sri Lanka. She is working on the reworking of myth in Indian writing. Co-editor of *Literary Constructs of the Self:*

Socio-Cultural Reflections, Nanda has participated in several national and international conferences.

Ameena Kazi Ansari teaches in the Department of English, Jamia Millia Islamia, a Central University in New Delhi. She has worked and published in the areas of literary translation and postcolonial literature. Apart from articles and reviews, she has published two books—*English-Canadian Literary Canon: Emergence and Development* (2004) and *Partitions* (2006), a translation of Kamleshwar's award-winning Hindi novel, *Kitne Pakistan*. She has also co-edited two volumes—*Translation/Representation* (2008) and *Indian English Women Poets* (2009).

Urmil Talwar is in the Rajasthan Education Service, presently on a postdoctoral fellowship in the University of Rajasthan working on Border Poetics. She has worked on public schools in early 20th century British writing and is the co-editor of *Literary Debates: Essays by R.K. Kaul, Contemporary Indian Drama: Astride Two Traditions* and *Gender, History and Culture: Inside the Haveli*. Interested in diaspora writing, Dr Talwar has participated in several national and international conferences. She is also a translator, translating from Hindi into English.

Indubala Singh is an Associate Professor in English and is presently teaching in a college in Chandigarh. She has published *Gender Relations and Cultural Ideology in Indian Cinema* and has written a play 'The Elusive Heer' and various academic articles. She is also a documentary filmmaker and has made documentaries on an orphan disabled girl suffering from cerebral palsy who earns her own livelihood; on blind children and slum children who study on account of the *raddi* donors, and one 'Hope for Peace through Preet'. Dr Singh is also trained in Bharat Natyam.

Divya Walia is working as an Assistant Professor in the Department of English of the IIS University, Jaipur. Her area of specialisation is ELT and she has been in the field for more than six years. Dr Walia has also done Nipun (M.A.) in Music (Vocal) from Bhatkhande Sangeet Vidhyapeeth, Lucknow.

Samina Khan is an Associate Professor in the Department of English, Aligarh Muslim University, Aligarh. Her areas of interest and research include Modern British and Indian Drama, Comparative Literature and Culture Studies and Poetry in Urdu and Hindi. She presently teaches Drama, Criticism, Communicative Skills and ELT.

1

Introduction

Jasbir Jain

Culture surrounds us and inhabits us in its invisibility, yet it is a term difficult to define. The evident signifiers, externally traceable are associated with our daily practices, customs and rituals. But its deeper inheritance and hold on us is through language and thought, through our inherited pasts and our identification with a way of living. It manifests itself in our code of behaviour and traditions that we have accepted or gradually evolved. Despite all the load of the past the word carries, it is subject to external pressures emanating from religion, economics and politics. Thus tossed around between the past, the socio-historical forces and the individual will, it continues to remain elusive. What we study, when we study cultural practices, is the intricacy of their shifts as they travel or are transplanted in different societal formations.

The idea of organising a seminar on 'Representation of Muslim Culture in Indian Cinema', generated a lot of debate. Both the plus and minus points were discussed. Why separate 'the Muslim'? was one question. But on the other hand, there was a larger support for closely examining the way Muslim culture, language, religious philosophy, poetry and film folk themselves have shaped and projected the culture of a community.

Films have a three-way relation with society. Firstly, the media derives its strength, its themes and inspiration from socio-historical environs. Secondly, it depends on reception by the audiences. The film medium needs an immediate response. And thirdly, subtly and artistically, it can introduce change. A political aspect was the declining graph of Muslim representation and the corresponding rise in stereotyping the Muslim. Even whilst we support the concept and ideology of secularism, the focus on the way a section of our society is represented is important for everyone. It acts as a mirror; allows us to see the prejudices and the flow of historical forces much more clearly than passive, uncritical viewing. It also draws us towards the artistic, a realisation of the unusual, of the sensitive and of the agony of being marked. Moreover it is a shared area. Further, it allows us to become aware of the immense debt the industry owes to the inputs of Muslim culture. Some of our best lyrics are in Urdu. Yesterday I was viewing an old film, Kishore Sahu's *Hamlet*. Shakespeare's poetry lends itself easily to the Urdu translations. Several of the essays in this collection focus on the above issues, the various aspects of culture and the manner in which it is seen and framed. Some of these essays were presented at the seminar IRIS organised in April 2010.

While the categories of culture and Muslim present their own difficulties, the word 'representation' is not any easier. It too involves a great deal which escapes words such as depiction and presentation. It works through the processes of selection and interpretation; it also brings in perspectives and ideological leanings and becomes in itself an act of stereotyping or of contesting stereotypes. As the medium of the film is a team-based venture, which despite its centrality in the director moves, at times, outside this centre to include other shades. Often, we as ordinary viewers, consider the director the principle organising figure. But the cinematographer and editor, and at a later stage, the censors also have a role to play, no matter how marginal.

A review of the Hindi films of the last seventy years or more does reveal a varied picture and sadly enough, a sliding graph which needs serious attention by both the makers and the viewers. Films of the 40s worked with the Muslim ethos without in the least being conscious of it. Hindustani and Urdu ghazals were woven in as they were true to the life in most of North India, UP and Bihar. Urdu was read, spoken and understood. The early scriptwriters and dialogue writers were Urdu speaking people, right from Agha Hashr Kashmiri, Rajinder Singh Bedi, Saadat Hasan Manto, F.R. Mirza to K.A. Abbas. There were lyricists such as Sahir Ludhianvi, Kaifi Azmi and music directors such as Ghulam Haider and Naushad, singers such as Suraiya, Noor Jehan, Mohammed Rafi and Talat Mahmud. A large number of directors were rooted (and educated) in Muslim culture such as A.R. Kardar, Mehboob and Kamal Amrohi. Names in themselves do not indicate all. A number of people from Punjab whether Hindu or Sikh and from UP were soaked in the culture of the language and its accompanying heritage. Together they constitute a sizeable number even today. Culture is thus freed from a purely regional or religious affiliation. As for instance, the Yash Chopra film *Waqt* (1965) is about a Punjabi-Hindu family but their dress and language affiliations reflect the regional culture, which is Muslim-Pathan, rather than a closed Hindu culture. Furthermore, this is not an artificial frame. The film is located in Quetta and the family is dislocated and dispersed because of the earthquake. The dialogues are heavily laced with Urdu, the music reflects a similar resonance. The group song, *Ai meri zohra jabeen, tu abhi tak hai haseen aur main jawan, tujh pe qurban meri jaan* (dearly beloved, you are still beautiful and I am young), was interwoven into another song in *Dilwale Dulhania Le Jayenge* (1995). The latter film, made several years later, also reflects a similar culture in the rural setting, the same lifestyle, the same patriarchal authority which was widespread in the north-western region, irrespective of religious faith.

It is difficult to identify the distinguishing border lines from one culture to another. They blur, overlap and merge into each other. The distinctions become visible more clearly within enclosed spaces through a variety of symbols, frames, interiors and customs. It is the 'puja houses', the idols displayed or the photographs placed on the walls, the domestic spaces, dress and then ceremonies, which become the external signifiers of difference. At a deeper level it is the religious belief and the pull of the community's socio-religious traditions.

Returning to the 40s, one realises that cultures slided more comfortably into one another and the process was affected largely by two factors: one was increased urbanisation and the other was the spirit of nationhood. A nation had come together to take a common stand against the British. The lyricist Pradeep's patriotic songs spawning the 40s–60s bring the whole nation together. In Bombay Talkies's *Kismet* (1943), we have the song *Aaj Himalaya ki choti se phir humne lalkara hai, dur hato ai duniyawalon, Hindustan hamara hai.* The lines I wish to emphasise are, *Yahan hamare mandir-masjid…* (Today we have once again proclaimed to the world that Hindustan is ours… here we have our religious places of worship of all faiths.) There is oneness. A couple of years earlier, in another Bombay Talkies's film *Bandhan* (1940), there is the village schoolmaster's geography class which points to the territorial boundaries.

Another factor which perhaps leads to this coming together of various strands was the idea of romantic love which was associated, in the popular mind, with the Urdu ghazal, with the mystery of the beloved, with 'virah' or separation and the consequent languishing and suffering. Romance was not frivolous, but something demanding loyalty, absorption, fidelity and sacrifice. The heart-rending lyric *Tu purdahnashin ka aashiq hai, yun reh reh kar faryaad na kar, dil jalta hai to jalne de, yun name wafaa badnam nan kar* (Your beloved observes purdah, do not complain of separation, even if your heart is restless, be careful, do not bring disrepute to the idea of fidelity), says it all (*Pehli Nazar*, 1945). Restraint, protection, purdah all are brought in, in one breath. The song implies that complaints of separation may bring her disrepute.

Legendary romances of sacrificing love relationships ending in tragedies were rooted in Sufi culture or in Iraq or in Punjab. Right from the late 20s to the mid-80s, we have several films being made on the romantic legends of *Heer Ranjha, Laila Majnu* and *Sohni Mahiwal*, some of them in Tamil, Malayalam and other Indian languages as well. Titles differed at times: *Heer, Heer Syal, Heer Ranjha* and such like, but the narrative had an undying appeal. One needs to realise that films ran for longer durations at the cinema hall than they do now, that it was one of least expensive forms of entertainment, specially for the front rowers. These romantic tales of devotion and sacrifice, and of dying either pining for the lover or in his arms, served several purposes all at once. They evoked emotional response, absorbed one in a distant story, different and perhaps unrealisable, preached both restraint and rebellion in the same breath and brought different cultural segments together. The language they used was Urdu as the environs were dominantly Muslim. The language also leant itself more easily to the idea of romance.

The nation has been comfortable with histories of the past, accepting, recounting and presenting both its victories and defeats; basking in its glory and also sharing the agony of defeat. We have a range of historical sagas, as well as portrayals of upper class Muslim aristocracy with all their social grace, sophistication and poetry. Perhaps the arrogance as well. A whole range of films such as *Mere Mehboob* and *Bahu Begum* surfaced in the 70s. There was space enough for everyone. Film titles were displayed in three or four languages. In 1983 Manmohan Desai's film *Coolie* apparently Muslim-centred, has the well-known song *Mubarak ho tum ko 'Hajj' ka maheena* proclaiming the miracles wrought by faith. Though Rajadhyaksha and Willemen comment that 'is also Manmohan Desai's most aggressively communal film', the point is not very clear. They link it up with Bachchan's election as an MP in 1984 (459). If the term aggressive is positively implied then Desai like Yash Chopra, has looked closely at some of the complex edges of religions which do not weld together. Chopra's *Dhool Ka Phool* (1961) looks at how religion and upbringing are connected and highlights the humanistic aspects in every religion. A similar theme had been explored in another pre-partition film *Hum Ek Hain* (1946) where an elderly woman brings up three orphan children of different religious faiths and encourages them to follow their individual faiths without letting it interfere in this foster-sibling bonding. The film expressed a desire for national unity. Similarly, *Dharmputra* (1961) goes on to examine the turn of religion into hardened fanaticism. As already mentioned, Chopra's *Waqt* absorbs the dominant north-western culture of the country.

Manmohan Desai's *Chhalia* (1960) problematises the case of women who had been abducted during the partition, and when brought back to India were placed in refugee camps to await restoration to their families. In this film, Pran plays the role of a Pathan who is caring and paternally protective of the Hindu girl and extends her all help. And Desai's 1977 *Amar Akbar Anthony* registers the relationship of brotherhood desired by the subconscious of the nation. One wonders at what point the cracks began to surface and violence, crime and mafia took over leading to a whole range of stereotyped figures. But fortunately, there has always been the redeeming figure of the 'good' Muslim, religious, human and humanistic, and able to distinguish between right and wrong. Prayer is not misused and men are not pushed over the bridge. The figure of the 'good' Muslim interrupts the mainstream hysteria to make a significant point. Faith, righteousness and nation all come together in the good man.

In *Vastaav* (1999), we have Paresh Rawal, in the role of a Muslim agent Suleimani Bhai, but when the hero comes to him for help, he does not hand him over to his enemies because he believes it would amount to treachery. That is the moment when he was saying his namaz and the essence of his faith surfaces in his act. Similarly, in *Ghulam-e-Mustafa* (1997), Nana Patekar's role is cast as a member of the underworld. His Hindu neighbours, especially the women folk, hold him not only in suspicion but also in disapproval. But his role in protecting them from anti social elements reveals his sense of values. Once the neighbours recognise this, he is more than welcome in their house. By narrowing down the love-hate relationship and the purity-impurity of 'difference' from a community to a neighbourhood relationship, the film emphasises the importance of these.

Sarfarosh (1999), amongst other things, takes up two cases of Muslim identity. One is the case of the singer who has migrated to Pakistan but is a muhajir, an outsider, looked upon with suspicion and consequently distrusted. He is asked to prove his loyalty by becoming instrumental in acts of spying and smuggling. He is a divided and an alienated man, no longer at home anywhere. The other case is of the Muslim police officer, who is an Indian and who is similarly placed in a situation of defence, required, in so many invisible ways, to prove his loyalty. His hurt and frustration at being branded marginal and untrustworthy is obvious and reflects on societal insensitivity. Later on, in the film, his worth is recognised both as a loyal citizen and as a capable police officer.

A more recent film *Fanaa* (2006) has a double discourse, one of terrorism and the other of love. Once again nationhood and the loyalty it demands come into play. The choice between the two is governed by one's upbringing, values and environment. The self has to rise above personal desire in order to make the right choice. Ironically, the terrorist-lover likewise rises above personal desire in order to obey his commandant. As the two lovers confront their inner personal conflicts, the balance is clearly in favour of being true to oneself, to be able to live with the decision for a lifetime. The terrorist is engaged in bargaining with himself: once this mission is fulfilled, he will abandon that road. Not so the woman. Her choices are clearly spelt out—either this or that. There is no bargaining of time or before and after. And she is the one to win a moral victory.

The case of the 'good' Muslim is directed towards breaking stereotypes, and compels the viewer to think in terms of the 'human', in terms of values, belonging and trust. Similar portrayals are there in *Mission Kashmir* (2006) and in a more recent film *Road to Sangam* (2010). The Muslim inspector, his Hindu wife, their adoption of a Muslim orphan narrate their own story of conflict, sacrifice and struggle in *Mission Kashmir*. *Road to Sangam* is a title loaded with symbolical significance. It is a remarkable tale of one man's loyalty to his job and to Gandhian principles, magnifying themselves into a national duty, a devotion to the past and thus leading a whole community to come out together in support of a society bound together in respect and trust, not divided along communal lines. 'Sangam', besides meaning merger or coming together, is also the place where in Allahabad the rivers meet and the ashes of the dead are immersed. The occasion also has the background of national history; the mechanic is entrusted with the task of reconstructing the several decades' old car in which Gandhi's ashes had been carried in 1948, for the observation of the 50th anniversary. The whole community imposes a ban on all its members in order to observe a bandh as a protest to some political decision and calls for a closure of all shops, workshops and business houses owned by them. The mechanic is caught between these two loyalties but finally transcends his loyalty to the religious community and performs his task towards his commitment to Gandhian ideals.

In many earlier films also, even as early as *Deewar* (1975), the good neighbour, guardian and friend was a Muslim character. Pran's role in *Deewar* illustrates this. The message is especially underlined in post Babri-Masjid films such as *Bombay*, which sends out a very positive message, specially when the two grandfathers save each other's religious scriptures and learn to live together in their children's home, when they are visiting them and the '93 riots take place. How easy it is to shed prejudices and extend a hand of friendship, once one makes up one's mind to do so! The film stresses that interaction alone can lead to understanding and harmony; from the good neighbour, the shift here is to marriage and kinship.

The poor in society have often attracted attention. They hail from all communities, but a phase did come when the Muslim was seen as the socially marginalised due to lack of education, unemployment and related poverty. A classic film analysing these three aspects together is Saeed Mirza's *Salim Langde Pe Mat Ro* (1990). In this, there is a hint as to why the underdog turns towards revolution. *Gaman* (1978) and *Bazaar* (1982) project a range of problems, such as divided families due to husband's/son's search for a job, lack of employment opportunities and in *Bazaar*, the film takes in its purview the bride market, where women become objects for sale and purchase, money changes hands and man-woman relationships are reduced to bare sex. Similar films dealing with bride purchase and have also been made with non-Muslim characters and female prostitution has had its own attention. *Bazaar*, as it is set in Hyderabad, draws attention to the Dubai market.

The off-tossed remark that sufficient interest has not been taken in the portrayal of the Muslim character, is not true in its essence. True, several social problems are approached as social texts in many movies; there are also several depictions of stereotypes. But for that matter the Pathan as a benign person, sensitive and helpful has, by being repeated, also acquired the semblance of a stereotype. There are certain qualities such as courage, sense of adventure and loyalty which are associated with the Pathan image. What we do not have is sufficient attention to people from different parts of the country and very often when a representative figure from a regional or a religious minority is projected such as a Sikh or a South Indian, semiotically he is treated as a symbol and comes to represent a stereotype.

The space may have shrunk in recent years because of the shift in the political scenario but many representations acknowledge the cultural past and India's debt to it; they also go further to explore conflictual dimensions of the Muslim as a member of society and present individualised characters. Their societal role and desire for harmony are also reflected. The culture of Chandni Chowk, as depicted in *Delhi 6* (2009) as well as in the earlier *Kabhi Khushi Kabhi Gham* (2001) project these mixed communities. Many films focus on the prejudices harboured by the rest of the community and by drawing attention to them create enough material for the viewer to self-reflect. Hidden as an undercurrent in many of these projections, is the desire to see the return of harmony, belonging, security and friendship; to go beyond good neighbourliness to belong as kin, as one of a family, as human beings and as co-partners in the making of our reality. There is a great deal that a surface representation presents through its semiotics.

In the present collection of essays, the individual writers have approached many of the issues either discussed or hinted at above. Right in the beginning we have excerpts from Saeed Mirza's *Ammi: Letter to a Democratic Mother*. The extracts bring out different facets of Muslim culture. This piece of creative writing is by a filmmaker who has made several sensitive films on the lives, psychologies and compulsions of people from the margins. The biography is multi-ranging and above other things also presents the biography of a nation. His most recent film is *Naseem* (1995) in which Kaifi Azmi performed the role of the grandfather, during his own illness. *Naseem* tells the story of a Muslim family and its being crowded in by fear and insecurity.

Anisur Rahman's essay on the Urdu language in Bombay cinema details the finenesses and the contribution of the Muslim culture, language and the resonance that it creates in memory constitute the strength of communication, poetry and the emotions it evokes as well as the sophistication and courtesy involved in it. The canvas is wide and the perceptions offer fresh insights. Later on in the volume, Urmil Talwar also works with the theme of language in her essay on *Muhafiz*, where the poet Nur's life is placed under the scanner. Based on Anita Desai's *In Custody*, the film depicts Urdu's losing battle against the dominance of Hindi portrayed by juxtaposing on one hand the poet's sliding into oblivion, and on the other, the Hindi teacher's effort to record his voice end in naught.

Music, like language, is another significant contribution. We have two full-length essays on Sufi poetry and the qawwali, followed later by an individual essay on *Sardari Begum*. Rashmi Attri, Madhuri Chatterjee and Divya Walia have located their perceptions in the history of music, in Sufi mysticism and in the personal struggles of an artist in that order. Gita Viswanath's essay is on Shahrukh's career graph. By locating it in cinema history, she presents a meaningful analysis of the interaction between act, film media and audience reception as they work within the political and social contexts.

An overall theme of Hindu–Muslim love relationships and the legality or otherwise of these is explored by Santosh Gupta when she takes up mixed marriages and the children born out of wedlock. The emotional burden that films such as *Zakhm* carry is overlaid with political meanings. The essay shifts its focus from 'motherland' and the 'nation' tropes, to talk of failed fatherhood and failed responsibility. Simultaneously, the abstract sanctity of the Hindu marriage also comes into question. In the aftermath of the partition, the government had adopted a patriarchal role towards women; these films record the failure of the patriarch to protect even his sons.

Films, like history and narrative, move backward and forward. Jasbir Jain looks at two films made two decades apart, *Mirza Ghalib* and *Shatranj ke Khiladi* which take up the years

1856–1857 and are about the last phase of Nawab of Oudh's and Bahadur Shah Zafar's rules. They portray the state of the nation at a critical time in India's history, the failure of the intellectuals, the apathy on part of the land-owning class, the priorities given to self-interest over the larger interests of the country and study the dynamics of power.

It is difficult to ignore history and it is even more difficult to forget partition, when we talk about projections of Muslim culture. Like the notion of romance living in the relationship of two lovers, the idea of culture invades an inter-relationship be it violence, love, hatred or forgiveness. Charu Mathur presents a sensitive analysis of *Pinjar*, a partition film and the *Flight of Pigeons* as projected in *Junoon,* a film about 1857. The events of the two, placed as they are a century apart, both concern themselves with relationships across community boundaries, with slow-developing realisation that the other is human and is extending a warm affection.

There are other two-film essays, where through parallel discourses and through juxtapositions and contrasts, a number of issues as well as films are discussed by Bandana Chakrabarty, Mini Nanda and S. Asha. Chakrabarty works with *Umrao Jaan* and *Pakeezah*, projecting the compulsions of the nautch girl and the societal rejection that follows despite her not being at fault. Mini Nanda works with two Benegal films *Zubeida* and *Mammo.* As she examines the directorial connectivity, she also proceeds to look at both the historical and autobiographical elements as the conflicts between desire and social acceptability are projected. Asha looks closely at the issues of purchase marriage and impulsive divorce in her analysis of *Bazaar* and *Nikaah*. Hooking on to social debates in the 80s, these films work with the woman's point of view—her sexuality, desire, need for freedom as they work within economic and religious compulsions.

The notion of romance as it had caught the imagination of the 60s and 70s, and framed by a romantic lover himself in reflected in Ameena Ansari's study of *Chaudhvin ka Chand*. She makes good use of the cinematic frames to substantiate her analysis. There is no denying the fact that everyone loves a lover, no matter how tragic the end. It brings back the vibrancy and desire of youth; but beauty can turn into molten beauty frozen in its self-absorption. Love, after all, exists *between* the two lovers, not in the mind or heart of any one of them. *Chaudhvin ka Chand* with its backdrop, interior settings, songs and music, and the beauty of language, fills up a necessary memory slot.

Another love story, located in rural Punjab and concerned with both the dislocations and the trauma of the partition is discussed by Indubala Singh in her analysis of *Train to Pakistan*. As both the films discussed by Charu Mathur and the one by Indu Singh are based on novels, the two writers also bring in an additional dimension to their work as they examine the problematics of transference from text to image.

The iconology of the 'nautch' girl is so vividly presented in *Umrao Jaan* that it is the subject of another article. Samina Khan takes up a study of the two versions of 1981 and of 2006, in order to work on the finer differences in their presentation a quarter century apart.

This brings me to the second term 'representation', a word which is implicit in the title and which concerns us. Is representation just framing or selection? Or lifting it from the written word to the body of the actor and communicating with an audience? Or does it involve a more comprehensive act of concern, interpretation, philosophical and ideological issues? This is a serious concern, especially when we are discussing the art form of the film, which involves inputs of various kinds: story, dialogue, songs, music and at times embedded performances such as dance plus a number of people working with the mechanics of production. Thus, it is never and cannot become a complete frame in itself; if it is serious and has something to say, it actually unfolds itself during the process of reception in order to continue its many journeys in multiple directions, into many homes, several generations and social circles to continue to disseminate its viewpoint, ideology and philosophy.

Films entertain, but they do not only entertain. They are like gentle reminders to our historical memory, and work at times, as the projection of the subconscious ideals we desire. They occasionally prod our consciences. Amidst the potboilers, there is always a sizeable number of classic literature. Similarly, several of the films we have discussed have been directed by serious directors, have interacted with their contemporary political environs and many of them have been recognised for their contributions to culture and art and won many prestigious awards.

Together, these essays support the validity of our project which we had begun with some trepidation and, at the same time, a great deal of excitement, as if embarking on a journey. It has engaged us intensely and seriously and somewhere or the other, it has opened a number of doors and windows.

Work Cited

Rajadhyaksha, Ashish and Paul Willemen. *Encyclopaedia of Indian Cinema*. New revised edition. New Delhi: OUP, 1999.

Filmography

Amar Akbar Anthony. Dir. Manmohan Desai. Prod. MKD Films. Perf. Vinod Khanna, Amitabh Bachchan, Rishi Kapoor, Neetu Singh, Shabana Azmi, Parveen Babi, Nirupa Roy, Pran. 1977.

Bandhan. Dir. N.R. Acharya. Prod. Bombay Talkies. Perf. Leela Chitnis, Ashok Kumar, Suresh, Shah Nawaz, Purnima Desai. 1940.

Bombay. Dir. Mani Ratnam. Prod. S. Sriram. Perf. Manisha Koirala, Arvind Swamy, Tinnu Anand, Sonali Bendre. 1995.

Bazaar. Dir. Sagar Sarhadi. Prod. Vijay Talwar. Perf. Smita Patil, Farooq Sheikh, Naseerudin Shah. 1982.

Chhalia. Dir. Manmohan Desai. Prod. Subhash Films. Perf. Raj Kapoor, Dev Anand, Rehman, Shobana Samarath, Pran. 1960.

Coolie. Dir. Manmohan Desai. Prod. MKD Films. Perf. Amitabh Bachchan, Kader Khan, Rati Agnihotri, Rishi Kapoor, Waheeda Rehman. 1983.

Deewar. Dir. Yash Chopra. Prod. Gulshan Rai. Perf. Amitabh Bachchan, Shashi Kapoor, Parveen Babi, Iftekar, Nirupa Roy, Aruna Irani. 1975.

Delhi 6. Dir. and Prod. Om Prakash Mehra. Perf. Abhishek Bachchan, Sonam Kapoor, Om Puri, Waheeda Rehman, Rishi Kapoor, Anil Kapoor, Divya Dutta. 2009.

Dharmputra. Dir. Yash Chopra. Prod. Yash Raj Films. Perf. Shashi Kapoor, Mala Sinha, Rehman, Manmohan Krishna. 1961.

Dhool ka Phool. Dir. Yash Chopra. Prod. B.R. Films. Perf. Mala Sinha, Rajendra Kumar, Ashok Kumar, Manmohan Krishna Leela Chitnis, Daisy Irani. 1959.

Fanaa. Dir. Kunal Kohli. Prod. Aditya Chopra. Perf. Aamir Khan, Kajol, Rishi Kapoor, Kirron Kher, Tabu, Shruti Shah. 2006.

Gaman. Dir. Muzaffar Ali. Prod. Integrated Films. Perf. Farooque Sheikh, Smita Patil, Nana Patekar, Jalal Agha. 1978.

Ghulam-e-Mustafa. Dir. Partho Ghosh. Prod. P.G. Srikanth. Perf. Nana Patekar, Paresh Rawal, Raveena Tandon, Aruna Irani. 1997.

Hum Ek Hain. Dir. P.L. Santoshi. Prod. Prabhat Films. Perf. Durga Khote, Kamala Kotnis, Dev Anand, Rehman, Ram Singh, Baby Usha. 1946.

Kabhi Khushi Kabhi Gham. Dir. Karan Johar. Prod. Yash Johar. Perf. Amitabh Bachchan, Jaya Bachchan, Shahrukh Khan, Kajol, Hrithik Roshan, Kareena Kapoor, Rani Mukherjee, Farida Jalal. 2001.

Kismet. Dir. Gyan Mukherjee. Prod. Bombay Talkies. Perf. Ashok Kumar, Mumtaz Shanti, Shah Nawaz, V.H. Desai, Mubarak. 1943.

Mission Kashmir. Dir. and Prod. Vidhu Vinod Chopra. Perf. Sanjay Dutt, Hrithik Roshan, Preity Zinta, Sonali Kulkarni, Vinod Sharma. 2000.

Naseem. Dir. Saeed Akhtar Mirza. Prod. NFDC. Perf. Kaifi Azmi, Mayuri Kango, Kulbhushan Kharbanda, Kay Kay Menon, Surekha Sikri. 1995.

Pehli Nazar. Dir. Mazhar Khan. Perf. Motilal, Veena, Munawar Sultana. 1945.

Road to Sangam. Dir. Amit Rai. Prod. Amit Chheda. Co-Pro. Sunil Sharma. Perf. Paresh Rawal, Om Puri, Javed Sheikh, Pawan Malhotra, Yusuf Hussain, Masood Akhtar, Vijay Mishra. 2010.

Saleem Langde Pe Mat Ro. Dir. Saeed Akhtar Mirza. Prod. NFDC. Perf. Pawan Malhotra, Vikram Gokhale, Surekha Sikri, Sudhir Pandey, Neelima Azim, Ajit Vachani, Nishiganda. 1990.

Sarfarosh. Dir. John Mathew Mattan. Prod. Anil Arora. Perf. Aamir Khan, Sonali Bendre, Naseerudin Shah, Pradeep Singh Rawat. 1999.

Vaastav. Dir. Mahesh Manjrekar. Prod. Deepak Nikalje/AFI. Perf. Sanjay Dutt, Namrata Shirodkar, Sanjay Narvekar, Reema Lagoo. 1999.

Waqt. Dir. Yash Chopra. Prod. B.R. Films. Perf. Balraj Sahni, Sunil Dutt, Raaj Kumar, Shashi Kapoor, Achala Sachdev Rehman, Sharmila Tagore. 1965.

Zakhm. Dir. Mahesh Bhatt. Prod. Mukesh Bhatt and Pooja Bhatt. Perf. Ajay Devgn, Pooja Bhatt, Sonali Bendre, Ashutosh Rana. 1998.

2

Ammi *

Saeed Akhtar Mirza

'Nusrat Beg,' said Amanullah Khan, 'two nights ago my younger brother asked for my daughter's hand in marriage on your behalf. I had said no.'

Amanullah Khan paused, looked around the room and then addressed Nusrat again.

'But today, I have decided to rethink my decision. Before I do so, however, I would like my entire family to listen to what you have to say. We all would like to know more about your family and its history. I know we have your sister in our midst, but we never thought to ask her this because our brother had already made up his mind. With you, it is different. We would also like to know what you plan to do and how you will be able to support a family. We ask you all this because it has to do with the future of my daughter.'

Nusrat was taken aback. Even though he had had an inkling of what could happen at dinner, he had not imagined it would

---

* Excerpts from *Ammi: Letter to a Democratic Mother*. Chennai: Tranquebar Press, 2008.

turn out this way. Here was the entire extended Khan family—men, women, boys and girls and smaller children—all waiting for his reply. It was like an open court with everyone invited. He turned to look at Jahanara. She was leaning against a doorway that led to an inner room and she was looking directly at him with a steady gaze, almost as if to tell him she was the one who really wanted to hear him out. He turned to look at the women who sat near the kitchen. They were all staring at him. He shifted his gaze to his sister. She nodded and smiled encouragingly. Nusrat took a deep breath and began to speak.

'Khan Baba, your clan has an illustrious history and can trace its roots all the way back to the time of Shah Babar. I know it has a record of that. I also know that your clan believes that a man's worth can be judged by his family, his tribe and his roots. I respect that. But I belong to a family that has lost its history. I have no roots like you do. All I know is that the story of my family begins with Wali Beg. That is what my father told me. Mirza Wali Beg was from Samarqand and he, with a band of worries, moved from Samarqand to Kabul seeking glory. It was an age for adventures. And it was in Kabul that he joined the grand alliance of Ahmed Shah Durrani that was marching on to fight the new rulers of Delhi, the Marathas. Though the war was eventually won, Wali Beg's band was decimated in the first two hours of battle because it was at the helm of a cavalry charge. The charge was a fiasco. After the truce Wali Beg did not return home. Maybe he felt that he would not have the courage to face the mothers or widows of the men who had died in the field. He stayed on in the land of Hind where he was given a small jagir near a town called Najibabad, just north of the city of Delhi. That was seven generations ago. It was here that Wali Beg met other rootless Mughals, Turkmen, Pathans, Afghans and Persians, all of them casualties of an era of endless wars. He married the daughter of one such casualty. After the death of Wali Beg, the links with his history and his roots got weaker and were slowly erased, so that by the time of my grandfather, Mirza Akbar Beg, they were entirely lost.'

Nusrat stopped speaking. There was silence around the dastarkhwan.

'What happened to the land?' asked the matriarch.

'We had it for four generations until it was seized by the British after the bloody uprising of 1857. After the loss of the land my grandfather, Akbar Beg, decided to teach. He was scholar of Arabic and Persian texts. He began to teach in the courts of Lahore and Rampur. His son, Safdar Beg, followed in his footsteps. Only, he added English texts to the Persian, Urdu and Arabic ones. He was a travelling scholar who tutored the families of the rich and the powerful across the Punjab, in Delhi and in Avadh. It was in Quetta that he met Jamal Khan. So all I can say is that for three generations, we have been scholars. Our family has always been small. We have no links with larger clans and tribes and therefore we can claim no history.'

There was silence in the room once again.

'Since you have no land and no inheritance, how will you support my daughter?' asked Amanullah Khan.

'I have a job as a teacher in the government school at Sibi,' said Nusrat.

'Will that be enough?' asked the matriarch.

'It's start,' said Nusrat. 'As for the future, I have faith in myself.'

'What makes you so confident about your future?' asked Amanullah Khan.

'Because I have gambled on it,' said Nusrat confidently.

There was a murmur in the hall. Nusrat knew it had to do with his choice of the word 'gamble'. He looked at Jahanara. She didn't look away. Her gaze held steady.

It was the eldest brother, Attaullah Khan, who asked the next question.

'What do you mean, "gambled on it"?'

'The world is changing rapidly,' said Nusrat. 'And I am on the side of change. There have been revolutions in France and Russia. Mighty storms have swept away old histories and values. Kings and queens do not matter any more because all men are equal. And I believe that from now on, men will be judged not by who they are, what their families own or where they come from, but by what they can do. Look at the decrees of Kemal Atatürk! In one stroke, he has changed the destiny of his people and his country. Look at what electricity, the telephone and the motor car have done to the world! There are even airplanes in the sky! Every day something new is being discovered. That is the world I have gambled on. That is the world I believe will shape the future. We have a choice. Do we want to live in a well from which we can see only a patch of sky, or do we want to live outside the well and see much more? I want to live outside the well. That is the way I want to see the world.'

Nusrat paused and looked around the room. All eyes were on him. Jahanara was still looking at him steadily. Attaullah Khan broke the silence.

'You talked about Russia. It is said they don't believe in God there. You talked about that Turk. He has forbidden women from wearing the veil. He has persecuted priests. What have you to say about that?'

'About Russia, I do not agree with all that they have done, but I do believe that they are on the side of the poor. For the first time in the history of mankind, the poor have a voice.'

'Do you believe in Allah, Nusrat Beg?'

'I do. I most certainly do.'

'Then why do you take up for that Turk?'

'Because he believes in Allah too,' said Nusrat. 'But he was tired of seeing foolish priests harm the progress of his country.'

(36–39)

***

the tale of the veil that disappeared

I am trying to imagine that moment. The year was 1938 and you had been wearing a burqa ever since you were thirteen years old. What went through your mind that made you decide that you were not going to wear it anymore? It was such an incredible decision. In a way I believe that this particular moment would be fixed forever in your mind. Am I right? What did Baba do or say when you shook your head? I believe he smiled. What did you do with the burqa that was in your hands? I was told that you folded it and put it around your arm and walked home? There must have been hundreds of people who passed you by on the streets that evening and who, perhaps, even looked at you. Did you look back at them? Or, did you look down at the road as you walked? Later, you folded the burqa and put it away in a trunk at home, almost saying to the world and, perhaps, to yourself too, that a chapter was closed. You then joined Baba at the dining table and smiled. I was told that Baba looked at you and smiled too.

It was perhaps the quietest revolution ever because it seems you and Baba never talked about your decision again. And here I am, so many years later, still wondering about a story that should have made the headlines, that should have been trumpeted from rooftops, but was instead silently hushed up in a rented apartment on Cuffe Parade. I am not suggesting that you had turned into a revolutionary because I do know you were a devout Muslim all your life and you even prayed five times a day. But I still wonder.

(153–154)

***

the day I became a Muslim

It was in 1952 and it was Eid. As was your usual practice you prepared the bowls of sheer korma that you had made at home. Along with the bowls you included plates of mithai that you had bought. The bowls and plates were put on trays that were covered in embroidered malmal cloth and sent to our neighbours. This was done every year but that year something strange happened. Our neighbour next door came back with the bowl of sheer korma looking embarrassed and he apologized profusely. He told Baba that his mother from Punjab was visiting and she would not touch anything that was made in a Muslim's house. And, since she was there, the rest of the family couldn't eat it either.

'What about the mithai?' Baba asked.

The neighbour, still embarrassed, tried to explain that since the mithai was bought from a Hindu shop his mother would accept it. Baba listened silently as the man pleaded his case.

'She is seventy years old, please forgive her.'

Baba didn't say a word. He took the tray back and gave it to you. You took bowl of sheer korma and put it away. Talat was furious.

'Why didn't they throw it in the sink and pretend they'd eaten it?'

'Let's get the mithai back,' said Aziz angrily.

You had said nothing. It was later that I asked you about the incident.

'Why did she refuse it, Ammi?'

'I don't know.'

'She said she will not eat anything made in our house.'

You nodded and kept silent.

'Are you feeling bad about it?'

'I am.'

'I think she is a stupid old woman.'

'Saddu, people don't want to be rude. She and her family have come from Pakistan. I don't know what happened to them there and that could be a reason. Could it not?'

It could have been a reason. I knew the partition of India had led to terrible acts of mass violence and the old lady may have been a witness to those times. But there is another reason for recalling this incident, which occurred when I was perhaps just nine years old. For the first time in my life the fact that we were Muslims had been underlined. And maybe something else was defined too. Was it hate? Or revulsion at 'eating food made by hands that were unclean and impure'? Whatever the rationale, it was used to define an entire community. It happened such a long time ago but I still remember the feeling of confusion, a peculiar emptiness inside and anger.

(167–168)

***

A woman in the midst of men. This brings me to the other reason for recalling those evenings.

Just below our house and on the steps of the entrance to our block sat other married women of Fonseca Mansion. Sometimes there would be seven or eight of them and sometimes about four or five. They would gather every evening at around six-thirty and quietly talk to each other till about eight. Then they would head back to their homes and serve dinner to their husbands and children. You never joined them on those steps Ammi, not once. I always wondered why. I got an answer from you in 1968.

'I did not give up the burqa a long while ago to sit on those steps and moan and groan about my problems.'

'Why did you give it up?'

'I didn't know, but definitely not for that.'

I believe you, Ammi. It was definitely not for that. I believe that you gave up the burqa to be able to participate in journeys and not be a spectator. I also know that when your 'manufacturing phase' collapsed it was you who convinced Baba to write for films. Baba finally relented because he had run out of other ideas and money. And when Baba did begin to write, another journey began. It was you who would be the first to listen to his ideas and make your comments. Then he would further develop it into a story. By 1960 Baba was a famous filmwriter though he did have a reputation for not being 'open to ideas and change'. It was incredible. Baba was a famous filmwriter who didn't get much work. But he wrote his stories anyway, whether they got sold or not. What very few people knew was your role in the writing of these stories. You did it for thirty-five years. In fact both of you went on with it even when the producers and directors had stopped calling years ago. By the early 1970s the calls got fewer and by the end of the decade they had stopped. I remember those times when I would drop by for a chat and Baba would be ready by ten in the morning, pen and paper in hand, and you would join him by eleven after completing the cooking. The help in the kitchen had gone years ago and there was only Asha who would come twice a week to do the sweeping and scrubbing.

I would observe both of you as you settled down for the day's work. I know it mattered to both of you that there was no producer waiting in the wings, but there was something else that I think you also realized: this was what Baba was really cut out for and so were you. Both of you could create stories and dreams. The only problem in this journey was that Baba had an unusual faith in his stories and that is why he protected them so obstinately. So many of his stories were almost sold but rejected at the last minute. That is also the reason why the times of plenty in our home were not too often and financial uncertainty constantly lurked around the corner. The price of this uncertainty was borne by you because you had a home to run and Baba knew this too. Maybe those were also the times when he stretched out his hand to you and you held it.

(169–170)

3

Language, Culture, Bombay Cinema

Reflections on Cinematic Representations of Muslims*

Anisur Rahman

Language, Culture, Cinema: A Prologue and Three Interrogations

If language is a medium of expression and culture a mode of life, then creative representation may quite justifiably be read as their metaphor. The medium, the mode and the metaphor are inseparable in all texts—verbal visual, and written. They complement each other to grow into a form worthy of critical cognisance. In its ultimate configuration, this form becomes an index of a people's behaviour, their ways of communication, and finally, their identity. Taking my cue from this, I would posit that reading a filmic text is like reading a form in its verbal and visual manifestations that represent the major marks of a given culture.

All creative arts, including films, represent various stages in the development of this matrix of medium, mode and metaphor.

* Revised version of the plenary delivered in IRIS Seminar on *Representations of Muslim Culture in Indian Cinema*, Jaipur, April 23–25, 2010.

This becomes all the more significant in a multilingual, multicultural, multiethnic and multireligious site like India where various cultural clusters contribute towards the emergence of a broad Indian reality. When put on the screen, this reality is best appreciated in terms of arts and artefacts, myths and metaphors, social and political responses, ritual and spiritual practices. As such, films create their own iconographies through their stock or experimental modes of representation.

A community or a group of people, who constitute a part of the medium-mode-metaphor matrix, and who configure a larger nationalist paradigm, may be appropriately and broadly identified with reference to their cultural marks and linguistic behaviour. In the case of cinematic representation, however, this matrix needs to be problematised differently as cinema acquires its strength from the plausibility and concrescence of visuals as re-constructed for the screen. Here, the spoken language broadens its frontier to incorporate both gesture and music in its fold. This theoretical basis may be applied to discuss the cinematic representation of the Muslims who have been prominently visible on the Indian screen, and have represented a certain cultural pattern and a certain linguistic taste. As the Bombay cinema carved a definite space for Muslim cultural marks and the language used by them, it also remained influenced, in turn, by these very marks. It remained so for several decades, especially till the emergence of a cinematic diction that drew its life from the linguistic habits of the masses, and which could not be assigned to any particular class or community of people. These issues may be appreciated in a critical perspective by interrogating at least three essentialist positions that have evolved over a period of time and have been reiterated incessantly. As these positions bear directly upon our reading of the cinematic representations of the Muslims, it would be proper to examine them and develop a paradigm to appreciate the issues involved.

First, is there anything called 'Hindi cinema'? While one may understand what is meant by regional cinema, or even

Hindustani or Indian cinema(s), one may not identify the so-called Hindi cinema with the same confidence. We are aware that the question of categorisation is a problematic one in the Indian context, as it may be variously approached in terms of regions, languages, cultures, apart from genres, forms and techniques of representation. This constraint should not, however, help one language appropriate over other language(s) as it is quite liable to create a map of misreading. Developing an entirely objective view of the issue, I may posit that irrespective of the long-drawn and irreconcilable stances adopted regarding Urdu, Hindi, and Hindustani,[1] Hindi cinema is clearly a misnomer as it has subsumed several other linguistic and geographical spaces without ascertaining its own position in the larger imagination of the people. Unlike the regional cinemas which use given languages, the so-called Hindi cinema, which Yves Thoraval has discussed in great detail to establish its 'supremacy', has unhesitatingly appropriated the benefits of hegemony that a national language is supposed to exercise over the entire length and breadth of a country, which Hindi does not obviously do. This cinema found its home in the Bombay of yesteryears and appropriated the space even of that cinema which was decidedly Urdu in its language, culture and essential make up.[2] In the years that followed, this cinema used a language that was commonly understood and negotiable even though it was not so commonly or uniformly adopted or spoken.[3] Although Bombay emerged as the centre of this so-called Hindi cinema, it broadly produced the cinema *of* and *for* the northern part of India[4] which is the home to the Indo-Aryan group of languages. As northern India speaks in different languages, this cinema also absorbs and evolves its own language for different levels of reception. Today, this cinema speaks in Hindi now, now in Urdu, in Hindustani now, now in Hinglish, in Bombaiyya now, and now in an argot of a mixed variety, and all of these are passed under the broad identity of Hindi, with the final seal put over it by Central Board of Film Certification of the Ministry of Information and

Broadcasting. This mixed linguistic baggage of Bombay cinema, as may be testified, creates a variety of impressions—serious, comic, plebeian—either by turns or even simultaneously, and constructs diverse Indian discourses in turn.

Second, what is 'Bollywood' and what does it signify? To put it precisely, Bollywood is a queer construct, a fashionable pictogram, a bizarre hybrid that seeks its identity through a lingering hangover for Hollywood on the one hand, and our loyalty to the mythical Bombay of pre-Thackerite days, on the other. It is a self-defeating exercise in carving a unique identity for one's own self. It is yet another misnomer, after Hindi cinema, which needs serious contestation. It relegates the major postcolonial questions, reiterated ceaselessly, regarding history, identity, indigeneity, and the contexts of power, language, and image. In spite of a host of filmic texts, narrating the nation in distinctive terms, Bombay cinema has been unquestioningly and ubiquitously canonised as Bollywood cinema. With the silence of film critics and historians on this issue,[5] as also on the other issue of Hindi cinema, Bollywood stands authenticated as a term of reference for Bombay cinema, and it has become a part of the larger Indian imagination in spite of its being too priggish and self-conscious. Even if it is re-incarnated in future as Mollywood cinema in response to the compulsions of a segment of contemporary local politics, it would remain a portmanteau of Mumbai cinema. It would not be too remote to imagine that in spite of this, it would carry the burden of the canonised and overpowering Hollywood. It needs to be asserted that this is the very Bombay or Mumbai cinema[6] of our own make and mix that has remained the citadel of authentic cultural configurations of the larger part of north India of which Muslims, being the largest minority of India with a population of more than a hundred million, form a significant part.

Third, like the two problematic identifiers mentioned above, there is yet another identifier—'Islamicate'—that seems to have emerged as a category to discuss the representation of Muslim subjects in Bombay cinema ever since Marshall Hodgson, a historian of repute, used it to associate Muslims with Islam, and Mukul Kesavan, Rachel Dwyer, Ira Bhaskar and Allen Richard appropriated it for the same purpose in the context of films, and to designate all motifs and manners associated with Muslims as 'Islamicate'.[7] To put it in a perspective, I may ask as to what is Islamicate, and how can this be possibly used as a category to study the representation of Muslims in Bombay cinema? I would posit that like Hindi cinema and Bollywood, Islamicate is another misleading label that has not only gained currency in reading filmic texts with Muslims as their subject, but it has been presumably done with certain academic justification although the justification does not hold well. All the pleas put together by a more informed set of critics, however, fail to erase one seminal line of distinction that a religious faith and a people that follow it, do not necessarily and compulsively need to be taken as inevitable constituents of one, or single formation. Like all religious faiths and their followers, Islam and Muslims are also linked but all constructions relating to Muslims are not to be assessed in terms of their religious identity. The thesis advanced by those projecting the Islamicate category, thus, crumbles as it fails to take note of a simple distinction that Islam is a faith while Muslims are the followers of that faith, and the two are not necessarily the one and the same for all possible reasons. Muslims are a people in a social matrix and live as simple or complex a life as anyone else to deserve a cinematic representation. While they profess one faith, they speak many languages and reflect many cultures. As such, equating a people only with their faith and not contextualising them in a complex cultural formation is negating their legitimate space for larger participation in life's various manifestations. It would, thus, be grossly unjust to designate all of their actions and responses to history and society under the category of the Islamicate. It would be as unfair as equating the responses of Hindus with Hinduism, or of Christians with Christianity. As

Muslims represented in the Bombay cinema are a part of the larger Indian reality, they have to be viewed as such rather than shown to be representing a separate category in conformity with their religious identity. Categorising all subjects related with Muslim life and culture under the broad label of the Islamicate, would be stereotyping and essentialising a people and their socio-cultural identity of which religious faith is only a part and not the whole. I would, thus, assert that Islamicate may be used with great profit in areas where studies focus on faith, its history, religious practices, rituals and other related manifestations, rather than social practices and cultural norms.

With this, I go back to my argument about cultural representations of a people. And with this, I pose yet another set of questions in relation to the representations of the Muslim culture. What are the signs of this culture, let me ask? Is it mujra, or mushaira; ghazal, or qawwali; or is it simply the skull cap, or lungi/tehmed, or domes, or minarets? Is it not civility and refinement that also distinguish this culture; or is it not a modest and modernist outlook as well that could identify these people known as Muslims? One could also ask: are Muslims essentially decadent, or are they simply incapable of looking forward? Further, do they act and react, write and speak, relate and respond differently from others? My contention is that the critical readings of filmic texts, conducted by some perceptive critics who have engaged with the idea of the Islamicate, have grossly overlooked the layers of implications carried in the three contestable categories—Hindi cinema, Bollywood and the Islamicate—even though the Bombay cinema has chosen to address the issue of Muslim representation in some of the most imaginative ways. Let me take you on a tour.

Bombay Cinema: A Tour

With the 1930s began the history of the Bombay sound film,[8] and it began with *Alam Ara* (1931), a Muslim cultural representation, which also happened to be a commercial success. The decade also saw on screen, films of the same genre in *Lal-e Yemen*, *Char Dervesh* and *Pukar*. Four out of the eight films related with 'Muslim Subjects' or 'Muslim Representation'—two neutral expressions I choose in preference to 'Islamicate'—produced during this significant colonial decade, underlined an important thesis that the subject was considered worthy of attention, and that it had a respectable number of viewers in the market. The 1940s followed with five more of the type: *Mumtaz Mahal*, *Zeenat*, *Shahjahan*, *Omar Khayyam* and *Najma*. These five figured in a list of less than two dozen films produced during the decade. The dwindling number of Muslim representations in the 40s, as compared with the 30s, did not suggest anything against their reception except that this decade made way for the production of some of the most remarkable films such as *Bandhan*, *Anmol Ghadi*, *Jugnu*, *Nadiya Ke Paar*, *Mela*, *Barsaat*, *Andaz* and *Mahal*. In other words, the decade sought its character at a broader level of reception, and a more holistic representation of the Indian society and culture, which the subsequent two decades sharpened further.

The 50s and the 60s could best be described as the golden period of Muslim representation on the celluloid. The 50s saw the production of approximately two dozen films that dealt with Muslim subjects, although it was *Mirza Ghalib* that stole the show. The 60s produced about three dozen Muslim subject films for an ever-growing number of viewers and it produced some of the classics such as *Chaudvin ka Chand*, *Mughal-e-Azam* and *Sahib Bibi Aur Ghulam*.[9] These films became a part of the collective memory of those who lived during this period, and indeed many of them grew with these films over the years. It would be significant to note that most of the films produced during this golden period were character-plot centric, and that they drew upon history and places although they did not necessarily succeed at the so-called box office. A particular geographical location that engrossed the attention of the filmmakers repeatedly and, by implication, of the viewers, was

Baghdad. The mythic and real characters that caught both their fancy and imagination included Ali Baba, Alif Laila and Laila Majnun, among several others, on the one hand,[10] and Jehangir, Akbar, Anarkali and Mirza Ghalib, and many more of this type, on the other.[11] All these showed a typical hangover for romantic themes, plots, characters and situations. They seemed to have the potential to engage the viewers, and hold them in spell for three hours of cinematic entertainment.

Bombay films started developing new genres, new modes, and new techniques in the 70s which has continued with remarkable success ever since. While the thief of Baghdad and Ali Baba still held a limited space in the common imagination of the filmmakers and viewers, the 70s showed a general decline in the representation of Muslim subjects. As the age of celebrating the regal splendour, kings, queens and princesses had gone by, and as these subjects had also been fully exhausted, newer subjects caught the attention of filmmakers. Films such as *Lal Patthar*, *Pakeezah*, *Shatranj ke Khiladi*, *Noorie* and *Garm Hawa* appeared as the new classics of the age, and they offered a new dimension to the classics of the golden period mentioned above. Among these, *Shatranj ke Khiladi* and *Garm Hawa* were new additions to the common imaginary of the Indian viewers, as these films spoke a new language, and premiered new concerns. In the 80s, *Umrao Jaan*, *Nikaah, Tawaif* and *Salim Langde Pe Mat Ro* emerged as yet other modern classics, and extended the concern manifested in earlier films such as *Pakeezah.* Films as varied in form and content as *Henna, Train to Pakistan, Sardari Begum* in the 90s, and *Mission Kashmir, Refugee* and *Fiza,*[12] among others, in the first decade of the 21st century, problematised the scenario of Muslim representation still further.

This tour through the Bombay cinema affords me with a way to assess its essential nature and character. While I have gone on in a chronological order underlining the hallmarks of this cinema through the eight decades of its development, I have refrained from offering neat classifications to trace the trajectory of this cinema. Classifications are tricky; they are limiting and lead to oversights and slippages. While some effort has been made to study Bombay cinema with this methodology by Ira Bhaskar and Richard Allen,[13] I would desist from doing so as a number of remarkable films representing socio-political issues, ideological shifts and rebuttal of stereotypes cannot be properly appreciated if they are viewed from fixed perspectives. Similarly, there are films that reconstruct Indian history with Muslims playing their part in it, as there are films on cross-cultural representations, resistance, fear, exploitation and marginalisation. Then, there are films that engage with issues that concern religious faith and problematise gender, language, rural-urban divide, or in other words, a cluster of motifs and icons spread over time and space. If needed, one could place these films in more secular and common-sensical categories such as epicals, musicals, chronicles, romances, courtesanates, masals, melodramas, parallels, mafiates, comedies, satires, thrillers, religious, etc. rather than put them under an unjustifiably fanciful, broad and misconceived category of the Islamicate.

I would, therefore, suggest that more important than sticking to the neat categories of Bombay cinema and arriving at tidy conclusions, are the issues concerning the very emergence and development of this cinema that may tell us about its types and stereotypes. This cinema has emerged out of the multiple influences of the Indian epics, the Sanskrit drama, the theatrical conventions and traditions of North India, the Parsi theatre and finally, the inescapable Hollywood. Early Bombay cinema went back to Parsi theatre for all its theatricality and its high-flown style of the Urdu verse. The reasons were obvious: Urdu could reach out to masses as it was a descendant of the Persian language, an heir apparent so to say, that had been used as the language of literature and administration during the British rule. For at least four decades ever since the consequential 30s, Bombay cinema has used Urdu as its prime language, even though it was popularly branded as Hindi cinema in almost all descriptions and entries on individual films. Let me also posit that the Bombay cinema of today is not worried about Urdu, or Hindi, or Hindustani as its language; it is concerned basically with an idiom that makes good sense to the common people who are composed of an extremely mixed variety of viewers. It is concerned, to a very great extent, with how this cinema may secure a safe place for itself in the market. This thesis finds further explanation through certain cinematic representations in terms of their dialogues and lyrics which call for a closer look.

Language as Gesture

Language acquires a variety of forms in filmic texts. Apart from verbal appropriation, it is also used as gesture, or as a way of expressing a mood. Depending on its nature, every film discovers its own schema of expression. Even though Urdu has been stereotyped both as a language and a culture, it is in the films that it has acquired its most remarkable strength. Although the grace of the Urdu language and the cultural legacy associated with it, helped create an environment for the film, it was the strength of the given plot and the resilience of the characters that combined to make a dramatic impact on the viewers. Strong deliveries helped them become a part of the common memory as it happened in the case of *Mughal-e-Azam*. It could be possible with the available talent who nurtured a linguistic culture and created a register that appealed to the literary and the popular imagination together. One could underline the strength imbued in some of the narratives and dialogues only to show that language performs many a role as a tool of expression, a gesture or a mood. This could be well borne out by the kind of language appropriated in *Mughal-e-Azam, Mere Mehboob, Umrao Jaan, Lal Patthar, Pakeezah* and many others films like these. It was not only the language, however, that played the magic but the right accent and intonation, the quality of speaker's baritone and style of delivery as it came from masters such as Prithviraj Kapoor, Dilip Kumar, Raaj Kumar and several others in a variety of films.[14]

In Bombay cinema, Urdu language could be used in many of its avatars—as the language of love, war, court, diplomacy and of the common day-to-day interaction. It must also be noted that many Urdu writers, lyricists, producers and directors of significance such as Agha Hashr Kashmiri, A.R. Kardar and K. Asif,[15] and many more who formed a league and practised their arts at that point of time, or joined them in subsequent years, were well aware of the rich and expressive conventions of the Urdu language. They worked from behind the scene to create an auditory and visual culture in a series of memorable films ever produced. They also helped create a condition for a broader reception by recharging the language and making it accessible. Beginning with the 1930s, Urdu stayed as the lingua franca of the Bombay films at least till the 70s when other linguistic and dialectic traditions found their way and a new argot for the new filmic tradition was created. It only strengthened the idea further that Bombay films could well develop their own medium of expression, keeping in view the shifting paradigms of life and culture. Bombay could well realise, more than ever before, that language alone could not do the trick; it was the camera also that spoke a language of its own, and the commercialisation of the age that dictated the nature of language. The age of romantic exuberance was gone where language could be charged emotionally and made to sound romantic and husky; language was now a tool in hand to support the complex scheme of filmmaking.

This thesis may also be borne out by looking at the kind of titles that are chosen for the new films. Depending on the nature of the film, the titles were sometimes in Urdu such as *Hazaron Khwahishein Aisi, Shola aur Shabnam* and *Aashiqui*[16] and sometimes in Hindi such as *Ankur, Nishant* and *Swades.*[17] At the third remove, there were titles that were neither Urdu nor Hindi but simple Hindustani that could echo the heart beats of the general viewers and reflect their simple joys of life, love and romance. Here are some interesting examples with emphasis on 'dil', as in *Dil Hai ke Maanta Nahin, Dil Waley Dulhania Le Jayenge* and *Dil to Pagal Hai,*[18] and others with emphasis on 'pyar', as in *Pyar to Hona Hi Tha, Hum Hain Raahi Pyar Ke* and *Aur Pyar Ho Gaya.* The changing trends of communication have made good space for both English and Hinglish in the recent past. Some English titles that make practical sense and find ready appeal include *Luck by Chance, Rock On* and *What's Your Rashee.*[19] Yet another variation on this liberal trend may be seen in the use of Hinglish which is also equally and totally acceptable as a part of common parlance in India today. These include *Love ka Tadka, Jab We Met* and *Pyar Impossible.*[20] These titles succeed like success with the new groups of viewers who book their seats on internet and watch the movies in multiplexes. This thesis may be extended and justified further if one chooses to look closely at the language used by the characters and the general atmosphere created in the film to hold the attention of the viewers.

Language as Music

Bombay films present the richest possible variety of lyrics written in varied registers for an immensely varied audience. Like the titles that we have surveyed above, there are lyrics that also come from various linguistic traditions and registers such as Urdu, Hindi, Hindustani, Hinglish, and the common parlance of the day. These lyrics live their short and long lives, depending on how imaginatively they are composed and sung. They combine the linguistic traditions of Urdu and Hindi with themes ranging from religious to secular, and from secular to profane. Let us take, for example, some of the Urdu lyrics that are devotional in nature and also fall in a literary tradition. These include *Bekas pe karam kijiye sarkar-e Medina* (have mercy on this poor soul, O lord of Medina); *Aaqa Saleem Chishti, Maula Saleem Chishti* (O my lord Saleem Chishti, O my saviour Saleem Chishti) and *Khwaja mere khwaja* (saviour, my saviour). It reflects the tradition of the religious/mystical poetry of the Perso-Arabic tradition, as carried over in the Urdu language. The same language, when used in a romantic context evokes nostalgia, suffering and pangs of love. We may note this in examples such as *Mili khak mein mohabbat/jala dil ka ashiyana* (my love's ruined, my heart's abode lies tattered), *Jurm-e ulfat ki hamein log saza detey hain* (the world punishes me for I loved my love) and *Rang aur noor ki baraat kisey pesh karoon* (whom shall I offer this grand gift of colours and light).[21] Both kinds of lyrics—spiritual and romantic—have had their acceptance with huge clusters of audiences and have stayed in public memory ever since they were sung and enacted on the screen. Bombay films proved a major channel through which the worth of this tradition could be passed on to the common people who could internalise them and hum at leisure to ameliorate the pains and pleasures of their life and living.

Another facet of audience-language negotiation may be seen in some of the Hindi lyrics that develop a different idiom. It harks back to the indigenous literary traditions of the most secular kind which is completely different from the Perso-Arabic religious/mystical and romantic traditions mentioned above. This may be marked in lyrics such as *Mohe panghat pe Nandlal chhed gayo re* (my love has teased me by the banks of the river), *Thaade rahiyo o bankey yaar* (wait O my love, wait a while) and *Chandan sa badan, chanchal chitwan* (the body like sandalwood, the looks so wanton).[22] Yet another facet of an extremely popular variety of lyrics may be seen in romantic love songs. This is a novel variation that may, for the sake of convenience, be called Hindustani in its linguistic make up. Examples of this kind may be marked in lyrics such as *Hawa mein udta jaye mera lal dupatta malmal ka* (my red muslin scarf waves in the wind), *Jaane kya tu ne kaha* (don't know what you said) and *Chhod do aanchal zamana kya kahega* (please let go my *aanchal*, what will the world think).[23] Lyrics of this kind turn into pure romantic dramas in duets such as *Aap yun hi agar mujhse milte rahey, dekhiye ek din pyar ho jayega* (look, I'll fall in love one day, if you meet me like this so often). A fine illustration of this variety may be found in *Hum aap ki aankhon mein is dil ko basa dein toh?* (what if I carve a home in your eyes?). Let us see how this delicate dialogue of love develops in dramatic terms:

Male: *Hum aapki aankhon mein is dil ko basa dein toh?*
(What if I carve a home in your eyes?)

Female: *Hum moond ke palkon ko is dil ko saza dein toh?*
(Then what if I shut my eyes and punish your heart?)

Male: *In zulfon mein gundhenge hum phool mohabbat ke*
(I will string the flowers of love in your tresses)

Female: *Zulfon ko jhatak ke hum yeh phool gira dein to?*
(Then what if I jerk my tresses to drop your flowers?)

Male: *Hum aapko khwabon mein aa aa ke satayenge*
(I'll get into your dreams and tease you no end)

Female: *Hum aapki aankhon se neendein hi uda dein toh?*
(Then what if I steal the sleep from your eyes?)

Male: *Hum aapke qadmon pe gir jayenge ghash kha kar*
(I'll faint and fall at your feet, my love)

Female: *Is per bhi na hum apne aanchal ki hawa dein toh?*
(What if I don't soothe and help you back to breath?)

This is a fine example of sheer romance, fun and playfulness. These couplets of hardly any literary worth sung on the screen decades ago, find an echo in the hearts of young lovers even today. What makes it so is the combined magic of language, music, voice and tonal variations. This is a stock example of many such romantic lyrics that stay in our memory essentially because of their intense musicality and instant appeal to popular imagination. These lyrics came from a phase of popular romantic movies which had soon to be replaced by more earthy ones, written in the popular parlance of the market. The new age defied much of the rhyme and reason that characterised the earlier lyrics. Even though the new lyrics had shorter lives, they reflected the contemporary popular culture which was prone to changes at a much faster pace than ever before. These lyrics were funny, witty, dramatic and purely entertaining, and were aimed at a larger audience of an extremely mixed variety. These qualities of the downright popular lyrics could be marked in *Khai ke paan banares wala* (chewing the betel leaves of Benares), *Aati kya Khandala?* (aren't you coming to Khandala?) and *Chal chhaiyyan chhaiyyan* (move in shade, the thick shade).[24] These lyrics take a whole lot of people to sing as if in a rote, without ever running the risk of being pooh-poohed. To bring this discussion on lyrics to an end, let me also refer to the Hinglish incarnation of the Bombay lyrics. There is nothing odd, nothing forbidden in this domain of the significant absurd. Listen to these, for example: *Love ka tadka rey, Hotty naughty baby in town* and *Give me some sunshine.*[25] This is the idiom of modern India, the lingo of the new nation carving its identity each day in yet another way, and revising it at a faster pace than ever before. Considering the immense variety of Bombay lyrics, I may propose further that they have been composed in diverse linguistic registers and sung in an amazing variety of tone and tenor, representing almost all the nine *rasas*. Most of them represent *shringar, hasya, veera, karuna* and *shanta* but they are not entirely devoid of *bhayanak, raudra, vibhatsya* and *adabhut*. The only occasions when lyrics or even dialogues fail to hold the popular imagination are those when they are unable to synchronise with the tone and tenor of the age for which they are composed. A stock example of this may be seen in the lyric that begins thus: *Priye praneshwari! Yadi aap hamein aadesh karein to prem ka hum shri ganesh karein* (My dear, the breath of my heart! If you so order me, I will just begin to love you).

Let me bring my argument to an end with reference to a film called *Dil Dosti Etc.* (2007) that interrogates stereotypes and reflects iconoclastic aspirations of some young Indian boys and girls who constitute the major cast of this film. They are in search of their distinct individual identities and an idiom for themselves;

they nurse their own aspirations and speak their own kinds of lingo. One of the characters, played by Imaduddin Shah, speaks a pure and Sanskritised version of Hindi which only evokes laughter although whatever he says, deserves serious critical attention. The intention is not to pooh-pooh a language but to portray the character as a type, who is one of the many other types, as well a queer part of the whole. This film represents a way of life that the young generation in India prefers to live today. It reflects their predominant attitudes, their world view and their special manners of speech. It stands as a major signpost of contemporary India, and it also accounts for the long distance covered in terms of India's emergence as a nation state, marked by severe odds and pleasant evens, since the production of *Alam Ara* (1931). During the eight decades between the two films—*Alam Ara* and *Dil Dosti Etc.*—Bombay cinema has configured and re-configured itself again and again; it has created liberal space for scripting the histories of the nation, initiating significant socio-political discourses, negotiating with languages and cultures, and re-inventing appropriate medium, mode and metaphor.

On being asked once in an interview on what was more important—pure communication or expression of one's ideas—Shyam Benegal answered that the film was nothing else but only a communicative medium of ideas, and that the success of a film depended on the kind of language one chose to make it. This brings me to mention a recent film called *Ye Saali Zindagi* (2011), and to reflect on why this could not have been called *Ye Saala Jeevan*. Even though the bare intents remain the same in both the titles but the impacts they create are decidedly different. More than a matter of language, or choice of words, *Ye Saali Zindagi* hits the popular imagination instantly, which the other possible title could not have even touched. As suggested earlier, the Bombay film today is not so much concerned with matters of linguistic chastity or choice, as it is concerned with its commercial viability, which comes from making right thematic, linguistic and stylistic preferences. Filmmaking is an industry today; it is a profit-making concern involving high stakes, and it faces threat from the small screen, new art forms and international challenges in filming. One has been hearing of the demise of Urdu language and *tehzeeb* for long; one has already lamented that Uttar Pradesh, the so-called citadel of the growth and development of Urdu, has turned its back on this language, and one also knows that the younger generation in Uttar Pradesh fights shy of its complete ignorance of the Urdu alphabets. This may well be an appropriate story for a Bombay film but even that film will have to speak in its own language and discover its own form. Films that sustain themselves do so through imaginative reconstructions of a given society and culture. They do so also by discovering a new medium of expression, which, in today's scenario, would neither be Urdu pure, nor Hindi absolute, not even Bombaiyya pucca, but just a new verbal construct which is ever ready to be revised with each turn of history, and with each imaginative leap that catches its reverberations.

Notes

1. Much has been written on this issue from social, political, literary and linguistic angles, as also on the issue of script and its acceptability. Some of the works include: Christopher Schackle and Rupert Snell, *Hindi and Urdu Since 1800: A Common Reader* (London: School of Oriental and African Studies, 1990), Christopher King, *One Language, Two Scripts: The Hindi Movement in Nineteenth Century India* (Delhi: Oxford University Press, 1994), David Lelyveld, 'Zuban-e Urdu-e Mu'alla and the Idol of Linguistic Origins,' *Annual of Urdu Studies*, 9, March 2003; Alok Rai, *Hindi Nationalism* (Hyderabad: Orient Longman, 2001), Alok Rai, 'The Persistence of Hindustani,' *Annual of Urdu Studies* 20, August 2005.
2. While Mukul Kesavan considers Urdu to be the 'bedrock' of Bombay cinema, Harish Trivedi develops an opposite view in favour of Hindi. These opposite views may be seen in Mukul Kesavan, 'Urdu, Awadh, and the Tawaif: The Islamicate Root of

Hindi Cinema,' *The Ugliness of the Indian Male and Other Propositions* (New Delhi: Black Kite, 2008) and Harish Trivedi, 'All Kinds of Hindi: The Evolving Language of Hindi Cinema,' in Vinay Lal and Ashis Nandy (eds.) *Fingerprinting Popular Culture: The Mythic and the Iconic in Indian Cinema* (Delhi: OUP, 2006).

3. Yves Thoraval presents a detailed account of the rise of the so-called Hindi cinema beginning with a brief historical-cum-political survey from 1940 to 2000. He goes on to discuss other aspects as well, such as colour film, the commercial cinema, the golden age of Hindi cinema, the star system, along with a discussions on music, dance, producers, directors, actors and some major films. See Chapter 3 entitled 'The Supremacy of Hindi Cinema' in *The Cinemas of India: 1896–2000* (Delhi: Macmillan, 2000).
4. The linguistic map of India is clearly divisible between the Indo-Aryan and Dravidian languages spoken in the northern and southern parts of India, respectively. Even though North India comprises diverse linguistic states (Jammu and Kashmir, Himachal Pradesh, Punjab, Haryana, Uttarakhand, Uttar Pradesh, Rajasthan, Bihar, Jharkhand, Madhya Pradesh, Orissa, West Bengal), the so-called Hindi is commonly understood although it is not so commonly spoken except in the Hindi heartland. Even if it is spoken in other states, it is spoken in a way that it may not be designated as Hindi in a strict sense.
5. 'Bollywood' has engaged the attention of a large number of writers who accept this hybrid nomenclature without ever interrogating it. Taking it as it is, they have only reiterated the basic spirit of the colonial discourse even further. A quick glance at the title of some of the books published during the last one decade would bear it out quite amply that 'Bollywood' has been unhesitatingly and unabashedly adopted as a favourite name for the Bombay filmdom, and there is no stopping or interrogating this phenomenon. The books that may be mentioned in this regard include: Vijay Mishra, *Bollywood Cinema: Temples of Desire* (2001), Jonathan Togovnik and Nasreen Munni Kabeer, *Bollywood Dreams* (2003), R. Dawar, *Bollywood: Yesterday, Today, and Tomorrow* (2006), Derek Bose, *Brand Bollywood: A New Global Entertainment* (2006), Robert James Elliott and Nicholas R. Bradley, *Bollywood: Behind the Screens, Beyond the Stars* (2007), Mihir Bose, *Bollywood: A History* (Gloucestershire: 2007), Anandam and Aswan Punthambekar,

Global Bollywood (2008), Rachel Dwyer, *100 Bollywood Films* (2008), Anwar Jamal and Saibal Chatterjee, *Hollywood Bollywood* (Hindi, 2009), Rajendra K. Dudra and Jigna Desai, *The Bollywood Reader* (2009), Ajay Gehlawat, *Reframing Bollywood: Theories of Popular Hindi Cinema* (2010), Anustup Basu, *Bollywood in the Age of New Media: The Geo-Televisual Aesthetics* (2010).

6. A brief note on why I call it 'Bombay Cinema' would be relevant and central to the argument that I am trying to build. I call it so because India is a complex site with two thousand dialects, 800 distinct languages, and twenty four official languages. As far as films are concerned, we have regional cinemas in India (which cater to identified linguistic and regional groups), and all of them taken together, can be considered to be the various faces of Indian cinema. Since 'Indian Cinema' is a an amorphous body to me and signifies, at best, a broad spectrum, I consider it proper to designate it as Bombay or Mumbai Cinema which (in spite of also being the ite of production of Marathi cinema) is traditionally associated with the so-called Hindi cinema that caters to larger number of people than other cinemas.

7. The expression 'Islamicate' was first used by a historian, Marshall G.S. Hodgson, in his book *The Venture of Islam: Conscience and History in a World Civilisation* (Chicago: 1974). In the first volume of his book, *The Classical Age of Islam,* he uses it as a term to associate Muslims with Islam. The impact of this nomenclature proved infectious as it was later overstretched by some others to discuss all Muslims subjects in the category of the 'Islamicate'.

   This term was later appropriated by another historian, fiction and non-fiction writer, Mukul Kesavan, in 'Urdu, Awadh, and the Tawaif: The Islamicate Root of Hindi Cinema', The *Ugliness of the Indian Male and Other Propositions* (New Delhi: Black Kite, 2008) to extend his thesis on the representations of Muslims in Indian cinema. Although he offers many explanations regarding why he chose to use 'Islamicate' to discuss Muslims subjects, he ultimately ends up by reiterating a stereotype that necessarily equates a people with their faith rather than the socio-cultural motifs, manners and a number of other eminently possible identifiers.

   Rachel Dwyer in Chapter 3 entitled 'The Islamicate Film,' in *Filming the Gods: Religion and Indian Cinema* (New York: Routledge, 2006) also follows the same pattern and uses the term 'Islamicate' without much critical justification for doing so. In summing up her argument, she says that in the films that she has discussed, Islam forms the basis of a culture with reference to language, literature, music, clothing, etc. and that these films 'do not usually include any mention of religion as belief beyond devotion and as practice'. (129)

Ira Bhaskar and Richard Allen follow Kesavan without much justification in their book *Islamicate Cultures of Bombay Cinema* (New Delhi: Tulika 2009) and use 'Islamicate' to refer to the socio-cultural aspects of the Muslims, the followers of Islam.

8. The history of Indian cinema begins with *Raja Harishchandra*, a silent film by Dadasaheb Phalke in 1913. This paper does not, however, consider the era of silent films although it may offer important clues towards the understanding of the Muslim cultural configurations.
9. The following may also be added: *Mere Mehboob, Taj Mahal, Ghazal, Jahan Aaraa, Qawwali ki Raat, Bahu Begum* and *Mere Huzoor.*
10. More characters of this nature that grappled the imagination of filmmakers included Char Dervish, Alauddin, Sindbad, Hatimtai, Gul Sanobar, Laila Majnu and Rustam Sohrab.
11. Other historical figures chosen as subjects were Babar, Jehangir, Akbar, Shahjehan, Anar Kali, Noor Jehan, Mumtaz Mahal, Jahan Aaraa, Razia Sultan and Nawab Sirajuddaula.
12. Some others in this category are *Gadar, Zubeida, Tehzeeb, Veer Zara, Maqbool, Jodha Akbar, Iqbal, Shaurya, Bombay, Zakhm, A Wednesday, Fida,* and *My Name is Khan.*
13. See for example, Ira Bhaskar and Richard Allen, *Islamicate Cultures of Bombay Cinema* (New Delhi: Tulika, 2009). They study Muslim subject films under four neat categories: Muslim Historical, Muslim Courtesan Films, Muslim Socials, and New Wave Muslim Social and After. They discuss *Pukar* (1939), *Mirza Ghalib* (1957), *Mughal-e-Azam* (1960), *Jodha Akbar* (2008) under Muslim Historical; *Pakeezah* (1971), *Umrao Jaan* (1981), *Tawaif* (1985), *Sardari Begum* (1996), *Umrao Jaan* (2006) under Muslim Courtesan films; *Najma* (1943), *Chaudhvin ka Chand* (1960), *Mere Mehboob* (1963) under Classical Muslim Socials; and *Garm Hawa* (1973), *Salim Langde Pe Mat Ro* (1989), *Fiza* (2000) under New

Wave Muslim Social and After. Another reference may be made to Rachel Dwyer, 'The Islamicate Film,' *Filming the Gods: Religion and Indian Cinema* (New York: 2006).

14. There are other remarkable voices to be heard in Madhubala, Meena Kumari, Nargis, Nimmi, Noorjehan, Waheeda Rehman, Rehman and Iftekar.
15. A number of talented literary figures to boost this tradition included Rajinder Singh Bedi, Saadat Hasan Manto, Khwaja Ahmad Abbas, Kamal Amrohi, Mehboob Khan, Abrar Alavi, Jan Nisar Akhtar, Sahir Ludhianvi, Akhtarul Iman, Kaifi Azmi, Shakeel Badayuni, Majrooh Sultanpuri.
16. Consider tiles such as *Fanaa, Bekhudi, Gardish, Jazbaat, Tapish, Aeteraz, Qayamat, Aks, Fareb, Elan, Jurm, Nigahbaan, Qurban, Lamhey*
17. More in the category, such as the following, may be mentioned: *Lakshya, Abhay, Yuddh, Aakrosh, Drohi, Mrityu Dand, Yugandhar, Shaurya, Khalnayak, Mithya.*
18. More films exploited the popularity of 'dil', as in, *Hum Dil De Chuke Sanam, Dil Jaley, Dil Chahta Hai, Dil Se, Dil Dosti Etc.*
19. Some more examples may be seen in *Karthik Calling Karthik, Don, LOC Kargil, Gang, Refugee, 1942: A Love Story, 1947 Earth, Duplicate, Yes Boss, Singh Is King, My Name Is Khan, 3 Idiots, Paa, Family, Race, Krazzy 4, All the Best, Black Friday, Welcome to Sajjanpur, Well Done Abba, Idiot Box, Trump Card, Hide and Seek, Chance Pe Dance, Life Partner, Wanted, Wake Up Sid, The Warrior, Monsoon Wedding, Black Friday.*
20. The following also fall in this category: *Aao Wish Karein, Oye Lucky Lucky Oye, Dil Mange More, Right Ya Wrong, Namaste London, Love Aajkal.*
21. There is a huge number of memorable lyrics that have formed part of the collective consciousness of the audiences. Some more of them are *Waqt ne kiya kya haseen sitam* (how tyrannical has the time been), *Wo jab yaad aaye bahut yaad aaye* (my ruminations go endless, whenever I ruminate), *Phir wahi sham wahi gham wahi tanhai hai* (it's again the same evening, the same misery, the same loneliness), *Banda parwar, thaam lo jigar, ban ke pyar phir aaya hoon* (love! Be happy, have heart, I'm here once again), *Ye kya jagah hai dosto, ye kaun sa dayar hai* (what place is this my friends, what

abode), *Dil cheez kya hai aap meri jaan lijiye* (not to mention my heart, I offer you my life) and many more, as the list is endless.

22. To add further to this category of lyrics, one could also mention *Ab ke baras bhej bhaiyya ko babul* (send me my brother, I am all alone my father), *Kahe ko byahi bides* (why did you marry me off to one in an alien, far off land), *Bhaura bada nadaan rey* (the bee is just too innocent), *Man re tu kahey na dheer dharey* (why don't you have patience, my poor heart), *Piya to se naina lagey re* (my love, my glances meet yours and, yours mine), *Poochho na kaise main ne rain bitayi* (don't ask me how I spent the dark night), *Mere naina sawan bhadon* (my eyes are streams; they shower like rains), *Tum bin jeewan kaisa jeewan* (what a life! What a life is this without you), etc.
23. One naturally recalls to mind some more lyrics such as *Pyar kiya to darna kya* (why fear, I have loved, and say so), *Teri zulfon se judai toh nahi mangi thhi* (I hadn't asked for separation from your tresses), *Chura liya hai tum ne jo dil ko* (you have stolen my heart, my love) *Dekho rootha na karo* (don't sulk, my love), *Abhi na jao chhod kar* (don't leave me yet), *Tumko dekha to ye khayal aaya* (it occurred to me as I saw you), *Chehra hai ya chand khila hai* (is that your face, or has the moon shown up), *Ek ladki ko dekha to aisa laga* (I saw a girl, I felt as if), *Ghar se nikalte hi/kucch door chalte hi* (stepping out of the house, walking forth a few steps).
24. These numbers may also be mentioned along this line: *Beedi jalai le* (light your beedi), *Yara sili sili* (O friend, sili sili), *Ibn-e Batuta baghal mein jota* (Ibn-e Batuta tucks his shoes by his side), *Gum sum gum sum sum kyun ho tum* (lost, all lost, why are you so lost).
25. Comparable numbers of this kind are *Zoobi doobi zoobi doobi, Hu tu tu* and *Tara rum pum* that sound like jingles.

Works Cited

Bhaskar, Ira and Allen, Richard. *Islamicate Culture of Bombay Cinema.* New Delhi: Tulika. 2009.

Dwyer, Rachel. *Filming the Gods: Religion and Indian Cinema.* New York: Routledge. 2006.

Hodgson, Marshall G.S. *The Venture of Islam: Conscience and History in a World Civilisation.* Chicago: The University of Chicago Press. 1974.

Kesavan, Mukul. *The Ugliness of the Indian Male and Other Propositions.* New Delhi: Black Kite. 2008.

Thoraval, Yves. *The Cinemas of India: 1896–2000.* Delhi: Macmillan. 2000.

Filmography

Aashiqui. Dir. Mahesh Bhatt. Perf. Rahul Roy, Anu Agrawal, Deepak Tijori, Tom Alter. 1990.

Alam Ara. Dir. Ardeshir Irani. Perf. Master Vitthal, Zubeida, Jilla, J. Shushila, Prithviraj Kapoor. 1931.

Andaz. Dir. Mehboob Khan. Perf. Dilip Kumar, Raj Kapoor, Nargis, Murad, Cuckoo. 1949.

Ankur. Dir. Shyam Benegal. Perf. Anant Nag, Priya Tendulkar, Shabana Azmi, Sadhu Meher, Dilip Tahil. 1974.

Anmol Ghadi. Dir. Mehboob Khan. Perf. Surender, Suraiya, Noor Jehan, Murad. 1946.

Aur Pyar Ho Gaya. Dir. Rahul Rawail. Perf. Bobby Deol, Anupam Kher, Aishwarya Rai, Shammi Kapoor. 1997.

Barsaat. Dir. Raj Kapoor. Perf. Raj Kapoor, Nargis, Prem Nath, Nimmi. 1949.

Char Darvesh. Dir. Prafulla Ghosh. Perf. Angurbala, Kanan Devi, Benoy Goswami. 1933.

Chaudhvin ka Chand. Dir. Mohammad Sadiq. Perf. Guru Dutt, Rehman, Waheeda Rehman, Johnny Walker. 1960.

Dil Dosti Etc. Dir. Manish Tiwari. Perf. Shreyas Talpade, Imdad Shah, Nikita Anand, Smriti Mishra, Ishita Sharma, Dinesh Kumar. 2007.

Dil Hai ke Maanta Naheen. Dir. Mahesh Bhatt. Perf. Aamir Khan, Anupam Kher, Pooja Bhatt, Tiku Taslania. 1991.

Dil to Pagal Hai. Dir. Yash Chopra. Perf. Shahrukh Khan, Madhuri Dixit, Karishma Kapoor, Akshay Kumar, Deven Verma, Farida Jalal. 1997.

Dilwale Dulhania Le Jayenge. Dir. Aditya Chopra. Perf. Shahrukh Khan, Kajol, Amrish Puri, Farida Jalal, Anupam Kher. 1995.

Fiza. Dir. Khaled Mohammad. Perf. Karishma Kapoor, Hrithik Roshan, Neha, Bikram Saluja, Jaya Bachchan, Sushmita Sen. 2000.

Garm Hawa. Dir. M.S. Sathyu. Perf. Balraj Sahni, Farooq Shaikh, A.K. Hangal, Jalal Agha. 1973.

Hazaron Khwahishein Aisi. Dir. Sudhir Mishra. Perf. Kay Kay Menon, Chitrangada Singh, Shiney Ahuja. 2005.

Henna. Dir. Randhir Kapoor. Perf. Rishi Kapoor, Zeba Bakhtiar, Ashwini Bhave, Saeed Jafri, Farida Jalal.1991.

Hum Hain Rahi Pyar Ke. Dir. Mahesh Bhatt. Perf. Aamir Khan, Juhi Chawla, Dalip Tahil. 1993.

Jab We Met. Dir. Imtiaz Ali. Perf. Shahid Kapoor, Kareena Kapoor. 2007.

Jugnu. Dir. Shaukat Hussain Rizvi. Perf. Noor Jahan, Dilip Kumar, Agha, Shashi Kala. 1947.

Lal-e Yemen. Dir. J.B.H. Wadia. Perf. Jal Khambata, Karimja, Padma, Feroze Dastur. 1933.

Lal Patthar. Dir. Sushil Majumdar. Perf. Raaj Kumar, Hema Malini, Vinod Mehra, Raakhi, Ajit. 1971.

Love ka Tedka. Dir. Gautam Adhikari and Rajan Wagdhare. Perf. Nauheed Cyrusi, Samir Dattani, Bakhtiar Irani, Satish Kaushik. 2009.

Luck by Chance. Dir. Zoya Akhtar. Perf. Rishi Kapoor, Dimple Kapadia, Juhi Chawla, Hritik Roshan, Isha Sharvani. 2009.

Mahal. Dir. Kamal Amrohi. Perf. Ashok Kumar, Madhubala. 1949.

Mela. Dir. S.U. Sunny. Perf. Dilip Kumar, Nargis, Jeevan, Rehman, Noor Jehan. 1948.

Mere Mehboob. Dir. H.S. Rawail. Perf. Rajender Kumar, Sadhna, Ashok Kumar, Nimmy, Pran, Johnny Walker, Amita. 1963.

Mirza Ghalib. Dir. Sohrab Modi. Perf. Bharat Bhushan, Suraiya. 1954.

Mission Kashmir. Dir. Vidu Vinod Chopra. Perf. Sanjay Dutt, Hrithik Roshan, Preity Zinta, Jackie Shroff. 2000.

Mughal-e-Azam. Dir. K. Asif. Perf. Prithvi Raj Kapoor, Dilip Kumar, Madhubala, Durga Khote, Ajit Murad. 1960.

Mumtaz Mahal. Dir. Kedar Nath Sharma. Perf. Khursheed, Madhubala, Chandra Mohan, Yakub. 1944.

Najma. Dir. Mehboob Khan. Perf. Ashok Kumar, Veena. 1943.

Nikaah. Dir. B.R. Chopra. Perf. Raj Babbar, Deepak Parashar, Salma Agha. 1982.

Nishaant. Dir. Shyam Benegal. Perf. Shabana Azmi, Naseeruddin Shah, Smita Patil, Anant Nag, Amrish Puri, Satyadev Dubey, Kulbhushan Kharbanda. 1974.

Noorie. Dir. Manmohan Krishna. Perf. Farooque Sheikh, Poonam Dhillon, Madan Puri, Iftekar. 1979.

Pakeezah. Dir. Kamal Amrohi. Perf. Ashok Kumar, Meena Kumari, Raaj Kumar, Veena Sapru, Nadira. 1972.

Pyar Impossible. Dir. Jugal Hansraj. Perf. Uday Chopra, Priyanka Chopra, Anupam Kher. 2010.

Pyar To Hona Hi Tha. Dir. Anees Bazmi. Perf. Ajay Devgn, Kajol, Om Puri. 1989.

Pukar. Dir. Sohrab Modi. Perf. Chandra Mohan, Naseem Bano, Sohrab Modi. 1939.

Refugee. Dir. J.P. Dutta. Perf. Abhishek Bachchan, Kareena Kapoor, Sunil Shetty, Jackie Shroff. 2000.

Rock On. Dir. Abhishek Kapoor. Perf. Farhan Akhtar, Prachi Desai, Arjun Rampal, Luke Kenny, Purab Kohli. 2008.

Sahib Bibi aur Ghulam. Dir. Abrar Alvi. Perf. Guru Dutt, Meena Kumari, Rehman, Waheeda Rehman. 1962.

Salim Langde Pe Mat Ro. Dir. Saeed Mirza. Perf. Pavan Malhotra, Makrand Deshpande, Nilima Azeem, Ashutosh Gowarikar. 1989.

Sardari Begum. Dir. Shyam Benegal. Perf. Kirron Kher, Amrish Puri, Rajit Kapur, Rajeshwari Sachdev. 1996.

Shahjahan. Dir. A.R. Kardar. Perf. Rehman, P. Jairaj, K.L. Saigal, Nasreen, Ragini. 1946.

Shatranj ke Khiladi. Dir. Satyajit Ray. Perf. Amjad Khan, Richard Attenborough, Sanjeev Kumar, Saeed Jafri, Shabana Azmi, Victor Banerjee, Farooque Shaikh, Tom Alter. 1977.

Shola aur Shabnam. Dir. Ramesh Saigal. Perf. Dharmendra, Tarla Mehta, Abhi Bhattacharya, Vijayalakshmi, M. Rajan. 1961.

Swades. Dir. Ashutosh Gowarikar. Perf. Shahrukh Khan, Gayatri Joshi. 2004.

Tawaif. Dir. Aleem Mansoor. Perf. Rishi Kapoor, Poonam Dhillon, Rati Agnihotri, Ashok Kumar, Kader Khan. 1985.

Train to Pakistan. Dir. Pamela Rooks. Perf. Nirmal Pandey, Rajit Kapoor, Mohan Agashe, Smriti Mishra, Divya Dutta. 1998.

Umrao Jaan. Dir. Muzaffar Ali. Perf. Rekha, Farooque Shaikh, Naseeruddin Shah, Raj Babbar. 1981.

Ye Sali Zindagi. Dir. Sudhir Mishra. Perf. Irfan Khan, Arunoday Singh, Chitrangada Singh, Aditi Rao Hyadri, Saurabh Shukla, Sushant Singh. 2011.

Zeenat. Dir. Shaukat Hussain Rizvi. Perf. Noor Jehan, Yakoob, Bibboo, Karan Dewan. 1945.

4

Qawwali

A Mode of Representation of Muslim Culture in Bollywood

Rashmi Attri

Qawwali, a vibrant musical tradition is a poetic performance, a traditional genre of Islamic devotional music popular in India and Pakistan. It is rooted in Sufism, a mystical school of Islamic thought, originally performed at Dargah or Shrine of respected Sufi saints. Though Sufism emerges from Islam, it is also a response to orthodox Islam. Sufism while affirming distinction between creator and created, strives to attain oneness with Divinity, through the dynamic force of love (Mohabbat). Mystical love, its central concept is to be cultivated spiritually and aroused emotionally through recollection of God's name called *Zikr*, and listening to the spiritual music called *Sama*. Sufi listener of the divine message of *sama* is called *mushaikh* (plural of Shaik), singer of this mystical song is called qawwal, i.e., 'one who says' and qawwali is the divine message or song.

Qawwali came to the Indian subcontinent in the 11th century from Persia. It is the Chishti school of Sufism, which propagated qawwali in India and Pakistan. Shaikh Nizamuddin

Aulia and his followers used music in their devotional gatherings. Amir Khusrau, of this Chishti order of Sufism is credited with fusing Persian and south Asian musical traditions to create its contemporary form in the late 13th century. Qawwali can be categorised as Hindustani semi-classical music set to mystical Sufi poetry in Farsi, Hindi, Punjabi, Urdu and Persian. Recent/present-day qawwalis are mostly in Urdu as Urdu serves as cultural lingua franca of Muslims all through the Indian subcontinent.

Qawwali songs consist of Sufi poetry rendered in ghazal form, which is regarded as an ideal vehicle for the mystical experience (Schimmel 162). Ghazal like other Sufi songs explores metaphysical and abstract questions regarding the nature of God, universe and love. Ghazal is multivalent in its resonance with its intense emotional and meditative registers expressed in a form which is lyrical, metaphoric and reflective at the same time. It becomes easily adaptable for qawwali songs. Its repetitive monorhyme or *radif* can serve to reiterate a central word, phrase or concept in the manner of *zikr*, principle (Schimmel 81–82). Qawwali assemblies are seen as royal courts of saints.

Qawwali songs deal with mystical love, devotion, longing of man for the divine. These qawwali Sufi songs like Bhakti poetic tradition use the metaphor of love to speak of the divine love. God is synonymous with the Beloved (Mehboob). The occasion for qawwali songs can vary from celebration of the saints, the divine being, to expression of abstract mystical thinking. Though qawwali song is conceived to be spiritual in meaning, its lyrics can sound passionately secular. Sufism aligned with the Bhakti tradition of India, is a philosophy of love for humanity at large. Lyrics are the most important part of a qawwali.

As an art form, qawwali is a group song/performance with one vocalist, the qawwal, leading and his supporting vocalists joining in. A typical qawwali begins with a song in praise of God. Harmonium, dholak, tabla, hand clap pings are the traditional musical instruments to be used with fast dadra beats of qawwali.

If the dadra taal is played fast, it produces a hypnotic beat. Qawwali gatherings are mixed and composed of a heterogeneous group. Listeners also become participants here. Qawwali follows a typical psychological process: the song begins, some words and lines are repeated with variations in tunes to suggest the deeper meaning of the lyrics, soon the repetition and fast beat become so intense that both the qawwal and the listeners enter a state of trance (*hal*), which leads to spiritual enlightenment, sense of mystical delight (*kafiat*), and finally to the state of ecstatic dancing (*raqs*).The qawwal's main aim is to evoke spiritual enhancement of its listeners leading to the mystical arousal and ecstasy. Both the lyrics and the music play crucial roles in this enlightenment and communicate at several levels simultaneously.

The devotional Sufi qawwali has faced many ups and downs. Qawwali flourished during the Mughal period, along with the Hindu religious songs called bhajans. Throughout the centuries qawwali was not only used by Sufis, but also performed at Mughal courts. But Aurangzeb, who could not tolerate Sufism and its liberal tradition, found it an attack on his fundamental beliefs. The final blow, however, came with the establishment of the British East India Company, as qawwali singers lost their patrons and gradually disappeared.

Then the emergence of the Indian film industry, mainly Hindi cinema, popularly known as Bollywood in the middle of the 20th century, gave it a new lease of life. Bollywood revived qawwali as an art form and there was a time when having at least one qawwali was a must for a formula Hindi film. The 1960s and 70s turned out to be the Golden Age for the qawwali. Right from its beginning till date Bollywood has given its audiences many hit qawwalis which not only add spice to the film music but also portray Muslim culture. Since *Mughal-e-Azam*, there have been qawwalis in Hindi films such as *Barsaat ki Raat, Chaudhvin ka Chand, Bahu Begum, Amar Akbar Anthony, Nikaah* and even in as recent films as *Fiza, Veer Zara* and *My Name is Khan*. Right from the beginning of Indian cinema, qawwali was transformed to the secular needs of the new medium. The style was retained but the focus shifted more towards romance from the purely mystical. Soon qawwali became popular in secular festivals and concerts all over the world overcoming racial and religious boundaries. Its music became a bridge between Hindu and Muslim communities. By 1940s commercialised stage versions of qawwali also emerged. As an art form, it has been redefining and reinventing itself with a dash of modernity subject to the needs of the times. This paper makes a modest attempt to explore the different ways in which qawwali as musical performance is introduced in Hindi films to represent Muslim culture.

Use of qawwali in a film is dependent on its theme. Mostly qawwali is related to Muslim subjects or characters in Hindi films. It is one of Bollywood's favourite devices of invoking Islamicate/Muslim culture or ethos in cinema (Qureshi 82). Hindi films, woven around Muslim cultural life definitely include qawwali form. We find qawwali in Muslim historicals, socials and also in New Wave cinema. *Zeenat,* released in 1944, was the first Hindi film to introduce this Sufi musical form. Filmy qawwali is to be seen in the context of the popular (secular) and traditional (devotional) qawwal. Both types of qawwalis manifest the deep influence of Islamic culture on Hindi cinema. Filmy qawwalis act as ambassadors of Muslim culture. Its use of Urdu language, in the ghazal form creates Muslim ethos.

Mughal-e-Azam directed by K. Asif, released in 1960 starring Prithviraj Kapoor, Dilip Kumar and Madhubala in the lead roles is based on the Mughal ruler Shahenshah Akbar. It has a very famous qawwali *Teri mehfil mein kismet azma ke hum bhi dekhenge* written by Shakeel Badayuni composed by Naushad and sung by Lata Mangeshkar and Shamshad Begum. This qawwali is in a form of battle between two groups of female singer. It is a debate on love between Anarkali (court dancer), Salim's beloved and Bahar, her rival. Its lyrics are secular and deal with love. Bahar sings: *Mohabbat karne walon ka bas yahi hai afsana, tadpna chup chup ke anhen bharna, ghut ghut ke mar jana*. To this

Anarkali, who is ready to subsume in love responds: *Mohabbat humne maana zindagi barbaad karti hai/ya kya kum ki Mar jane pe duniya yaad karti hai/Kisi ke Ishq mein dunyia luta ke hum bhi dekhenge. (*Bahar: Suffering and longing are the inevitable fate of every lover, they are smothered in their own sighs and die. Anarkali: Agreed that love ruins one's life, but is it not enough that when lovers die, the world remembers them, I too want to bestow my love on some one.)

This qawwali reflects the cultural life of the Mughal court, like the poets' gathering, known as mushaira, articulates the values of the Muslim elite and evokes the splendour and grandeur of the Mughal era thus projecting the rich cultural and artistic traditions of the Mughal empire. Besides being inherently secular in its Sufi message, this qawwali also suggests the rich cultural world of Akbar's court affirming Hindu/Muslim solidarity.

Barsaat ki Raat, a 1960s film, also has a very popular qawwali, *Na to carvan ki talaash hai*, highlights the universality of love. Performed at the shrine of Ajmer Sharif, the tomb of the great saint Muinuddin Chishti, which is the Mecca of all the qawwals, it is a combination of two qawwalis and brilliant example of qawwali in praise of love, where earthly love is equated with the spiritual experience. This qawwali is also in a form of competition between male and female groups. Bharat Bhushan, its main protagonist, seeks relief from the pain of love in the first part, while in the second part, Shyama along with her crew, sings of love elevating it to the divine state by proclaiming the supreme power of Ishq (the passionate self-effacing love), in these words:

> *Allah Rasool ka farman Ishq hai/Jaane Hafeez Ishq hai, Qurran Ishq Hai/Gautam ka aur Maseeh ka arman ishq hai/Ye kaynat Ishq hai aur jaan Ishq hai/khak ko but aur but ko devta kar de Ishq/Intehan ye hai ki bande ko khuda kar de Ishq.*
>
> (God's, Prophet's command is love, Love is protector, scripture is love, Gautam and Messiah desire love, this life is love and creation is love, the limits are that love can sculpt out of dust and raise a statue to the status of God.)

Ishq here is secular in nature. *Ishq Azaad hai Hindu na Musalman hei ishq.* Its Sufi inflected couplets also reach the higher level of mysticism pointing towards religious unity by referring to famous Krishna and Gopi myth.

This qawwali can be interpreted both at romantic and devotional levels. Ishq literally means love without lust. In Urdu, Ishq means love for any person, object or even God. The use of Urdu, Punjabi and Hindi khadi boli is typical of a Sufi qawwali. The use of such musical instruments as harmonium, dholak and tabla brings it very close to the traditional qawwali, the only departure being the introduction of the female singers.

While talking of great qawwalis of Hindi films we cannot bypass a famous qawwali of *Chaudhvin ka Chand, Sharma key youn sab purdahnashin kyun chehre ko chupaya karte hain/Kuch aisi nazar wale bhi hain jo chup chup ke nazara karte hain.* (Some maidens shy away behind purdah/there are those also who persist in peeping at them from behind the curtains.) Translated thus into prose, the romance of hide and seek does not come through but the film deals with the Nawabi culture and the purdah system of Muslim social life. Set in 19th century Lucknow, it deals with the drama of recognition and mistaken identity in the purdah system. The practice of purdah forbids women to show their face to men outside their immediate family members. The handling of the theme has both comic and tragic dimensions that provide structure to its plot of misunderstanding and misidentification. Nawab Pyare Mian, a sophisticated Lucknawi Nawab, is thunder-struck by a glimpse of Jameela, the heroine's face when she lifts her veil. This qawwali takes place when the women gathered for Pyare Mian's sister's wedding notice him peeping at the women in his attempt to locate Jameela. These women tease Jameela and sing this qawwali. It is a simple, playful and romantic qawwali growing out of the narrative. The film displays sympathy for both the genders, as the purdah creates chaos by involuntary infringements of its code. Still the film upholds the purdah institution prevalent among Muslims and reaffirms the need to follow the social norms. In its presentation it is close to traditional qawwali, which had travelled out of the dargah and the Mughal courts to be performed at Muslim weddings.

This discussion on qawwali in Hindi films remains incomplete, without mentioning the qawwali of *Amar Akbar Anthony*, a 1977 film. Akbar, the qawwal, the youngest brother of the trio, is dressed in a sparkling costume and the entire set is a scene of spectacle. In this qawwali, which is in the confessional mode, Akbar is requesting his beloved to reveal her face. The lyrics are so powerful and intense in passion that the burqa-clad heroine, (played by Neetu Singh) removes the purdah from her face, against all social norms and even the wishes of her father.

> *Khuda ka shukr hai chehra nazar to aya hai, hayaa ka rang, nigahon mein phir bhi chaya hai/Purdah hai purdah hai, purde ki peeche purdanashin hai, purdahnashin ko bepurda na kar doon to Akbar mera naam nahin hai/Purdah hai purdah.*
>
> (Thank God, the face is at last unveiled, the shyness lingers in her glances/the veil is there and behind it the woman/My name is no Akbar/If I don't compel her to unveil her face.)

These lyrics are both emotional and passionate combining the tones of request and anger. Though it is categorised as fun loving romantic, the qawwali picturised on the Muslim character Akbar has referential meaning, as literally 'purdahnashin' is Akbar's beloved wearing a burqa, metaphorically it could also refer to God Almighty. Akbar like a committed devotee is determined to find this Divine power, through his intense love. This qawwali represents the purdah system of Muslim culture, without critiquing it in any way.

Hindi films have also picturised qawwalis at dargahs highlighting its devotional aspect, though the situation still remains romantic, as in *Pardes* and a recent film *Veer Zara*. In both the films, qawwalis have been used as denouements where the high drama unfolds during and within these qawwalis. Its declamatory nature and emotionally driving rhythm serve to evoke intense feelings needed for the scene. Though in *Pardes*, a 1997 film directed by Subhash Ghai, starring Shahrukh Khan, Amrish Puri, Alok Nath and Mahima Chowdhary, we do not have a Muslim theme or Muslim characters still the qawwali is not a misfit as it speaks out the conflict in the mind of the protagonist, who is seeking the help of God Almighty in taking the right decision. The following lyrics by Anand Bakshi and composed by Nadeem Sharvan are sung by Alka Yagnik and Sabri brothers:

> *O Rabba, ye mohabbat bhi ek Ibadat hai aur ye Ibadat bhi ek mohabbat hai, ye bhi deewangi hai, Woh bhi deewangi hai, ye bhi dil ki lagi hai woh bhi dil ki lagi hai, Ab waqt faisle ka nazdeeq aa gaya hai, kya faisla karun mein dil to ye kaha hai, jeene ka hai shauk to marne ko ho ja tayyar.*
>
> (Oh God, this love is also worship and worship is also love, that's madness and this too is madness, this is an attachment, that too is an attachment. Now the time has come to take a decision, what shall I do? My heart says if you have the desire to live, be prepared to die.)

It has confessional tone where love is being equated with worship.

In *Veer Zara,* a film directed by Yash Chopra, starring Shahrukh khan, Preity Zinta and Rani Mukherji in lead roles, there is a qawwali occurring at a very dramatic moment, when Zara Hayat Khan, daughter of a Pakistani politician but in love with the Indian Veer, is to be engaged with a son of a Pakistani politician chosen by her father. Veer Pratap Singh, appears at this critical time. Qawwali lyrics with Madan Mohan's music are sung by Hussain brothers and express Veer's deep love for Zara, his beloved, for whose sake he has crossed the border. The qawwali becomes the lover's voice:

> *Jo bandishen thi zamane ki tod aaya hoon Main tere vaste duniya ko chod aaya hoon. Aaya tere dar par deevana, ye hai tera hi haar sandaayee… tera hi shahdayea.*

Tere ishq mein Isse marjana hai ... Jaan aur dil vaar doon main.
Zindagi doon mein jaise shamma pe marta hai parwana.

It is a story of a true lover in search of his lost lady love. Its lyrics even as they express the Sufi saint's desire to be united with his God, also convey Veer's true love and devotion towards his beloved Zara. In the lines above, the lover proclaims that he has broken all bonds, has left his world behind to unite with his love. The qawwali carry a message of love: I am your devotee and your worshipper, lost in you and prepared to die for my love, just as the moth destroys itself on the light of the candle. This qawwali is an example of an authentic qawwali, in terms of its Sufi message and in terms of its performance at a dargah, with dholak, tabla, harmonium and hand clap pings. It portrays Muslim cultural language used on the occasion of a wedding.

Though the qawwali had disappeared from Hindi films during 1970s, it has again been revived in recent years by such music directors as A.R. Rahman, Shankar Mahadevan and others. These directors have highlighted its Sufi message of peace, tolerance, universal secular love and pluralism. As against the dogmatic and fundamentalism of Islam increasingly predominant in media and recent Hindi films, misrepresenting Muslims as terrorists and equating Islam with violence and terrorism, these qawwalis laced with Sufism act as a bulwark against the fundamentalism linked with Islam. The Hindi film *Fiza* (2000), directed by Khalid Mohammad, starring Karisma Kapoor, Hrithik Roshan and Jaya Bachchan in lead roles serves as an example. Set in the aftermath of Bombay riots of 1993, the film projects how Muslim youth were trapped in the cycle of violence by two powerful social agents: politicians and professional militant groups.

Here 'Haji Ali Qawwali' composed by A.R. Rahman and sung by Mustafa, Murtaza Ghulam Mustafa and Srinivasan is like a soothing balm for tense nerves. This qawwali foregrounds a positive view of Islam while encouraging music as a way of deepening one's relationship with God Almighty. The qawwali is in praise of God, written in chaste Urdu, where Haji Ali is called

Shane Samandar Ibne Haider. It is an example of devotional performance in devotional space where the lyrics of praise, faith and obeisance invoke faithful relationship with Divine power. Haji Ali Dargah on the sea front in Bombay is seen as an iconic site to evoke Sufiana mystical peace loving and devotional aspect of Islam. In a way, it counters the effects of much publicised Islamic links with terrorism. Secular and generous spirit of Haji Ali is conveyed in this which prays to God to protect all human beings, from all races, none of them should live in fear. Almost the same effect is achieved by the Sufiana qawwali of *My Name is Khan*, a film which deals with the misrepresentation of Muslims as terrorists. Set against the background of 9/11, it poignantly depicts the pain of being a Muslim in a world which does not trust one; as a result its main protagonist Rizwan Khan, suffering from Asperger syndrome, is suspected to be terrorist, has to cry out 'My name is Khan and I am not a terrorist'. It has two beautiful qawwalis. One sung by Richa Sharma has Sufi-based lyrics penned by Niranjan Iyengar *Rome rome tera naam pukare, Ek huye din rain hamare* (every pore in my body calls your name, I have lost all sense of time). These lyrics in Urdu, Hindi and Punjabi, sung to the accompaniment of rubab, shahnai and dholak, express complete submission, which in a spiritual qawwali is the metaphor for the spiritual quest. The beloved is seen as an outward aspect of God. In Sufi poetry, every attribute of the beloved becomes a specific metaphor for the divine (Qureshi 135–139). This qawwali enhances both the emotional and devotional feelings. In its philosophy of oneness with the divine, this Sufi-based qawwali has secular connotations. Being in praise of God, it is in the spirit of *Tasawwuf* (eternal blessedness). It is present in the film as a background song during the wedding ceremony of Rizwan with Mandira. This film has one more qawwali which is essentially Sufistic and devotional, a sort of chanting of God's name, in order to attain oneness with God. Where the devotee is in love (Ishq) with God and in a state of ecstatic delight: *Kaise ishq se saj gayeen rahein, jab se dekhi hein teri nigahein, ya khuda, mein to tera ho gaya.* (The path is strewn with love, ever since I saw your eyes, My God I am all yours.) This Qawwali truly a *tasawwuf* depicts the protagonist's absolute surrender to the Almighty. This devotional mood conveyed with the help of Sufi-based Qawwali reaches its peak with *Noore Khuda* sung by Adnan Sami with Indian musical instruments. This qawwali is an intense prayer on part of the protagonist to help humanity at such critical times. God is referred to as light in this dark hour and is requested to remove this darkness and enlighten the distracted humanity and guide it towards the path of love:

Noore khuda, Tu kahan hai chhupa tera milta nahin pata
Yun na humse nazrein fira
Zakhme dilon faryaad karen tera milta nahin hai pata.

It is a prayer to God Almighty to shower peace and harmony on humanity: Why have you turned away from us. We, injured and wounded, search for you everywhere, but are unable to find you. All these qawwalis, definitely establish an alternate image of Islam as a peace loving pluralistic religion.

We can say that popular Hindi cinema of mid-20th century became the major source of popularising qawwalis. The romantic lyrics and intoxicating music with fast beats made the form very popular in Hindi films. The very fact that God is treated as a beloved in Sufi poetry led to its adaptability in Bollywood. What started in dargahs and mazars turned out to be a formidable art form gaining acceptability amongst the people of different communities. Qawwali embodying the power of the community through devotion, love, romance, ishq and undying devotion, and with its layered discourses has an immense seductive charm. This form is a major representation of Muslim culture weaving in the religious, the spiritual, the worldly and the romantic all into one.

Works Cited

Morcom, Anna. *Hindi Film Songs and Cinema*. UK: Ashgate Publishing Ltd., 2007.

Courtney, David. 'Islamic Devotional Music'. www.chandrakantha.com-Music of India. Accessed 20 June 2011.

Rajadhyaksya, Ashish and Paul Willemen. *An Encyclopaedia of Indian Cinema*. Revised edition. New Delhi: Oxford University Press, 1999.

Bhaskar, Ira and Richard Allen. *Islamicate Cultures of Bombay Cinema*. New Delhi: Tulika Books, 2009.

Qureshi, Regula Burchardt. *Sufi Music of India and Pakistan: Sound, Context and Meaning of Qawwali*. London: Oxford University Press, 1995.

Schimmel, Annemarrie. 'An Islamic Literature of India' in J. Gonda. Ed. *History of Indian Literature*, viii 3, Wiesbaden: Harrassowitz, 1975.

——. *Mystical Dimensions of Islam*. Chapel Hill: N.C. University of North Carolina Press, 1978.

Subham, Johar A. *Sufism, its Saints and Shrines: An Introduction to the Study of Sufism*. Lucknow: Lucknow Publishing House,1960.

Filmography

Amar Akbar Anthony. Dir. Manmohan Desai. Prod. MKD Films. Perf. Vinod Khanna, Amitabh Bachchan, Rishi Kapoor, Neetu Singh, Parveen Babi, Pran, Nirupa Roy. 1977.

Barsaat ki Raat. Dir. P.L. Santoshi. Prod. R. Chandra. Perf. Bharat Bhushan, Shyama, Madhubala. 1960.

Chaudhvin ka Chand. Dir. M. Sadiq. Prod. Guru Dutt. Perf. Guru Dutt, Waheeda Rehman, Rahman, Johnny Walker. 1960.

Fiza. Dir. Khalid Mohammad. Prod. Pradeep Guha. Perf. Jaya Bachchan, Karishma Kapoor, Hrithik Roshan, Neha. 2000.

Mughal-e-Azam. Dir. K. Asif. Perf. Prithvi Raj Kapoor, Dilip Kumar, Madhubala, Durga Khote, Ajit, Murad. 1960.

My Name is Khan. Dir. Karan Johar. Prod. Hiroo Johar and Gauri Khan. Perf. Shahrukh Khan, Kajol, Jimmy Shergill. 2010.

Pardes. Dir. and Prod. Subhash Ghai. Perf. Shahrukh Khan, Amrish Puri, Alok Nath, Mahima Chaudhary. 1997.

Veer Zara. Dir. Yash Chopra. Prod. Aditya Chopra and Yash Chopra. Perf. Shahrukh Khan, Preity Zinta, Rani Mukherjee, Amitabh Bachchan, Hema Malini. 2004.

5

Performance, Politics and Piety of Sufi Music

Madhuri Chatterjee

The call to prayer five times daily, often broadcast over loud speakers from mosques and by the muezzin in public places, and the recitations from the Quran permeate Muslim communities. The Muslim music tradition is overwhelmingly vocal, instrumental accompaniment being occasionally banned. Sufi music exemplified by the drums/oboes and percussion, form another important component of Muslim musical culture. As a means of drawing closer to God, the Sufi *dhikri* is a quintessential Islamic vehicle but an unwritten polemic surrounds the Sufi music of the subcontinent and particularly the Indian cinema. Sufism is a mystical tradition within Islam wherein there is a heavy emphasis on having the practitioners singing and dancing with passion in order to express love for God or Allah. Sufism is best described as the spiritual path to mystical union with God. And, a 'dervish' is a person who has taken vows of poverty and austerity. They often follow ecstatic rituals and hence called whirling dervishes. Sufis share the universal values that are most closely shared with other religious traditions; as practical spiritual guides they engage common concerns of suffering and anxiety, the celebration of joyous rapture and the terror of confronting death in ways more profound than theologians or jurists. Kungle's book on *Sufis and Saint Bodies: Mysticism, Corporeality and Sacred Power in Islam* points out, 'Sufis address these issues with an intellectual satisfaction and mythopoetic imagination that makes their Islamic narratives accessible and vibrant for others outside the tradition' (7).

In the Indian subcontinent, the various ritualistic traditions of singing, chanting, dancing and music are also incorporated in the Hindu faith. The Brahmins (Hindu priestly class) divide music into two categories: *marga* sangeet that which is pleasing to the gods and is sacred music and *desi* sangeet that which is pleasing to humans and which is secular or profane music. But between the 8th and 12th centuries, the cultural exchange in music between Arabia and India was exemplified by the name of two ragas, the Yemeni and Kafi, which clearly indicate Arabic origins. The advent of Islam in India and particularly Sufism has left its mark on the musical scene of India forever. The Sufi contribution to music was so great that it created and enriched existing musical traditions in India. Throughout the centuries, the qawwali was not only used by the Sufis but also sung at Mughal courts. Qawwali thus became a part of the classical tradition in India and has also been recognised and is now a part of the national heritage of Pakistan. The popularity of the qawwali gained momentum with the coming of the Indian film industry, popularly known as Bollywood. Qawwali was no longer restricted to the Sufi shrines and the gatherings of the pious but became ever popular with people of all faiths and regions. The qawwali or group form of Sufi music has always been present in Indian film industry but recently there is an influx of solo strain of Sufi performances who have drawn liberally from the rich and all-inclusive heritage of Sufi poetry and music and redeployed it with a clear political edge within the space of cultural activism.

Often in community pageants and singing—both intimate and personal and with aural charm exuded by flowing grey beard and pensive eyes—any Sufi verse recited would by implication become Sufi. In fact, Bollywood has taken some artistic liberties and many of the scenes woven around the rites of passage and accompanied by overpowering music try to bring a Sufi element though the central fact remains some insane passionate love—it is often in the form of traditional love song which is not directed at Allah or God but expresses a human love interest. The core of Sufism is to leave ordinary life and be closer to God, truth and knowledge. There are various routes the Sufi may follow to bridge the gap between God and himself, love being intrinsic to each. Techniques vary but they have three things in common—rhythm, repetition and endurance. This is manifested in the use of chants, music and dance.

Before giving a list of these songs, one must recall the singing-masquerade--the contributors. What has been this singing for all these years? If Sufi music did not exist at all then what is received and feted by people as Sufi music? How can one reclassify the names of Mian Abu Bakar, Hazrat Amir Khusrau, the Qawwal Bachche; the singing of Ustad Fateh Ali, Mubarak Ali, Aziz Mian, Ustad Jaafar Hussain, Sher Ali, Mehr Ali, Ustad Nusrat Fateh Ali, Allan Faqir, Alim and Farghana Qasimov, Shajarian, ShahramNazeri, Tufail Niazi, Abida Parveen, Saeen Zahoor. The list could go on and on. Abida Parveen has performed a great service in the cause of popularising Sufi music but has escaped Bollywood movie sound tracks. Nusrat Fateh Ali Khan introduced Sufi music to Hollywood and later to the entire world with the exquisite *Sawariya* song from *Bandit Queen* (1994), Shekhar Kapoor's masterly biographical film about Phoolan Devi. Next, his nephew Rahat Ali Khan produced gems like *Mann ki lagan* from *Paap* (2003), *Jiya dhadak dhadak jaye* from *Kalyug* (2005) and *Aj din chadiya* from *Love Aaj Kal* (2009). The talented Kailash Kher came into the scene with *Allah ke Bande* from the film *Aisa Bhi Hota Hai* (2003). A.R. Rehman has also delivered many Sufi creations like *Tere Bina* (*Guru,* 2007), *Arziyan sari* (*Delhi 6,* 2009) and *Khwaja Mere Khawaja* (*Jodhaa Akbar,* 2008*)*. Besides these songs, *Ya Ali* (*Gangster,* 2004), *Maula Mere Maula* (*Anwar,* 2008), *Piya Haji Ali (Halla Bol,* 2007), *Ye Hausla* (*Dor,* 2006) and *Rubaroo* (*Maqbool,* 2005) have all been chartbusters. Singer Sukhwinder Singh believes, 'Music is the voice of God and Sufi music is dedicated to Him. When you sing from your heart, it turns out to be soul stirring'. While Kailash Kher strongly feels, 'Both Sufi music and Sufism convey the messages of true love. It is not about a love between man and woman but something beyond that' (in an interview to Jai Rajendra at IANS on 16 November 2009). All these above songs are of undying hope and deep despair, of unquestioning surrender and exuberant challenge, of mystical romance and desire to create, construct and shape a world around us. In the performance and picturisation of these numbers, an element of Islam or some communal element does enter. The devotional act of repeating God's name is a Sufi practice known as *dhikr* or *fikr* in Urdu. The repetition of a line or a word in the devotional Sufi music till the word loses its meaning and you become one with God is perhaps the idea taken from *dhikr*. Another well known practice is the whirling. The whirling dervishes of Turkey were famous for their dance like movement on music, wearing flowing robes and believed to reach divinity at the end of their whirling performance. This was recently demonstrated in the movie *Jodhaa Akbar* in the Sufi song *Khwaja Mere Khwaja* about Khwaja Moinuddin Chisti. Also the lead Zakir has induced a state of wajid in the listener during sama, when the listener loses all worldly bearings and moves into a state of spiritual unity with the one remembered in this popular number. The language of the song is usually modified to create locally viable devotional expression. Indeed, the boundary of the 'devotional' is not always easy to locate. Although, Muslim devotional expression infuses the musical traditions of many communities to the extent that it serves to preserve what is perceived as authentic culture in most parts of the Islamic world as well as the Indian subcontinent, forms it also part of the musical language of the community. Sufism, also known as Tassawwuf, is completed as 'shariat' (the path), 'tariqat' (the observation), 'haqeeqat' (the truth) and finally 'marfat' (the union or oneness with god). The various practices of Sufism such as *dhikr, murqaba*, whirling, singing of qawwalis and many others is where the music part comes in.

The journey of these songs begins with the Allana Iqbal's Hamad[1] (pre-composition in praise of God) before 1947—*lab pe aati hai dua ban ker tamanaa meri* (my desire comes to my lips in the form of a prayer)—a secular, warm and compassionate song which gradually became more strident and aggressive around 1960s with a decade of war with Pakistan. But in a paradoxical sense, the Sahir Ludhianvi qawwali in *Barsaat ki Raat* (1960)—*Ye ishq ishq hai*[2] had everyone participating in the true spirit of the Sufi *zikr* (a creative art of remembrance in a collective Sufi ceremony of listening known as *Samaara*)[3]. Also, Ishq is a concept central to all Sufi practices. The *takraar* or the argumentative element is common to qawwalis but the lines have been picked from prominent Sufi names.[4]

> *Ishq aazad hai Hindu na Musalmaan hai ishq* (Bulleh Shah).
>
> *Aap hi dhamar hai aur aap hi imaan hai ishq* (Ghulam Farid).
>
> *Allah rasool ka farman ishq hai* (Waris Shah).
>
> (Ishq, love, is free, it is not tied to any religion; in itself it represents conscience, it is God's and Prophet's command. Each line has been taken from a different well-known Sufi poet).

A significant body of Sufi heritage of Punjab seemed to have been seamlessly embedded in this song of radical connectivity. The Sufi songs have also always incorporated the idea of homelessness both in its celebrative and darker shades. Even during times of communal politics, the singers espoused a vision of radical plurality and sent messages of social repair and reconstruction and in a paradoxical sense, the Sufi Bhakti tradition created a vibrant space for much of the displaced and homeless creativity. This Sufi music truly understood, was originally meant to be a community experience where the rich and the poor would mingle freely and possibly without a sense of divisive socio-economic hierarchy. It was performed in a spiritually well-defined space for *khalq e khuda* (people of God) gratis. Now at this juncture, Rabbi Shergil's song *Bulla ki jaana mein kaun*[5] (How do I, Bulla (the poet) know who am I?) sends a very strong message. We also clearly see the formation of a new cultural persona, rejecting identity politics without even lapsing into a mode of surrender and in one joyous affirmation of self-hood, we witness the Sufi song move beyond the glorified capitulation of the self to an imagined ultimate subject. At times, the Sufi songs have been used as means of critiquing historical and social narratives of films and as a way of reaffirming religion.

But gradually the Sufi song has moved beyond generic confines and its eclectic energy has drawn liberally from diverse sources. Interestingly, Sufi music is not generically non-existent but this music has never been exclusively about music like Indian classical music which creates locally viable devotional expression through various ragas. It is driven by an etiquette of spirituality and its concomitant rituals where supplication is also one but today it is monitored by the Indian film and cultural industry as a fetish object on one hand and is espoused by radical cultural artists as a poignant tool of resistance on the other. Popular Sufi singer Hansraj Hans feels Bollywood music has taken a lot of liberty with this genre, 'The words and the essence of the kalaams (works) cannot change, only the orchestra can change', while Sukhwinder says 'this genre should not be over utilized in films. Too many Sufi songs would take away the true fragrance of purity from them, overuse would dilute them. Herd mentality is never productive' (IANS-Indo American News Service at Delhi International Music Festival). For Indian films, this combination of melody and lyric believed to make God accessible to the devotee, transcending all religious barriers becomes the formula for a box office hit. It is a genre so mystical that it makes materialism of any kind irrelevant but now Sufi elements find their way into every soundtrack—coming out of car stereos and cell phones—which always cannot be applauded. Even the group *Junoon* packaged their songs as Sufi. A wide range of idioms that are neither orthodox nor Sufi can be seen in the songs.

Filmmaker Muzzafar Ali, a strong advocate of Sufism, always quotes the great Sufi poet saint of the 14th century Amir Khusrau who, he believes, was an harbinger of sublime peace and whose multicultural pluralistic identity can heal the wounds of the world. He revived the *Jahane Khusrau* Sufi music festival and constantly works to promote Sufi artists. In an interview to Prashant Nanda, he stressed the point that, 'the Sufi alone can bridge the divide and bring the much needed peace to the continent'.

To conclude, there should be a balance between the commercial and purer purposes. No art form can remain static and therefore change is inevitable, but to brand a piece of music as Sufi because it is good marketing strategy is wrong. Can packaging and purity go together? The film industry has an answer to this— 'The philosophy might be profound but it is easy on the tongue' and as Prasoon Joshi says—'The listeners get the satisfaction of being religious without having to follow the associated rituals, it addresses the vulnerability in people, their need and desire to belong and seek comfort from some higher, superior power'. In this century, devotional expression has found many venues and listening itself constitutes devotional behaviour. A genuine Sufi song has many layers but Bollywood has married the sacred with the profane and experimented liberally with it. In *Maula mere lele meri jaan* from *Chak De! India*, a nation is addressed in the Almighty, while a plea to God politically happens in another lyric, *Sajda/Noor e khuda* in *My Name is Khan*.

The composite culture advocated through music became the prime instrument of inverting the communal construction of history. Now these songs reach out to touch humanistic themes. In a traditional Sufi congregation, the performing musicians and devout followers were supposed to be bound together in a highly coded etiquette of listening and spiritual bonding. It is essential for fakirs and qalandar in the dargah to be knowledgable in order to understand that phraseology is more important than the tune, but the age of fakirs has withered, the khanqahs and dargahs have receded. One can be a non-Muslim, even an atheist, and still enjoy Sufi music. The new exponents of Sufi music have emerged from chaotically diverse backgrounds of cultural fluidity, transgressions and musical lineage, providing new vocabulary to cross-cultural diaspora, travelling histories, global tourism, and parasitic film and cultural industries. In another sense, its creative reach has been stretched and has begun to extend well beyond the ambit of Islam or even what had been understood as Sufism in the popular perception. The very nature of Sufi music stands radically changed. In the light of these changes, a series of questions are bound to arise even as this cultural shift ushered in completely new and unexpected possibilities.

Perhaps the single most important fallout of this emergent phenomenon is that more and more people understand what they do of Sufism through what they receive as Sufi music. There is a clearer desire to reinstall Sufi music beyond the pale of religion, at times paradoxically within modes of cloned religiosity. In other words, there is perhaps a problematic but celebrative conflation of Sufi music with the idea of Sufism as imagined and experienced by people across linguistic, cultural and religious boundaries. The very idea of music changed in view of its growing dissociation from its spiritual history and the centres of spirituality in which it flourished and developed for almost a thousand years.

The ethno-musicological Sufi tradition of the Islamic world has now tended to focus on music as means of forging new local spiritual solidarities and bringing together people in unprecedented ways. The communication technology has not just disseminated Sufi music but also integrated it with the growing idea of cultural industry. Therefore, it will not be wrong to say that Sufi music and tradition in Indian films and beyond have also relocated and readdressed the very question of Sufism.

Notes

1. *Hamd*, in the Islamic tradition, is a poem/composition in praise of God.

   Lab pe aati hai dua banke tamanna meri
   Zindagi shama k isurat ho khudaya meri

   (A fervent wish keeps coming to my lips/My life may glow like an impassioned flame, O God!)

   Door duniyaka mere dam andhera ho jaaye
   Harjagah mere chamakane se ujaala ho jaaye

   (My deeds may dispel the world's darkness/With my sparkle may the entire world light up!)

   Ho mere dam se yoon hi mere watan ki zeenat
   Jis tarah phool se hoti hai chaman ki izeenat

   (Because of my deeds may my homeland dazzle/Just as a garden blossom) through its flowers.)

   Zindagi ho meri parwaane ki surat ya rab
   Ilm ki shama se ho mujh ko mohabbat ya rab

   (O Lord! My life may be the life of a moth/O Lord! May the flame of knowledge be my love)

   Ho mera kaam garibon ki himaayat karna
   Dard-mandon se zaifon se mohabbat karna

   (May all my deeds be supportive of the poor/May I forever the suffering humanity love.)

   Mere Allah buraai se bachaanaa mujh ko
   Nek jo raah ho us raah pe chalaanaa mujh ko

   (Protect me, O God, from the evil path/Make me tread the path of good deeds, O Lord!)

2. A mode of group singing associated primarily with Sufi music. Structurally, it consists of a *naghma* (melody) played on instruments, a *rubai* or a poetic verse that precedes the main composition cutting into the *naghme*, a *mukhra* or refrain which may be like the *antara* or the stanzas that follow by obsessive argumentation of *takraar* or may go out of the main song altogether to tie a knot outside, *girahlugaana*, and fortify a polemical loop before returning to the main song. Qawwali is often led by one or two main singers who are supported by a group who provide vocal and rhythmic

support by clapping their hands to fixed beat structures as in: *Na To Karvaan ki Talash Hai.*

3. *Zikr* is a creative act of remembrance in a collective Sufi ceremony of listening known as *sama.*
4. To pick a few examples from the poem at random, the following lines clearly invoke the poets whose names are parenthesised:

   Ishq aazaad hai, Hindu na musalmaạn hai ishq (Bulleh Shah)

   Aap hi dhamar hai aur aap hi imaan hai ishq (Bulleh Shah, GhulamFarid)

   Us haqiqat ka garajataa huaa ilaan hai ishq (Sultan Bahu, Bulleh Shah)

   Allah rasul ka farmaan ishq hai (Waris Shah)

   Yaane hafiz ishq hai, quraan ishq hai (GhulamFarid)
5. '*Na main Arabi na Lahori, na main Hindi shehar Nagaori, na Hindu na Turk Pashauri, Na main bhed mazhab da payana main aadam hawwa jayana koi apna naam dharaya, Avvala akhar aap nu janana koi dooja hor pacchana, Mai to na koi hor sayana, Bulleh Shah kharha hai kaun, Bulla ki jaana main kaun*'—*Baba Bulleh Shah.* (Neither do I come from Arab, nor Lahore, I am not Turk nor am I from a Hindi speaking area, I do not know any religion. Born of Adam and Eve, I have taken any name. Who is to know me. Some wise man has to distinguish what is pure and authentic, how do I know who am I?)

Works Cited

Joshi, Namrata. 'Mumbai's Mast Calendar'. *Outlook.* 15 February 2010.

Kungle, Scott. *Sufis and Saint Bodies: Mysticism, Corporeality and the Sacred Power in Islam.* Austin: University of Texas Press, 2007.

Nanda, Prashant. In an interview with Muzzafar Ali on Friday, 30 September 2005. (http://www.imdb.com)

Rajinder, Jai (interviewer). IANS-Indo American News Service at Delhi International Music Festival. 16 November 2009 (http://in.news.yahoo.com/jazz.delhi-20110405-html)

Filmography

Anwar. Dir. Manish Jha. Prod. Rajesh Singh. Perf. Siddharth Koirala, Nauheed Cyrusi, Manisha Koirala, Vijay Raaz. 2006.

Bandit Queen. Dir. Shekhar Kapoor. Prod. Bobby Bedi. Perf. Seema Biswas, Aditya Shrivastava. 1994.

Barsaat ki Raat. Dir. P.L. Santoshi. Prod. R. Chandra. Perf. Bharat Bhushan, Shyama, Madhubala.1960.

Chak De! India. Dir. Shimit Amin. Prod. Aditya Chopra and Yash Chopra. Perf. Shahrukh Khan, Vidya Malvade, Sagarika Ghatge, Shubhi Mehta, Seema Azmi. 2007.

Delhi 6. Dir. Rakeysh Omprakash. Prod. Rakeysh Omprakash and Ronnie Screwwala. Perf. Abhishek Bachchan, Sonam Kapoor, Rishi Kapoor, Waheeda Rehman, Om Puri. 2009.

Gangster. Dir. Anurag Basu. Prod. Mahesh Bhatt and Mukesh Bhatt. Perf. Shiney Ahuja, Kangna Ranaut, Emraam Hashmi. 2006.

Guru. Dir. Mani Ratnam. Prod. Mani Ratnam and Srinivas. Perf. Abhishek Bachchan, Aishwarya Rai, Mallika Sherawat. 2007.

Halla Bol. Dir. Raj Kumar Santoshi. Prod. Suresh Sharma and Abdul Samee Siddiqui. Perf. Ajay Devgn, Vidya Balan, Pankaj Kapoor. 2008.

Jodhaa Akbar. Dir. Ashutosh Gowarikar. Prod. UTV Movies. Perf. Hrithik Roshan, Aishwarya Rai, Kulbhushan Kharbanda. 2008.

Kalyug. Dir. Mohit Suri. Prod. Mahesh Bhatt. Perf. Kunal Khemu, Emraam Hashmi, Smilie Suri, Amrita Singh. 2005.

Love Aaj Kal. Dir. Imtiaz Ali. Prod. Saif Ali Khan and Dinesh Vaish. Perf. Saif Ali Khan, Deepika Padukone, Rishi Kapoor, 2009.

My Name is Khan. Dir. Karan Johar. Prod. Hiroo Johar and Gauri Khan. Perf. Shahrukh Khan, Kajol, Jimmy Shergill. 2010.

Paap. Dir. Pooja Bhatt. Prod. Pooja Bhatt and Sujit Kumar Singh. Perf. John Abraham, Udita Goswami, Gulshan Grover. 2004.

6

The Star, the Role and the Spectator

Shahrukh Khan's Recalcitrant Muslim Identity

Gita Viswanath

Shahrukh Khan (henceforth SRK) rose to fame after acting in television serials such as *Fauji* (1988) and *Circus* (1989) that won him immediate appreciation. His first film *Deewana* (1992) became a box office hit which went a long way in establishing him as a star to reckon with. His rise was meteoric with several awards to his credit, even if one of his early ones for *Baazigar* (1993) was shrouded in allegations of fixing. The Indian state also endorsed his popularity by awarding him with a Padma Shri in 1995. Although Indian stars such as Raj Kapoor long before him had won acclaim on foreign shores, none other than SRK received the kind of adulation of fans from UK and USA that he did. His international stature was legitimated with *Newsweek* naming him one of the 50 most powerful people in the world in 1998. According to his biographer, Mushtaq Sheikh, SRK's story is 'the story of a Delhi Boy who comes and becomes a phenomenon' (http://www.blockbusters.in/bollywood/hindi/still-reading-khan/#more-371, site visited on 3 July 2010). He has since moved on to endorsing products, owning production companies, hosting television shows and owning a cricket team.

After creating the image of a contemporary post-globalisation Hindu youth as Raj Malhotra and Rahul Raichand contended in his multiple identities as a diasporic Indian in his early films such as *Dilwale Dulhaniya Le Jayenge* (1995), *Kabhi Khushi Kabhi Gham* (2001) and so on, SRK plays the role of a Muslim character in two films, Shimit Amin's *Chak De! India* (2007, henceforth *Chak De*) and Karan Johar's *My Name is Khan* (2010, henceforth *MNIK*).[1] His popularity as Raj was comparable to that of Raj Kapoor's as Raju or Amitabh Bachchan's as Vijay. As Isani points out, 'The audience believed that Shahrukh was Raj. He became every girl's fantasy lover, every sister's brother, every mother's son. In short, a superstar' (2007).

In an interview in *The Telegraph*, SRK declared, 'I can sell anything but I'll never sell anything in the name of religion. I won't play a Muslim guy just to get a Muslim audience' (Pradhan 2007). I wish to examine the ways in which SRK's identity as a Muslim is implicated in his films in which he plays the role of a Muslim character. The on-screen conflict depicted in a film such as *Chak De* seems to have uncannily played out in an off-screen controversy before the release of his film *MNIK*, the title, at once evoking autobiographical connotations. Further, this paper will locate the reception of *MNIK* in the larger context of the media mobilisations of Muslim stereotypes. Thus, we may view the Indian Premier League (IPL henceforth) controversy in the same continuum as the role he played of the real life hockey coach, Mir Ranjan Negi in *Chak De*.[2]

Star Studies

Before I proceed with the analysis of the Muslimness of SRK, it would be in order to try to understand the dynamics of the making of the star and what constitutes star identities. The star system emerged as early as 1908 in the French film industry and around 1910 during the days of the studio system in Hollywood.

Stars were perceived as having capital value (Hayward 349–350). In India, although the star system existed even in the days of the studio, it actually consolidated itself with the collapse of the studio system.

The process of building stars out of actors involves several agencies such as the media besides the star him/herself. The publicity given to such processes in television programmes, fan sites on the internet and in gossip magazines that elaborate the methods deployed for the construction, representation, dissemination and consumption of star images constitute what Richard Dyer calls 'star texts' (qtd. in Orgeron 194). However, much of the scholarship on star studies ignores the labour that goes into the process of becoming a star. A star is one who remains a star even outside the domain of his performance, that is, the film. He needs to cultivate and build up an image that extends outside the realm of cinema in interviews, gossip magazines, public appearances and the like, which Daniel Boorstin calls 'pseudo events' in his book, *The Image: a Guide to Pseudo-Events in America* (1961). Spectators accept such a meticulously constructed image as the real. According to Christine Gledhill, stars who comprise three components—real, reel, persona—reach their audiences via their bodies (qtd. in Hayward 350–352). Thus, the star image relies heavily on its corporeality. The alteration of the body through cosmetic surgeries, implants, excruciatingly painful work out regimes and surgical procedures constitute a part of the labour that goes into the making of a star. Shahrukh Khan had received wide media attention during the time he was building his six pack abs for his role in Farah Khan's *Om Shanti Om* (2007).

Distance between the star and his/her fan is crucial for the star figure. Qualities of mystique and enigma were considered as defining for a star. A classic example would be Greta Garbo and in Bollywood, Rekha, both of who assiduously cultivated isolation. Although in contemporary times, there is the belief that stars do not exist anymore because they have become accessible to their fans through social networking sites, the star system is still built on an element of enigma. For instance, SRK posts a status on the hugely popular social networking site, Twitter, which confirms such a distance. He says, 'i am in a strange space when i act. like in a bubble. i can see outside but the world doesn't touch me' (Mar 28 via web Retweeted by imsrk). At the same time, he also hints at the capricious nature of the image, which may be modified by the star, in the following two quotes: 'many say be careful not to damage ur image. images r meant to be created broken torn rebuilt. the real should not be damaged is wot i believe' (Mar via web Retweeted by imsrk) . 'Who am I? I am what you would like me to be and still be someone you don't know well enough. I am an aspiring actor and fulfilled dad' (May 26, 2010, reproduced in *Times of India*, Ahmedabad, May 28, 2010).

Media and the Muslim

The problematic of Muslim identity is all the more fraught ever since the 9/11 episode.[3] The expansion of global networks of *jihadi* terrorism has exacerbated the problematic of interfaith harmony. Media discourses are major epistemological tools even as they contribute to the perpetration of ethnic, racial and communal stereotypes. Thus, it becomes imperative that we study the various media forms in order to open up the question of the representation of Muslims because as Youngs points out, 'Studying media is not an "add on" to understanding the constitution of public discourse on security, terrorism and suspect communities, but is intrinsic to the constitution of that discursive reality' (quoted in Manchanda 44). Lamenting about the representation and misrepresentation of Islam and Muslims in his *Covering Islam*, Edward Said caustically remarks, '... the media have therefore covered Islam: they have portrayed it, characterised it, analysed it, given instant courses on it, and consequently they have made it "known"(Introduction li)'. Cinema is one of the most potent producers of visual signifiers and as I have argued elsewhere, it is a powerful medium that constructs historical narratives.[4] For this reason, the paper focuses on one media form, namely, cinema. Speaking of Islam in the West, Said corroborates: 'for most Americans (the same is generally true for Europeans) the branch of the cultural apparatus that has been delivering Islam to them for the most part includes the television and radio networks, the daily newspapers, and the mass-circulation news magazines; films play a role, of course, if only because to the extent that a visual sense of history and distant lands informs our own, it often comes by way of the cinema' (47).

Muslim Actors and Controversy

It is not that SRK is the first Bollywood star who has been embroiled in controversies that are based on the fact of his being a Muslim. Even if the Muslim identity of the actors is apparently disavowed, it unquestionably forms an obvious subtext to the discourse. Dilip Kumar and the controversy over his award, Nishan-e-Pakistan, given by the state of Pakistan in 1998 also indexes the disdain of 'the other.' A year later, during the Kargil war, Shiv Sena chief Bal Thackeray raked up the issue by asking Dilip Kumar to return the award to protest Pakistan's 'blatant aggression on Indian soil' (http://profiles.incredible-people.com/dilip-kumar, site visited on 3 August 2010). Sanjay Nirupam, a Sena member[5] had called Dilip Kumar a Pakistani in the Rajya Sabha (*The Telegraph*, 15 December 1998). Dilip Kumar refused to bow down to such a belligerent extra constitutional power by saying, 'have worked for many years to bridge the cultural and communal gaps between India and Pakistan. Politics and religion have created these boundaries. I have striven to bring the two people together in whatever way I could. Tell me, what does any of this have to do with the Kargil conflict?' (http://profiles.incredible-people.com/dilip-kumar, site visited on 3 August 2010).

Similarly, when Aamir Khan made a statement about the rehabilitation of people affected by the Narmada dam project, it caused a furore especially in the state of Gujarat for which the Narmada dam is as much an affective issue as it is a developmental one.[6] His effigies were burnt and his film *Fanaa* (2006) was banned from being released in theatres in the state. His religious identity surfaced in several interviews and press conferences. Here is one example. To a question 'Do you think you are being targeted because you are a Muslim?' Aamir Khan replied, 'I am an Indian first. Some people call God *Allah* and some call him *Bhagwan*. If anyone kills a person in the name of religion, it is wrong. This issue is not about religion. It is about poor people who need rehabilitation. I have got the right to my opinion' (http://www.rediff.com/movies/2006/may/25aamir1.htm, site visited on 11 July 2010).

SRK's career too is dotted with such contentious issues from time to time. The recalcitrance of SRK's religious identity is evident even in his interactions with his fans on Twitter. For instance he says, 'dont take it personally but wot i eat & drink is really my business. get tired sometimes when ppl tell me how to follow my own religion' (Mar 21 via web Retweeted by imsrk, site visited on 12 July 2010). He was detained in Newark airport in the US as his name featured in the most common names list. He was also harassed by the underworld don, Abu Salem, for refusing to act in a film produced by a Muslim (http://specials.rediff.com/movies/2007/aug/08sd1.htm, site visited on 15 July 2010). Just before the release of *MNIK*, SRK who is the owner of the Kolkata Knight Riders Team (one of the IPL cricket teams) said that the Pakistani players should also have been considered for selection in the IPL teams. This led to widespread protests by the Shiv Sena who blocked the release of his film. He also had to cancel the Lux Cozy deal following the Todi brothers' controversy.[7] As we can see, his religious identity becomes a *cause celebre* for not just non-Muslims but Muslims as well.

The Muslim in Hindi Cinema

Javed Akhtar notes: 'When it comes to "the Hindu–Muslim problem," popular Indian cinema usually shuts its eyes and turns the page, unless [the film is] the kind of saccharine *bhai bhai* treatment [in which] the Muslim characters were unbelievably angelic' (Dryland in Ather, 2009: 185). Rahim Chacha in *Sholay* (1975), Sher Khan in *Zanjeer* (1973) and Zohra Bai in *Muqaddar Ka Sikandar* (1978) are all the stereotypical 'good' Muslims whose representation is imbued with piety.

According to Giddens, outsider representations are characterised by two themes, viz., romanticised and quaint or demonised as urban criminals (in Alia and Bull 2005: 3). Both kinds abound in Hindi cinema. The representation of Muslims in Hindi cinema transformed from the romanticised and lethargic Nawabs, Badshahs and nobles into demonic underworld dons until the image crystallised as that of a fanatic *jihadi*. Few exceptions exist however. Unlike most terrorist films of the 1990s, Pooja Bhatt's *Dhoka* (2007) does not seek to overly dramatise terrorist activities. Rather, it depicts poignantly the problematic negotiations of a minority community in the public sphere.

The scene that shows the arbitrary police checking of vehicles driven by Muslims reveals both statist compulsions in the face of terror and the inescapable fact of the general perception of Muslims as terrorists. The lead actor's (Muzammil Ibrahim) Kashmiri roots make his predicament and his dialogues that much more resonant. *Dhoka* does not show terrorism for secession. It shows it as a contemporary all pervasive, urban phenomenon triggered by fundamentalist groups that has ramifications for ordinary Muslims too. The important category of identity may be inscribed here. When Zayed says, 'this is my country too,' he stakes a claim to this piece of land called India as a Muslim who has every right as a citizen to live a life of dignity. Like Vidhu Vinod Chopra's *Mission Kashmir* (2000), this film too inserts the Muslim hero within the state machinery. (Both heroes are police officers.) From this vantage point, *Dhoka* explores the complexities of identities of people in such locations. Early in the film Zayed says in jest to his friends who ask him to join them for a drink, 'Paanch baar namaaz padne wale ko daru pilate ho?' (Are you going to offer a drink to a guy who reads his *Namaaz* five times a day?) This is a pointer to the fact that a devout Muslim is not necessarily a fundamentalist (as shown in Mani Ratnam's *Roja* [1992]) with loyalties to pan-Islamism rather than nation. Zayed can be devout and yet a secular, loyal and conscientious police officer. The film's secularism does not negate religiosity. We are shown images of Hindu and Muslim characters in the film in the act of prayer within the confines of their homes. Ideologically, the film seems to adhere to the western notion of secularism as separation of church and state by which religion is restricted to the private domain out of bounds to the state.

Films that deal with the partition of the subcontinent provide ample possibilities to study the representation of the Muslims. These films no matter what the main thrust construct the categories of state, nation, citizen and minority. Anil Sharma's *Gadar: Ek Prem Katha* (2001) indulges in two common typologies of depicting Muslims: one in which the Muslim is conflated with Pakistan and two, the caricaturing of a 'good' Muslim. The heroine's father who becomes a powerful politician after migrating to Pakistan is cruel, selfish and domineering. The hero's friend who appears with a tetchy wife and a dozen children reinforces the image of a Muslim as one who produces a number of children. He is also shown to be a true and loyal friend whose sentiments have survived the calamity of the partition and its spread of hatred. Thus, we see the Muslim characters in *Gadar* playing the roles of a villain and a comedian, roles that were necessary components of formulaic Hindi films.

Chak De and *MNIK* stand on the shoulders of such films which deal with the intersections of categories such as nation, state, Muslim, loyalty, insurgency. *Chak De* retrieves from the ashes of sports history, the tale of an obscure hockey coach and uses his story at a time when it would have resonance for audiences who live in a world that is negotiating the complex issues of communal identity, the secular-religious debates occurring worldwide and an upsurge of right wing conservatism. *MNIK* tells the story of Rizwan Khan who suffers from Asperger's syndrome. Circumstances take him to America where his foster son is killed because of the surname Khan. Rizwan Khan then sets out on a unique mission to meet the President of the United States and tell him that he is not a terrorist.

Chak De and *MNIK* may be analysed in the light of a tradition of representations of the Muslim in Bollywood. In doing so, I would stretch the analysis to include the real life controversies that SRK was involved in. We would need therefore to consider three components of SRK: SRK the star, SRK the Muslim and SRK the actor playing the role of a Muslim. These three identities collapse in the roles he plays in *Chak De* and *MNIK*. The paper seeks to problematise some of the following questions: Is his Muslim identity embedded in these roles? What does his Muslimness do to the reception of his films? Can the images of SRK then be collapsed as a victim in both the roles he plays and himself as public figure and revered star?

In the early scenes of *Chak De*, a photographer clicks a picture of Kabir Khan shaking hands with the Pakistan team's captain. It is common knowledge that this gesture is part of the routine of players leaving the field with the losing team members congratulating members of the winning team. But the photographer thought it would be a scoop if he could photograph the Indian Muslim captain shaking hands with the Pakistani Muslim captain. So the scandal is manufactured by the camera of a photographer who always already carries this distrust within him. Would he have clicked the picture had the captain been a Hindu? This is a moot question. What is striking is the entire controversy over Kabir Khan is manufactured in the realm of the hyperreal[8] through the lens of a camera. Subsequently, the scoop is blown out of proportion when the television channels conduct on-the-spot interviews of people on the streets. The interviewees demonstrate the prejudices and stereotypes that abound about the Muslims. For instance, one person interviewed says, 'such people should have left for Pakistan at the time of Partition.' The response clearly presages the popularly held belief that the Muslim is an obstacle to national unity. The content of the scene showing the television interviews therefore ties in with what Said has to say about the media's role in the representation and dissemination of images of Muslims as described earlier in the paper.

The Indian team, in the film, is self-consciously constituted through the incorporation of the region. Each player is a state representative before becoming a part of the national team. Shahrukh Khan as coach is not anchored in any particular region. In the beginning of the film, he is a cast out, disgraced in his neighbourhood as a *gaddar* (traitor). The scene, in which he locks the door of his house and leaves pushing his scooter with his mother walking beside, is staged as a shaming scene, whose length is extended by making him push the scooter when he could have ridden off on it with his mother as pillion. Instead it is spectacularised with the entire neighbourhood spilling out of their homes to watch and participate in the shaming. A sympathetic Muslim woman is restrained by her husband from giving them packed food for fear of reprisals. A father lifts his son on his shoulders to let him 'see' the *gaddar*.

Kabir Khan is missing both at the time of victory and triumph. The same question repeats in the beginning and end of the film. 'Kabir Khan kahan hai?' (Where is Kabir Khan?) It is the drama of an individual overcoming the trauma of being dismissed as a traitor and his recovery from it. All he wants is dignity. Not for him the laurels of resurrecting women's hockey in the country. His battle has been fought towards the erasure of the little child's writing on the wall.

The controversy over *MNIK* springs from a cause external to the content of the film. Unlike Mani Ratnam's *Bombay* (1995) which ran into trouble for its representation of Muslims, the opposition to the release of *MNIK* centred on the star SRK. What irked the rioters, in fact, had nothing to do with the film; rather it had something to do with that other obsession of the Indian masses—cricket, which along with Bollywood is commonly referred to as a religion in India. However, SRK's remarks about

Pakistani players called into question the Muslim as distrustful and unpatriotic with loyalty to a holy land outside the geographical borders of India. Kabir Khan, the character in *Chak De* and SRK, the star are uncannily subjected to similar persecution.

Since a Muslim's patriotism is constantly contested in India, let us first try to understand what this complex sentiment patriotism is all about. Given that the subtext of any controversy about Muslim stars also has to do with doubts about their loyalty to the Indian nation state, we need to have some background about this sentiment called patriotism. It is the most enigmatic of human sentiments and difficult to theorise. Abu-Lughod in her essay on the import and context of television serials in Egypt and the debates they generate on Islamists and the nation says, 'the arena is national and in this way contributes to an ongoing sense of the nation as the critical frame for all aspects of life, including the religious' (20).

What is patriotism? Is it love of one's birthplace or a space associated with early dreams and aspirations? Is it pure mystique? Patriotism is usually associated with something concrete such as land, territory and place of birth. It is, to Gilbert, 'love of one's country, whether one's country is thought of in nationalist terms or not' (5). The term, nationalism is used in relation to a more amorphous thing like the nation-state. According to Gilbert, it involves the 'proper object of patriotism' (5), i.e., the nation. The state deploys a series of symbols in the service of patriotism such as flags, anthems, parades, fleet reviews, etc.

At another level, it is related to the visual politics of performance. Patriotism involves a set of practices that display loyalty to the nation. These practices could emerge from within individual groups or could be imposed from above, i.e., from the state. Pinning a flag on one's dress on 15 August (Indian Independence Day) or flag-waving during a cricket match are some instances of the performative aspect of patriotism. Then there is patriotism at the level of representation. Cinema, advertisements and other popular cultural productions within the nation-space effectively evoke sentiments of patriotism through manipulation of images. Patriotism thrives on creating fictions of the other, such as a dangerously belligerent neighbour, culturally inferior other society and so on. Such beliefs are so cleverly engineered that they give rise to feelings of superiority towards oneself and disdain for the other.

The two films studied here and the controversies about SRK's statements during the IPL tournament address the issue of patriotism. In *Chak De*, Kabir Khan's patriotism is doubted and the narrative revolves around the retrieval of honour for which he strives to get the Indian women's hockey team to win the World Cup. In *MNIK*, patriotism goes beyond national boundaries. While *Chak De* is about Kabir Khan's loyalty to India, *MNIK* makes Rizwan Khan an emblematic figure embodying a 'universal other' by locating him outside India. Thus, the Muslim is no longer a traitor to the country of his birth and residence but he appears as a traitor to humanity itself. Indeed, Rizwan Khan is imagined to be the enemy of the entire human race.

My Name is Khan establishes in the beginning of the narrative a notion of goodness. When the mother explains to her son distressed by the rioting outside that there are only 'good' and 'bad' people in this world, she is creating an ethical discourse that transcends the murky politics of religious divides. Having imbibed this, the hero in the rest of the film sets out on a journey that brings him face to face with crises. Each time he is the sole person out there being 'good' by helping others—pumping out water in a flooded housing colony, moving in waist-deep water to bring aid to stranded victims of a storm, which is a fairly clear allusion to Hurricane Katrina. Bollywood appropriates American trauma in order to establish a notion of goodness that surpasses race, religion, ethnicity and all such divisions based on ascriptive identities. Rizwan's ability to stay uncorrupted in the big bad world arises out of his mental condition, due to which he retains a child-like innocence and simplistic understanding of the world.

In this sense, the film aligns itself with an older convention in Hindi cinema and that is the construction of the 'good' Muslim—Rahim Chacha in *Sholay*, Inayat Khan in *Mission Kashmir* and so on. *My Name is Khan's* character is more poignant as he has to tell the world and especially the powers that be that he is not a terrorist. Unlike Rahim Chacha in *Sholay*, just being good will not do; Rizwan Khan has to scream it from the rooftops, so to speak. Just the way SRK the star had to announce his patriotism in every interview he gave on television, to newspapers and magazines, on his blog and social networking sites to defend himself during the IPL controversy. As he put up on Twitter: 'My stardom is transient. my integrity in non negotiable...my being Indian unquestionable ... hope peace prevails' (http://timesofindia. indiatimes.com, site visited on 12 July 2010).

Issues that are usually central to narratives of interfaith marriages, sexuality and identity are non-issues in *MNIK*. The protagonists are located in the US, the epicentre of modernity. They are more or less neutralised of their religious identities. No explicit coding of body or otherwise marks them as Hindu or Muslim except for the names. However, there is a scene in which Rizwan wears his skull cap and kneels down to pray but his act generates only amusement in the onlookers, one of who even clicks photographs. Praying has somehow remained a persistent sign of Muslim identity, whether it is the militant leader, Liaquat Khan praying in the open in *Roja* or Inayat Khan praying in his house in *Mission Kashmir*.

What does SRK being a victim of Asperger's syndrome do to the narrative the global terrorism in the film? He is at the outset outside of mainstream society, an 'other' of the 'normal.' The otherness of the Muslim then is refracted through the otherness of Rizwan as a victim of Asperger's. Like the cosmetics he markets, which promise to remove surface blemishes, his acts of goodness and kindness are individualistic and have only a superficial impact. Indeed it is deplorable that he needs to go to such lengths to prove his good-naturedness, thereby assuring the US President that he is not a terrorist. Ultimately, his acts can only bring about a 'feel good' sentiment but can do nothing to change either the image of the Muslim or foreign policy. Such a moral/ethical excess found within the framework of melodrama can be pleasing and reassuring to the audience. *My Name is Khan* in this sense is similar to earlier films that dealt with the theme of terrorism in which the humanitarian scores over the political creating a narrative that is depoliticised.[9]

Conclusion

As far as the films go, the representation of Muslims has come full circle from the construction of the 'good' Muslim to underworld criminals to Pakistani agents to terrorists back again to the 'good' Muslim. In *Chak De*, Kabir Khan is unnecessarily sent into obscurity on the basis of a combination of prejudice and media hysteria and needs to work hard with a near defunct women's hockey team to prove his nationalist credentials. In *My Name is Khan*, once again an innocent child is victimised for having a surname like Khan. Rizwan Khan then sets out to undo the guilt of the gruesome act in a narrative that resembles the American road movie genre. Along the journey, he achieves the near impossible task of rescuing hurricane victims and also finally meets the American President. In both films, he plays the role of the victimised. This seems to be the only way in which Bollywood can image the Muslim in its attempt to give space to a Muslim other than that of the 'terrorist' accorded to him in the 1990s. The representation of the Muslim then necessarily swings between victim and perpetrator especially in the post-9/11 global scenario. In his real life, the star SRK's patriotism is in a permanent state of interrogation with the slightest remark from him resulting in public debates and sheer harassment of the star in both his personal and professional life forcing him to make statements such as: 'Nationality: Indian. Born in: Delhi. Owe everything to: Mumbai. Love: My country India, my family & freedom. Desire:

Entertain all...' (http://news.outlookindia.com/item.aspx?674448, site visited on 4 August 2010). The star and the roles he played in the two films studied here coalesce to contribute to a discourse on the vexed position of the Muslim in India and the world.

Notes

1. He also played a cameo role as a Muslim in Kamal Hasan's *Hey Ram* (2000).
2. The controversy was generated by SRK's statement regarding the inclusion of players from Pakistan in the various IPL (Indian Premier League) cricket teams. The Shiv Sena blocked the release of *My Name is Khan* by tearing down posters and burning effigies of the star.
3. 9/11 stands for 11 September 2001—the day when airplanes crashed into the twin towers of the World Trade Center in New York in a suicide mission allegedly master minded by Osama bin Laden. In the specific Indian context, the representation of and attitude towards the Muslim is further complicated by the events of the Gujarat carnage of 2002, in which thousands of Muslims were killed and property damaged as a purported reaction to the killing of *Kar Sevaks* travelling in the S-6 coach of the Sabarmati Express.
4. Gita Viswanath and Salma Malik. 'Revisiting 1947 through Popular Cinema: A Comparative Study of India and Pakistan.' *Economic and Political Weekly*, Vol. 44, No. 36, 5–11 September 2009, 61–69.
5. Nirupam subsequently joined the Congress party in April 2005.
6. 'These are the political parties who promise to take us ahead, these are the political parties who promise to look after us, these are the political parties who promise to look after our poor and needy. They are using force, they are trying to bully (me),' Khan said (http://www.dancewithshadows.com/society/aamir-khan-narmada-bachao-andolan.asp, site visited on 4 July 2010).
7. Ashok Todi and Pradip Todi are facing court trail for the murder of graphics designer Rizwanur Rehman, a Muslim, after he married Ashok Todi's daughter Priyanka. The Kolkata Knight Riders players were supposed to wear uniforms of their brands but SRK had to cancel the tie-up following the controversy. The Muslim groups and

civil societies of Kolkata fumed over Shahrukh's deal. Moreover, Rizwanur's mother had also requested Khan not to endorse a product owned by the murderer of her son. The deal was later struck off (http://www.bollywoodmantra.com/news/shahrukh-khan-cancels-endorsement-deal/5449/, site visited on 9 July 2010).

8. This is a term from Jean Baudrillard by which is meant that the represented has no relationship whatsoever to any reality.
9. See Gita Viswanath's 'Visualizing Terror: Nation, State and Woman in the Terrorist Film.' *Reflections on Theory, Literature and Criticism: Essays in Honour of Prof. P.C. Kar.* Eds. K.C. Baral, Sura P. Rath, D. Venkat Rao. New Delhi: Pencraft International, 2003, 254–267.

Work Cited

Abu-Lughod, Lila. *Local Contexts of Islamism in Popular Media.* ISIM Paper 6. Amsterdam: Amsterdam University Press, 2006.

Alia, Valerie and Simone Bull. *Media and Ethnic Minorities.* Edinburgh: Edinburgh University Press, 2005.

Boorstin, Daniel J. *The Image: A Guide to Pseudo-Events in America.* USA: Vintage, 1961.

Dryland, Estelle. 'Indian Muslims and the Free Press'. Farouqui Ather (Ed). *Muslims and Media Images: News versus Views.* Delhi: Oxford University Press, 2009, 167–201.

Gilbert, Paul. *The Philosophy of Nationalism.* USA: Westview Press, 1998.

Hayward, Susan. *Key Concepts in Cinema Studies.* London and New York: Routledge, 2004.

Isani, Aamna Haider. 'The Man Who Would be King'. (http://www.jang.com.pk/thenews/sep2007-weekly/nos-30-09-/instep/mainissue.htm, site visited on 14 July 2010.)

Manchanda, Rita. 'Media-mediated Public Discourse on 'Terrorism' and "Suspect Communities"'. *Economic and Political Weekly,* Vol. XLV, No. 15. Mumbai: Sameeksha Trust Publication, 10–16 April 2010, 43–50.

Orgeron, Marsha. 'Media Celebrity in the Age of the Image'. Robert Kolker (ed.). *The Oxford Handbook of Film and Media Studies.* Oxford: Oxford University Press, 2008, 187–223.

Pradhan, Bharathi S. 'No Religion Please, I am Shahrukh'. Calcutta: *The Telegraph*, March 18, 2007 (http://www.telegraphindia.com/1070318/asp/7days/story_7533222.asp, site visited on 2 August 2010).

Said, Edward W. *Covering Islam: How the Media and the Experts Determine How We See the Rest of the World* (Revised edition). New York: Vintage Books, 1997.

Note: References to Twitter sites are given within parenthesis in the text.

Filmography

Television Series

Circus. Dir. and Prod. Aziz Mirza. Perf. Shahrukh Khan, Ashutosh Gowarikar, Mita Vashisht, Renuka Shahane, Rahul Bhad. 1989.

Fauji (Soldier). Dir. and Prod. Colonel R.K. Kapur (Retd). Perf. Shahrukh Khan, Sanjay Taneja, Rakesh Sharma, Amina S. Kapoor, Manjula Avtar. 1988

Films

Baazigar (Gambler). Dir. Abbas-Mastan. Prod. Ganesh Jain. Perf. Shahrukh Khan, Shilpa Shetty, Kajol, Raakhee. 1993.

Bombay. Dir. Mani Ratnam. Prod. S. Sriram. Perf. Arvind Swamy, Manisha Koirala, Tinnu Anand. 1995.

Chak De! India (Go for it, India). Dir. Shimit Amin. Prod. Yash Raj Films. Perf. Shahrukh Khan, Vidya Malvade, Sagarike Ghatge, Chitrashi Rawat. 2007.

Deewana (Crazy in Love). Dir. Raj Kanwar. Prod. Mayank Arts. Perf. Shahrukh Khan, Divya Bharti, Rishi Kapoor. 1992.

Dhoka (Deceit). Dir. Pooja Bhatt. Prod. Mukesh Bhatt. Perf. Muzammil Ibrahim, Tulip Joshi, Anupam Kher, Gulshan Grover. 2007.

Dilwale Dulhaniya Le Jayenge (The Large Hearted one gets the Bride). Dir. Aditya Chopra. Prod. Yash Chopra. Perf. Shahrukh Khan, Kajol, Amrish Puri, Farida Jalal, Anupam Kher. 1995.

Fanna (Destroyed in Love). Dir. Kunal Kohli. Prod. Yash Raj Films. Perf. Aamir Khan, Kajol, Rishi Kapoor, Kirron Kher, Shiney Ahuja, Lara Dutta. 2006.

Gadar: Ek Prem Katha (Revolution: A Love Story). Dir. Anil Sharma. Prod. Nitin Keni. Perf. Sunny Deol, Amisha Patel, Amrish Puri, Lillete Dubey. 2001.

Hey Ram (Oh! Lord). Dir. and Prod. Kamal Hasan. Perf. Kamal Hasan, Shahrukh Khan, Atul Kulkarni, Rani Mukherjee, Hema Malini, Vasundhara Das. 2000.

Kabhi Khushi Kabhi Gham (At times Happiness at times Sorrow). Dir. Karan Johar. Prod. Yash Johar. Perf. Shahrukh Khan, Kajol, Amitabh Bachchan, Jaya Bachchan, Kareena Kapoor, Hrithik Roshan, Farida Jalal. 2001.

Mission Kashmir. Dir. and Prod. Vidhu Vinod Chopra. Perf. Sanjay Dutt, Jackie Shroff, Hrithik Roshan, Preity Zinta, Sonali Kulkarni. 2000.

Muqaddar Ka Sikandar (Conqueror of Destiny). Dir. and Prod. Prakash Mehra. Perf. Amitabh Bachchan, Rekha, Vinod Khanna, Raakhee, Amjad Khan. 1978.

My Name is Khan. Dir. Karan Johar. Prod. Hiroo Johar and Gauri Khan. Perf. Shahrukh Khan, Kajol, Yuvaan Makaar, Zarina Wahab, Jimmy Shergill. 2010.

Om Shanti Om (Chant of Peace). Dir. Farah Khan. Prod. Gauri Khan. Perf. Shahrukh Khan, Deepika Padukone, Arjun Rampal, Shreyas Talpade, Kirron Kher. 2007.

Roja. Dir. Mani Ratnam. Prod. K. Balachander and Pushpa Kandaswamy. Perf. Arvind Swamy, Pankaj Kapoor, Madhoo. 1992.

Sholay (Flames). Dir. Ramesh Sippy. Prod. G.P. Sippy. Perf. Sanjeev Kumar, Amitabh Bachchan, Dharmendra, Jaya Bachchan, Hema Malini, Amjad Khan, A.K. Hangal. 1975.

Zanjeer (Chains). Dir. and Prod. Prakash Mehra. Perf. Amitabh Bachchan, Jaya Bachchan, Pran, Ajit. 1973.

7

Absent Fathers, Abandoned Sons in the Divided Family

Hindu–Muslim Relations in Hindi Films

Santọsh Gupta

Indian cinema's contribution to the formation of popular culture is unquestioned since its influence can be seen in matters big and small. It moulds the hair style, dress sense and even the body language of the masses that throng the cinema halls. Films have made their presence felt in social and economic affairs of the country as well by focussing on such matters. Films that support, critique and question policies or ideology of the state or of dominant social groups contribute to the formation of a discursive space within the society. The diverse streams of cinema may work differently but their impact on the formation of different kinds of opinions is significant. Their pleasure-giving role works along with the discursive, reflecting the dreams, desires and unvoiced emotions of the masses. Bennett remarks that these different modes 'vie...with one another to secure the spaces within which they can frame and organize popular culture and experiences' (Bennett qtd. by Jones 126).

Amidst this heterogeneity of opinions and concerns, a persistent theme deals with the making of the nation as a secular, pluralist state with an inclusive, assimilative framework. Indian films, including the Hindi ones, have been engaged with the basic assumptions of the nation as it changed from a colonial to an independent sovereign state. The problems facing this new state, its achievements and failures have been the subject of many popular films. M. Madhava Prasad says, 'I study cinema as an institution that is part of the continuing struggle within India over the form of the state' (9). The shifts in relations between different communities living together reflect the constant reinventing, questioning and defining of the structure of the nation in films using tropes of divided families, absent fathers and separated family members. The attempts made by the nationalist leaders during the 1930s and 40s were grounded in idealism; the efforts, however, foundered as the partition took place. The fire, which has raged all over during the recent decades, continues to singe society's structure, taking in its toll the harmony among people. After the holocaust of the partition in 1947, it was the demolition of the Babri Masjid in 1992 that severely damaged Hindu–Muslim relations in India.

Both the ideals and the disturbed conditions have been portrayed with fervour and intensity in the art produced during this period. Literature, music, paintings and films have dealt with these changing experiences of inter-communal relations. Images of friendliness, trust and the nurturing protection that was provided to members belonging to the other community are found in some well-made films that became very popular at the box office, reflecting their appeal to the masses. Films such as *Dhool Ka Phool* (1959) and *Dharmputra* (1961) show how a character from one community takes care of an infant from another community and gives unrestrained love to the child. *Do Raaste* (1969) was an immensely popular film in which a Muslim neighbour is shown providing financial, moral and emotional support to an elderly woman whose younger son, Birju, has left her. After having received higher education abroad, this son deserts the mother and the elder brother with his (Birju's) family, as their financial condition is not very sound. The Muslim neighbour, simply called 'Khan' (Jayant), quietly comes to the help of this family sending anonymous money orders, knowing very well that the family would not like to receive help from anyone outside the family fold. Khan's quiet affection and the warmth of the mother's behaviour leave a lasting impression of true human compassion, unrestricted by boundaries of community and religious differences.

During this period, some films were made depicting the *tehzeeb* (culture), *sharafat* (decency) and *adab* (etiquette) of the refined Muslim culture. These films were very popular at the box office, where viewers from different classes among the audience responded to the different *masala*—handsome heroes and beautiful heroines, wearing gorgeous costumes, in richly decorated havelis, with mujras, rich poetry and melodious music. This eroticising of the Muslim community and culture gave way to a portrayal of multi-ethnic intermingling with Manmohan Desai's blockbuster *Amar Akbar Anthony* (1977) where the fairy tale plot structure first showed the members of an ordinary man's family separated, and then united, some 20 years later. The three young sons of this man grow up with three different families, belonging to different communities, Hindu, Muslim and Christian. Adult life brings them together when, finally, after melodramatic encounters with the wrongdoers, they meet their parents, smoothly forming one happy, united family and 'live happily ever after'. The film celebrated a golden jubilee at the box office in 1977 and continues to be popular with the TV channels.

The increasing rifts and collisions between Hindu and Muslim communities in the 1990s changed this image of easy going friendliness. Films made during the 1990s have shown these changes with remarkable alacrity and frankness, depicting the absence of a vocabulary of mutual trust and acceptance of the other which creates an impasse whereby the divided people/nation-as-a-family cannot be reunited easily. It is proposed to discuss some of these films where the Muslim characters interact with members from other communities, and the focus of the analysis will be on the emergence of conflicts and friction between communities, the renewed search for trust and goodwill, and the glimpses of such reconstructed trust, as and when it is seen. In some of these films, the depiction of the existing conflict is taken to a further point, expressing some hope of a revival of a better relationship, through new cultural insights. It is suggested that films play an important role in the production of values that are acceptable to dominant classes, creating hegemony in the Gramscian sense, controlled by business concerns, and popular films try to represent the values held by the dominating group. But, some films like *Zakhm* and *Kachche Dhaage* boldly take an oppositional stance, interrupting the hegemonic value system. By doing so, these films critique the prevalent stereotypes and foreground social disruptions. Such films thereby represent not only continuities but also disrupted cultural and social life, drawing attention to other discourses that exist within the country. Opposition of the dominating group's/majority's militant, aggressive and over-riding definitions of nation, national identity and its multi-cultural imagination, is not necessarily done through an overtly political subject or theme. 'Family' remains an important trope, as the films in the 1990s emphasise the divided, truncated family.

Some of the films which take up inter-communal relations to deal with the tearing apart of the social fabric, such as *Kachche Dhaage* (1999), *Zakhm* (1998), *Sarfarosh* (1999), *Rang de Basanti* (2006) and *Chak De! India* (2007), have looked into the doubts, suspicions and anxieties experienced by several minority groups, and their sense of alienation in the Indian society. These films open up the wounds festering the social political body of the country. They see popular sentiments towards the minorities and prevailing hate campaigns as the reflection of an increasingly domineering behaviour of the majority community which needs to look at itself in the mirror of the eyes of the other. The 'other' has been converted into a monster through calculated gestures, but these films try to look into possibilities of human relationships between the dominating and the dominated groups. They record the history of the changing character of the Hindus, Muslims and other groups. One of the outcomes of the wars with Pakistan has been the emergence of a zealous patriotism, generating a renewed frenzy of hatred against Pakistan and Muslims. When a film is set against the background of Indo-Pak enmity then often, in order to highlight the heroic deeds of the ordinary Indian,, Muslim characters are portrayed in demonic shades with the purpose of evoking a jingoistic patriotism, as in films like *Diljale* and *Fanaa.*

Moving away from such stereotyped images, there is, in some of the films, an attempt to deal more sensitively and in a balanced way with the alienation and angst felt by the minority groups in the country as they are frequently treated with suspicion by the members of the community in majority. These portrayals try to deconstruct the stereotypes cast in prejudice and the readymade perceptions. Films such as *Zakhm*, *Kachche Dhaage* and *Sarfarosh* express a concern at the chasm that has been formed between the Hindus and the Muslim communities. Through artistic devices of the trope of a divided family and incomplete relationships, these films try to sensitise the audience/public. These films question the dubious role played by the State's officials, judiciary and police in their ineffectiveness in containing the violence and, at times, fanning the violence to fracture the nation. Through this critiquing and through a questioning of prejudices, a discourse of religious and political tolerance is opened up and new terms are suggested. Part of the popular culture of cinema, these films neither 'celebrate' popular culture 'as the authentic expression of popular values, nor condemn it as the servant of the dominant interest' (Jones 126);

such films rather intervene in the popularly held views, encouraging the formation of a more progressive political approach.

In most of these films, the family becomes an important site for enacting the drama of disturbed relationship between the two communities. Both *Zakhm* and *Kachche Dhaage* are about strained relations between a Hindu father and a son born of a Muslim woman, hence treated as a Muslim by others, specially the other members of the man's family. Such strained relations reflect the difficulties that lie in the possibilities of mutual acceptance by the members belonging to the two communities. Despite having lived together in the same cities, colonies, mohallas, even buildings, on friendly terms, religion becomes an obstacle in any inter-religious marriage. In *Zakhm* and *Kachche Dhaage,* the Muslim sons live with the knowledge of a general hostility towards their mothers and are estranged from their father's Hindu family. Love does not recognise these barriers of religion or other man-made institutions. Yet, life in its totality is lived within a social space. The 'family' of father, mother and child—a natural unit—breaks down in the presence of divided space, separating the Hindu and Muslim lovers. The child and mother, not owned by the father and rest of his family, are compelled to face the stigma of illegitimate relationship, with all its shame, loneliness and deprivation and, at times, pretence.

Living all one's childhood in an atmosphere of hostility and in a separate household has a deep psychological impact upon women and children. As a child, Ajay Desai (Ajay Devgn in *Zakhm*) yearns for his father's visits with as much keenness as does his mother. Living alone makes them relate very closely, yet the child feels the pain of an incomplete family. Aftaab (Ajay Devgn in *Kachche Dhaage*) grows up a lonely and bitter, angry young man, who has lost opportunities of a good education and a respectable social status.

These films also depict the agony experienced by the women who are pressurised into either erasing their original Muslim identities and/or withdrawing into the darkness of anonymity. The mother in *Zakhm* changes her appearance, her lifestyle and even her mode of worship to such an extent that the sons remain ignorant of her Muslim identity. Ajay learns about it accidentally, when she chants the (Muslim) prayer after the death of her husband, Mr. Desai. Anand, the younger son, is carefully kept in the dark (the elder brother helps his mother in this part of Anand's upbringing). As a consequence, Anand is terribly shocked when he learns, after the mother's death, about her being a Muslim. In his ignorance, Anand has become a follower of the fundamentalist, Subodh Bhai and his Hindutva Party. For both the sons, this fact of their mixed parentage leads to obsessive personalities, moulding their social and personal lives. The mother had to hide her real self only for the sake of public acceptance and survival, both of her sons and of her ownself. Aftaab in *Kachche Dhaage* bears the stigma of illegitimacy (like Ajay in *Zakhm*). He is uneducated and has fallen in with smugglers and petty criminals. Consequently, the parents of the girl he loves consider him an unsuitable suitor. The discovery (by Aftaab) of his being the son of a well-to-do Hindu, who has a full-fledged second family is another big shock. For the two sons in these two films, the semi-orphaned and shameful position could have been avoided if only their fathers had owned them as their 'legitimate' heirs and acknowledged the relationship in public. Both these films are built around the failure of the father to own the son, the failure to give him his 'name'. The 'illegitimacy' that haunts the woman and the son becomes a reflection also upon the failure at the macro-level, when the majority community fails to accept the minorities, be they Muslim, Sikh, Christian or others, as belonging to India, having the same right to the home (land) as the others have. The death of the mother in *Zakhm* and of the father in *Kachche Dhaage* precipitates the crisis around which the issues are raised: of belonging to the nation/family, of the making of a secular state and of the role of state authorities in bridging these divisions.

After his mother's death, Ajay (*Zakhm*) insists on burying her as a Muslim, to keep the promise he had made her, for she had firmly believed that after her burial, she would be united with her lover in heaven. Ajay faces the irate younger brother, Anand, the fundamentalist Hindutva leader, Subodh Bhai and angry mobs who threaten to harm him and the 'dead body', in case he goes ahead with the stated intent. In this, he gets the full support of his friends of different religious groups who confront the crowd with boldness, an act which makes a very positive statement regarding love, friendship, religion and nation.

In the entire film, the woman who is the beloved of Mr. Desai (a film producer) and the mother of Ajay, who becomes a music director, is not addressed even once by her first name. She has lost her individual identity as she becomes a symbol of the un-owned wife and beloved to such an extent that she is known only as 'mother'. The son stands up to claim her religious identity only after she has been burnt by the rioters at the steps of a church. The film creates an Antigone-like situation where the state authority, represented by a corrupt police inspector, connives with the militant and illegal authority wrested by sheer bullyism by the Hindutva leader, Subodh Bhai (played effectively by Ashutosh Rana). Ajay's deep sense of satisfaction in having fulfilled his mother's wishes is conveyed through a scene in which, at the end, he imagines his parents meeting each other in a heavenly set up, suggested by clouds billowing all around. Their union brings together the brothers, with the knowledge of the true identities of the parents.

Individual temperament is shaped by social background and its predominant attitudes towards different religious and ethnic communities. The film *Kachche Dhaage* shows the impact of such social conditioning on the two sons of Mr. Pandit—Dhananjay (Saif Ali Khan), born of his Hindu wife, has had all the advantages of his father's affluence and social status, and Aftaab, the Muslim son, who lives in the conditions of poverty, deprivation and disadvantages. As they face each other at the time of their father's illness, they convey all the distrust, dislike and antipathy they feel for each other. Circumstances throw them together as they become embroiled in an anti-nationalist smuggling of arms and bombing. Their destinies are bound together when, symbolically, a handcuff fastens them together. In a couple of scenes, the two run, jump onto a running train and struggle with each other with their hands tied together. This handcuffing forces upon them a physical closeness that gradually undermines their mutual dislike of each other's proximity. They are together in their struggle to flee the police that is more interested in eliminating them, especially Aftaab, than in finding out the guilty. In this ordeal, they learn to see the goodness and human features in the other, who is accepted as a brother towards the end of the film. The failure of the parents to come together as a family is corrected as the young sons accept each other as brothers.

In the film *Dharm* (2007), again, the problem of a Hindu's difficulties of accepting a Muslim child as worthy of his love, is seen against the frame of religious orthodoxy. The central character, Pandit Chaturvedi (Pankaj Kapur), conveys all the shades of emotions that range from his initial reluctance to accept an unknown child (barely a few months old) left at his doorstep, to gradually learning to love it as a human child. He then is shocked when he learns that the child has Muslim parents. The drama of self-disgust and penance, leading to a realisation of a deeper meaning of a humanistic religion, give him a true sense of his *dharma*. All these emotions are enacted with a quiet intensity. The religious orthodoxy that he has adopted is given up by the Pandit when he goes on the streets where violent rioting is taking place and where Hindus are targetting the colonies and homes of Muslims. He walks straight into a house set aflame, in order to save the child he had forsaken. Rescuing the child, he takes him away, overcoming the prejudices created in the name of religious differences. Here, the adoption of the child with full recognition of its religious difference opens up a possibility of the family as one that can accommodate differences.

Alienation from the predominant majority group is part of the growing disillusionment among the Muslim youth—a sense of betrayal is felt when they share the country's history and geography yet continue to be treated as second class citizens, and, worse still, with suspicion. In *Sarfarosh*, the marginalisation of the honest and sincere police officer, Saleem, reflects the growing sense of humiliation and isolation he experiences when his integrity as a police officer is suspected by the other officers who might be less devoted and sincere than him in carrying out their duties. In one instance, he is unable to catch a Muslim smuggler (in Mumbai) and other officers in the department ask for his transfer from the case. When Saleem, in frustration, expresses his unwillingness to continue working for a country which rejects him on grounds of his faith, Ajay Rathore, the DCP, reasons with him that his duty alone is justification enough for him to work. But this constant suspicion in the minds of the majority, necessitating a constant need to prove one's loyalty to the nation, is felt by several Muslims. Another film that has raised this problem is *Chak De! India* (2007) where the Hockey Coach—Kabir Khan—is humiliated publicly as his team loses a match to Pakistan's team due to his mistake. He is labelled a *gaddar* and consequently ostracised. These two characters portray the pain felt by such unjustifiable mistrust. In both *Sarfarosh* and *Chak De! India,* the subtext of the Muslim characters' awareness of the lack of trust among the majority community lends their characters an emotional intensity, making them humanly touching. Their claim to national pride and sense of belonging are undermined within themselves too when they are looked upon and treated as guilty 'traitors'.

While *Chak De! India* focusses on Kabir's deep humiliation and pain to ignite his struggle to vindicate his lost dignity, *Sarfarosh* depicts several other aspects of the Muslim community's relations with the nation as well. In taking diverse kinds of responses to the issue of belonging to the nation, the film effectively dislodges the monolithic image of Muslims that exists in the common imagination. The monochronic 'other' is split and portrayed in different shades—of loyalty, honesty and betrayal. The complex emotional reasons for their stances are also discussed, revealing intensely felt emotions of pain, desertion and self-negation. The characters of Saleem and Gulfaam Sahib, the India-born ghazal singer who has migrated to Pakistan, cover a wide range of emotional responses. The loss of inheritance that Gulfaam experiences is also an inheritance of loss, for as he ruminates about his ancestral haveli, now turned into a deserted lifeless lacklustre structure, he feels his link with his history too has been severed. It was the whimsical political decision of a few individuals at the helm of affairs that has, he feels, suddenly destroyed the past as well as the future for millions of Indians. The deserted haveli symbolises the past grandeur and richness of life that hundreds of thousands were made to leave behind at the time of partition. It also represents the present-day marginalisation of that culture and tradition. Mughal architectural ruins are used in this film, as in some others, to heighten the sense of loss, emptiness and disruption.

The use of Mughal architectural ruins to depict the passing away of a rich culture is made highly effectively in some films dealing with the Muslim social life and characters. While *Chaudhvin ka Chand* (1960) is a comparatively earlier example of this imaginative use of the ruins (Taneja 38), there are films such as *Rang de Basanti* (2006) and *Fanaa* (2006) where the architecture of the Mughal period helps in emphasising the undercurrents of a violent past, loss of a culture and tradition, and also suggest a desire to reconnect with that tradition. Strangely enough, it also points to the Muslim as a member of society and to the Muslim participation in the nation. In the haveli of Gulfaam's ancestors, a cultural tradition of arts and courtesy was nurtured. But, in the aftermath of the partition, as Gulfaam expresses his pain, that link has been irrevocably destroyed. As a muhajir, he lives in a no-man's land, for he has disowned one country while the other does not accept him.

Gulfaam develops a friendship with Ajay Rathore (Aamir Khan) the DCP of Mumbai, who has been put on the case of cracking the network of illegal smuggling of arms, ammunition and drugs into India. As Rathore works on the trail of criminals, he reaches Gulfaam's haveli in Jodhpur. Having accepted him as a guest, Gulfaam refuses to kill the sleeping Ajay when he is told of the real purpose of Ajay's visit. When pressurised, Gulfaam is left with no other choice but to commit suicide.

The loss of this rich cultural tradition is common to both Hindus and Muslims. The composite culture of India, which developed right through the Mughal period in India, experimented with different ways of forging a common Hindu–Muslim tradition. In *Jodhaa Akbar* (2008), the director, Ashutosh Gowarikar, focusses on Akbar's early formative period as the king who soon gained the stature of a great Emperor. Gowarikar's film raised a controversy regarding the historical authenticity about the identity and life of the Rajput Princess whom Akbar had married. One interesting aspect to this controversy was that no such interest in this detail was shown in the 1960s and 70s when *Mughal-e-Azam* (1960) went on to become a blockbuster, a change that suggests how politicised the issue of Muslim–Hindu marriage has become within half a century.

Jodhaa Akbar dwells upon the young Akbar experimenting with different strategies to gain a moral and emotional right to rule over a populace that was largely Hindu, and who were therefore resisting subjects. His careful interactions with kings and advisors of Hindu and Muslim communities show his line of thought. In this film too, family becomes an important space where the king enacts the values of tolerance and respect for different religions and races. The film dwells upon the recognition of Princess Jodhaa's dignity, self-respect and intelligence by Akbar, as he observes her praying and walking about in the courtyard with her attendants. The episodes, in which he banishes her to her parental home and then woos her back, are perhaps totally imaginary; perhaps, the idea is to build up the formation of a genuine sense of the love developing between them, to emphasise that their relationship was not totally one of political convenience and lacked warmth. He treats her (in the film) with courtesy and respect as an equal human being, not as an inferior due to her gender or their different religious and political backgrounds.

Jodhaa Akbar looks into Akbar's efforts to create a secular political atmosphere as he holds discussions with the scholars of different religions. The film shows in one scene a discussion of the policy of imposing a special tax on the Hindus. Akbar encounters the anger of the common Hindu citizens towards this policy when he goes to the market in disguise. His decision to revoke this tax, even though the counsel of the Muslim ministers and advisors is to continue with the tax, indicates his desire to build better relations with the common people, who were predominantly Hindus. His steps may be seen as both democratic and secular.

These films move beyond the stereotypical limited and fixed images of Muslims which have taken on demonic shades in the recent times. While increased hostility now prevails among the diverse communities and even within sub-castes among the communities themselves, these artistic attempts open up the issue of a democratic set-up of the nation as the problems existing within the imaginary construct of the nation itself are foregrounded in many films made in the recent years. India's heritage of multiple ethnic and religious units living together in the spirit of belonging to one nation has survived as repeated efforts have been made, during different historical periods, to give it an adequate ideological and emotional framework. Now, perhaps, in the second decade of the 21 century, it requires us to think beyond, as Stuart Hall puts it, 'the traditional boundaries of the existing political discourses and their ever ready "solutions"' (Hall 219). And, he further observes, 'Difference and identity can be brought together on same grounds if an effort is made to recharge and renew the political vocabularies, recasting of words like liberty and equality, the "good" and the "right"' (Hall 235).

These films do not necessarily provide any solutions to the prevailing problematic conditions, but through individual characters, ideas and actions, posit some hope for better understanding among human beings as they touch a human chord in the viewer. In *Zakhm,* the strong resistance to the erasure of the Muslim identity brings together different persons to act against the rule of the mob. *Kachche Dhaage* brings the two separated brothers together, through their experience of fighting against the wrongdoers—whether from outside the country or within the domestic sphere. In *Jodhaa Akbar,* the historical context of the growing awareness of different religions existing together with respect and tolerance for each other is brought forth. Together, they attempt to connect history and the present.

Works Cited

Hall, Stuart. 'Conclusion: The Multi-cultural Question' in B. Hesse (ed.) *Un/settled Multiculturalisms.* London & New York: Zed Books, 2000. 209–242.

Jones, Steve. 'After Gramsci' in *Antonio Gramsci.* London & New York: Routledge, 2007, 121–133.

Prasad, M. Madhava. *Ideology of the Hindi Film: A Historical Construction.* New Delhi: OUP (1998), 2008.

Taneja, Anand V. 'Muslimness in Hindi Cinema'. *Seminar 578,* June 2009, 36–40.

Filmography

Amar Akbar Anthony. Prod. and Dir. Manmohan Desai. Perf. Amitabh Bachchan, Vinod Khanna, Rishi Kapoor, Nirupa Roy, Shabana Azmi, Nitu Singh, Parveen Babi. 1977.

Chak De! India. Dir. Shimit Amin. Prod. Aditya Chopra. Perf. Shahrukh Khan. 2007.

Chaudhvin ka Chand. Dir. M. Sadiq. Prod. Guru Dutt. Perf. Guru Dutt, Waheeda Rahman, Johnny Walker, Rahman. 1960.

Dharm. Prod. Sheetal Vinod Talwar. Dir. Bhavna Talwar. Perf. Pankaj Kapoor, Supriya Pathak, Hrishita Bhatt. 2007.

Dhool ka Phool. Dir. Yash Chopra. Prod. B.R. Chopra. Perf. Rajendra Kumar, Nanda, Manmohan Krishna. 1959.

Do Raaste. Dir. and Prod. Raj Khosla. Perf. Rajesh Khanna, Balraj Sahni, Prem Chopra, Veena, Jayant. 1969.

Jodhaa Akbar. Prod. and Dir. Ashutosh Gowarikar. Perf. Hrithik Roshan, Aishwarya Rai Bachchan, Kulbhushan Kharbanda, Ila Arun. 2008.

Kachche Dhaage. Dir. Milan Luthra. Prod. Ramesh Taurani. Perf. Ajay Devgn, Saif Ali Khan, Manisha Koirala. 1999.

Rang de Basanti. Dir. Rakeysh Om Prakash Mehra. Prod. Ronnie Screwvala and Rakeysh Om Prakash Mehra. Perf. Aamir Khan, Soha Ali Khan, Atul Kulkarni, Sharman Joshi. 2006.

Sarfarosh. Dir. and Prod. John Matthew Mathan. Perf. Aamir Khan, Naseerudin Shah, Sonali Bendre. 1999.

Zakhm. Dir. Mahesh Bhatt. Prod. Mukesh Bhatt and Pooja Bhatt. Perf. Ajay Devgn, Pooja Bhatt, Sonali Bendre, Ashutosh Rana. 1998.

8

Art and Power Dynamics

Mirza Ghalib and *Shatranj ke Khiladi*

Jasbir Jain

Made more than two decades apart, Sohrab Modi's *Mirza Ghalib* (1954) and Satyajit Ray's *Shatranj ke Khiladi* (1977) locate themselves in mid-19th century India—a period which marks both the high point of a cultural renaissance and the disintegration of the native power centres. It is a period of shifts which went on to affect language, culture, moral values and community equations. The first of these is ostensibly about Ghalib's life while the second about the two chess-players Mir and Mirza who in search of their chess-playing passion abandon home and city. But the royal houses portrayed in these films are the hub of culture and the measures of both power and powerlessness. Bahadur Shah Zafar, the Emperor of Delhi and Wajid Ali Shah, the Nawab of Awadh were both patrons and practitioners of art. Zafar himself a poet, held frequent mushairas in his court. He was also a calligrapher and a connoisseur of art. Wajid Ali was a composer, a poet and a dancer. Both observed all decorum where royal hospitality and behaviour were concerned and adhered to their side of the political bargain which however did not prevent the British from violating the treaties or the many encroachments they carried out on native power. Mid-19th century history raises (but does not answer) several questions about the inter-relationship between art and power. Were these rulers weak, and was their artistic sensibility unable to accommodate the ruthlessness demanded of power? Or was the aristocracy really and truly decadent, too self-engrossed and occupied with its own indulgences to provide and sustain a support system? These questions naturally surface when films are located in this period and, connecting the past with the present, they call for a rethinking on these issues and a self-reflection on our own times. These films work against the background of the years 1856–1857 and raise important questions about the role of the intellectuals as well as of the community. The making of *Mirza Ghalib* came at a time when Nehruvian idealism was still a driving force but one needs to note that the territorial disputes with China had begun while *Shatranj ke Khiladi* was made during the crucial years of the Emergency. These national and international political situations are significant because they too were about power and territory, and about passivity and indifference. At one level both the films are also about failure, exile and loss.

In *Mirza Ghalib*, the court mushaira appears very early in the film, just after the initial scene of the poet's preparation for the evening. It is to mark his entry into the intellectual milieu. Some of the best known poets of the period are present—Mir Taqi Mir, Momin, Zauq, Mufti—but Ghalib is far too different from them to win any acclaim. His 'newness' is not well received. Based on a selection of known and recorded facts about Mirza Ghalib, the film is scripted by Saadat Hasan Manto, the dialogues written by Rajinder Singh Bedi, and some of the ghazals are from Ghalib's own poetry. The poet inhabits a world centred around the court. There are at least four scenes around Bahadur Shah Zafar—the mushaira; the entertainment arranged to distract him from his anxieties when he is downcast and Chaudvin Begum is the one to sing one of Mirza's ghazals; there is then the resultant importance bestowed on the Mirza, elevating his status to the king's Ustad and the fourth scene is the one when Chaudvin Begum's appeals to the Emperor for help in order to free Ghalib from prison, where he is held on the charge of gambling. It is from the court that life flows into the streets as the palanquin-carried nobles move about and courtesans' songs can be heard and fakirs still earn their living through singing in the streets. The scenes shift from dark, domestic interiors, to the court, the streets and then the outskirts of the city, symbolically conveying a subtext.

Satyajit Ray made his debut in Hindi cinema in 1977 with *Shatranj ke Khiladi* based on Premchand's 1924 short story of the same name. Ray however gives an equal amount of attention to the embedded narrative in the story and develops it into a powerful centre of the film, rendering the Mir-Mirza story a secondary one. The Urdu title of Premchand's story, published some years later (in 1928), happens to be 'Shatranj ki Bazi,' a title which significantly changes the focus from the players to the game. The title has several layers of implications. One needs to recall that Premchand was deeply concerned with the socio-political situation and none of his work is free of a political viewpoint. Ray's film deviates in large measure from the text and his changes and additions shift the focus even further. For the main, he draws upon four brief references to the Nawab in Premchand's story: *Wajid Ali Shah ka samay tha* (It was the time of Wajid Ali Shah); *ha-ha-kar macha hua tha* (there was a great deal of unrest); then follows a reference to the recruitment to the king's army, and a final mention of his captivity. Cinematically, after a fairly all-embracing prologue, the film begins with the Mir-Mirza story, but having prepared the domestic ouster of the two friends, there is a ten-minute long scene where the Nawab makes almost a confession of his artistic inclinations, confronts his courtiers, examines the Company's proposal and rejecting it, orders recruitment. This scene has an embedded memory scene—adding another 7½ minutes—and close shots are given of his throne and the crown as he enumerates his reasons for having accepted the throne and the glory and glamour attached to it. Twice he points out, very much like Lear, that he had conceded the power of administration to the Company but not the symbol of authority, *hukumat di hai, masnad nahin di* and fondly caresses the jewel-studded knobs of the jewel-studded throne. Twice the camera shifts to the vacant throne as he climbs up the steps to occupy it—once in the present, once in the memory embedment which also contains his own sudden disassociation from outer reality and a counter-move into the world of poetry. The addition and elaboration of the four reference points shifts the story from the decadent parasitical and failed men, who are equally unable to manage their wives' sexuality as the affairs of the state, to the two contradictory strains in the Nawab's character. The events are compressed in 1856 even as the narrative moves to and fro outside this time frame. The two narratives however freely interact as the Munshi's visit to the chess-players first brings out the ingrained habit of hospitality and then the contrast between the British way of playing chess and the Indian way, the former foreshortens the game through manipulation and unpredictably, while the latter attempts to anticipate the opponent's move. This in itself connects the two narratives. The Nawab has come up against a checkmate as the British move has rendered him helpless. All the ingredients of the chess game are involved—the king, the minister, the queen (mother) and the soldier. It is the assessment of what to expect that goes wrong in the larger power game. The Nawab as well as his mother, the Begum, never expected the Treaty of Friendship to be violated unilaterally on false grounds.

Just as there are four scenes with the Emperor in *Mirza Ghalib*, there are four significant ones of General Outran, the British Resident: the first with his ADC, the second with the doctor, the third with the Begum and finally the fourth with the Nawab. In the first, there is an attempt to understand the nature of the Nawab's talent, this is an in-between area, the ADC is obviously sympathetic to native cultural practices, the General cautious as appreciation would undermine authority; in the second, the General expresses both his disapproval and abhorrence of the task in hand; in the third he is reduced to a worm squirming between his two officers, uncomfortable under the

Begum's questioning, and in the fourth both shocked and galled by the dignity of the Nawab's abdication. Each one of these scenes is played like a chess game. The body language of each player is important. In the two scenes with his subordinates, the General is seated; it is he who commands authority. His officers are standing and answerable to him, cautious and guarded in their views. In the scene with the Begum, he meets an equal and more powerful moral authority, while in the scene with the Nawab, his own betrayal stares him in the face, rendering him intensely aware of himself being a pawn in the larger game. Attenborough plays this role to perfection with his massive body while Amjad Ali Khan's heaviness is redeemed by his anguish, his poetic self and the genuine sense of betrayal. He wins a moral victory at the cost of his kingdom.

One may say there are two parallel narratives, but the break-away segments are more. The Nawab's artistic talents constitute an independent discourse reflecting the use of several art forms and languages. One of his compositions is, *Kaun desh gaye sanwariya* (where has my beloved gone). Wajid Ali was a composer in his own right, composing ragas—Jogi, Jushi and Shah Pasand—writing ghazals and thumris including the well-known *Babul mora nehar chhuta jaye* (My father's home is being left behind). Perhaps he also wrote the first play of our time, *Radha Kanhaiya ka Kanu* and revived Kathak. There is a scene when he is surrounded by the gopis. He was trained in vocal music under ustads such as Basit Khan, Pyar Khan and Jaffar Khan and learnt Kathak from masters such as Bindabin Maharaj and others. (internet ref. http://www.answers.com/topic/nawab-wajid-ali-shah: consulted 22 April 2010). Ray by interweaving his narrative with the Nawab's memories and artistic expression is foregrounding the richness of a culture that reflected the different streams that flowed, into it and redeems the Nawab's position by projecting his artistic contribution. Simultaneously, there is also a construction of the national culture which is inclusive and not divisive. In preparation for the film, Ray researched extensively both at home and abroad. Darius Cooper provides an account of his researches and Ray himself talked about this interpretation of Wajid Ali Shah in an article 'My Wajid Ali is Not Effete and Effeminate' (*The Illustrated Weekly of India*, 31 December 1976, 49–51). In fact, in refusing to condemn Wajid Ali, Ray came under a continued attack. By shifting the focus from Premchand's perspective, which literally holds the past responsible for our present woes, Ray creates a counter-discourse, at once more complex and balanced. He underlines the political context much more heavily than Premchand and brings out the ambivalences present in the Nawab's character. Nevertheless, the debate about masculinity and femininity has persisted and even Premchand's statement at the end of the narrative, where he clearly states that it was self-absorption and not cowardice which made Mir and Mirza indifferent to the power struggle has not ended this debate. They could stand up and fight and lay down their lives for their own honour. Vinay Lal returns to the debate in 1996 in his article, 'Masculinity and Femininity in the Chess Players' (*Manushi*, Nos. 92–93, January–April 1996). Ray's purpose was very different. His emphasis was on the moral element and not on general decadence. The two figures who stand in confrontation are Outran and the Nawab, and the larger issue is a power struggle between manipulation and trust. More than a century later with the facts consigned to history, one is left to debate the moral issues. Ray was focussed on presenting both feudalism and colonialism and to condemn both Wajid Ali Shah and Dalhousie, 'This was a challenge. I wanted to make the condemnation interesting by bringing in certain plus points of both the sides' (Dasgupta, 113).

A natural question to ask would be what was is it at this point of history, from 1954 to 1981, which attracted a number of filmmakers to turn to the mid-19th century milieu? *Mirza Ghalib* (1954), *Shatranj ke Khiladi* (1977), *Junoon* (1979), *Umrao Jaan* (1981) were all located in the years between the 1830s to 1850s and all have been award-winning films, honoured by the Golden Lotus, the Silver Lotus, Critics' Awards and Filmfare Awards, awards which testify to their cinematic excellence and in these cases even their popularity as their music was played and the tunes hummed all over the country. Each one of these films boasts of good lyrics, some taken from the pages of history—Amir Khusrau, Sant Kabir, Ghalib himself and others by some of the best lyricists of the mid-20th century, and music by composers such as Omar Khayyam, Ghulam Mohammed, Ray himself and Vanraj Bhatia. What was it that stirred the nation's imagination to take up the last days of the Mughal rule, the resistance that failed and the loss of a culture by yielding to a foreign domination? Nostalgia, a critical reviewing in order to set the balance straight, or an attempt at preserving what was worth salvaging and could help in laying the foundation of a composite culture after having faced the massacre of the partition? Or were these parallel narratives of intellectual betrayal and myopic nationhood?

I have already referred to the introduction to Bahadur Shah's court through the mushaira where the Mirza is also present to woo favour with the court and recognition from his peers (*Mirza Ghalib*). His admirers are few and critics many; one of the admirers is acting as a proxy and feverishly writes down every word that the poet speaks, thus becoming the medium of communication first to the *domni* Chaudvin Begum and then through her to the fakir in the streets. Thus art and its appreciation cross all class and social boundaries. The Mirza's poetry is highly Persianised as his emotional sophistication. His self-centredness is indicative of an indifference to religious rituals. The emperor himself is of Sufi inclinations. Wajid Ali Shah's court goes even further and is a living interaction between different cultures as it moves freely between languages and art forms. The Nawab's tastes are secular and extend to the music, rasleela and dance of the Vaishnava cult. Else the Hindu presence is limited in the films and is represented peripherally by the moneylender in one and the munshi in the other. The two however also represent characteristics essential to the wellbeing of a nation, the munshi is literate, hard-working, politically and socially aware, and shrewd while the moneylender, though feudalistic in his behaviour, is able to generate capital and has the money-power. These two figures comment on the parasitical behaviour of Mir and Mirza in Ray's film and on Ghalib's inability to earn money in Modi's film. (Ghalib was compelled by his financial circumstances to pursue his application for a pension from the British authorities which led to many compromises on his part and the suppression of his personal comments about the war of 1857, leaving a blank for posterity, except in his unpublished diary.)

The Kotwal's intended marriage to Chaudvin is an occasion for all marriage rituals to be foregrounded—the mehndi ceremony, the songs, costumes, jewellery and the bridegroom's procession, the floral sehra—all of it. It is impossible to trace any particular affiliations of these rituals. The Arabic word for mehndi's is hinna, but we have evidence of mehndi applications in ancient Hindu, Egyptian, Middle Eastern and Babylonian civilisations. Practices catch on, mehndi has its medicinal affects, and even if there is any religious significance, rituals cross boundaries. Amongst the jewellery, the side tika as an ornament for her hair is perhaps identifiable as Muslim way of wearing the 'tika' but that is about all. Social and cultural values are shared, even interior spaces are similar as they are dependent on social and gender hierarchy as well the notions of the supervisory role of the elders of the family. Ways of worship may be different but faith is common to all.

Other shared cultural reflections which locate the films in their background are betel-chewing, smoking the hookah, addiction to opium—some of which are encouraged by trade practices and some indicate self-indulgence—and absorption in community games such as pigeon flying, cock and goat fights. These are some of the preoccupations which can be seen running through communities, classes, regions and are present in several films, especially those projecting Muslim heritage or culture, even in a recent one such as *Delhi 6*.

Spatial strategies are used to great advantage in both the films in order to reflect the dynamics of power games, comment upon territory and territorial rights (through the metaphor of exile), and reflect upon personal loss and conflict. Space is also significant pointer to the construction of nation space. In Chaudhvin Begum's life, the staircase to her house forms an important symbol and centre of power shifts, conflicts between desire and compulsion, and the struggle between self desire and social subordination. The open entrance contrasts with the closed doors of Mirza's house, where two rooms have to be crossed to get to him, where his father-in-law sits like a sentinel and the poet is hedged in by a host of factors such as the dark interior, the uninspiring surroundings, the old furniture and most of all his non-appreciative and wife, whose very silence condemns.

Political space is marked by the courts which are gradually being circumscribed in area. When Bahudar Shah Zafar expresses his helplessness to Chaudhvin Begum in Ghalib's case, it is because his authority is limited to the premises of the Red Fort and does not go beyond. Similarly, the Nawab is out of touch with political reality occupied by his own artistic passions. In *Mirza Ghalib*, the ruins where Chaudvin meets her end and where the Mirza is searching wildly for her as he finds his way through the woods and the uneven surface, is a wilderness far from the city just as the mosque where Mir and Mirza find their way in *Shatranj ke Khiladi.* The mosque represents another wilderness. There are no utopias anywhere.

The skyscape is filled with minarets and domes, projections of Muslim architecture, just as the shifting landscape in both the films—*Mirza Ghalib* and *Shatranj ke Khiladi*—marks a shift to wildernesses, lost quests and displacement as the poet and the players move away from cities. Bahadur Shah is taken prisoner though the film, centred on the poet's biography, does not depict this and Wajid Ali hands over his ornate crown which was later exhibited in London. The soldiers are disbanded and the Nawab goes into self-exile. Both the rulers are exiled from the cities they love—Delhi and Lucknow—this exile marking their destiny when even their graves are far away. As Zafar was to write—*Do gaz zameen bhi na milin kuyen yaar mein* (Two yards of land was also not available in the land of my beloved).

No film is an end in itself and a film dealing with a historical period is even more firmly located in multiple frames: its origin, reinterpretation, projection and reception. To these add a layered fifth one—recollection, relevance and remembrance. How do we read these films today, filtered as they are through several layers of time? The question naturally arises what is it in the mid 50s and the late 70s that demands a reference to the past? Any casual search is likely to lead to the times of their making, even as it weighs culture and power constructs; *Shatranj ke Khiladi* made in the times of the Emergency, problematises the overreach of power when rebellion becomes inevitable and examines the impact of power conflicts on the people. *Mirza Ghalib* and *Shatranj ke Khiladi* critique the non-involvement of the intellectuals as well as of the landed aristocracy. They can be read as presentations of a composite past, where domination is human, but there is also an inherent sensitivity, where aspirations clash against reality, where individual loyalties and compulsions lend themselves to narrow concerns, but where certain very positive elements emerge of a very clear move from narrow religious bigotry, with faith as the ruling conscience and an art which brings us together but still falls short of nationhood. They remind us of our lost heritage.

Work Cited

Cooper, Darius. *The Cinema of Satyajit Ray: Between Tradition and Modernity*. Cambridge: CUP, 2000.

Dasgupta, Chidananda., ed. *Satyajit Ray: An Anthology of Statements on Ray and by Ray*. New Delhi: Directorate of Film Festivals, Ministry of Information and Broadcasting, Government of India, 1981.

Lal, Vinay. 'Masculinity and Femininity in the Chess Players: Sexual Moves, Colonial Maneouvres and an Indian Game'. *Manushi* Nos. 92–93. Jan–April 1996. 41–50. Internet source: http:/www.manushi.india/org/pdfs—issues/PDF%2092-93/TheChessplayers. viewed 10 June 2011.

'Nawab Wajid Ali Shah'. Internet ref.: http://www.answers.com/topic/nawab-wajid-ali-shah: consulted 22 April 2010.

Premchand. 'Shatranj ke Khiladi'. *Mansarovar* Vol. 3. New Delhi: Prakashan Sansthan, 2008. 193–201

Ray, Satyajit. 'My Wajid Ali is Not Effete and Effeminate'. *The Illustrated Weekly of India.* 31 December 1978. 49–51.

Varma, Pawan K. *Mirza Ghalib: The Man, The Times.* New Delhi: Penguin Books (1989), 2008.

Filmography

Delhi 6. Dir. Rakeysh Om Prakash Mehra. Prod. Rakeysh Om Prakash Mehra and Ronnie Screwwala. Perf. Abhishek Bachchan, Sonam Kapoor, Om Puri, Waheeda Rahman, Rishi Kapoor, Atul Kulkarni, Deepak Dobriyal, Divya Dutt. 2009.

Junoon. Dir. Shyam Benegal. Prod. Shashi Kapoor/PC Filmvalas. St. Ruskin Bond. Dia. Satyadev Dubey, Ismat Chughtai, Lyr. Yogesh Parveen, Jigar Muradabadi, Amir Khusrau, Sant Kabir. Perf. Shashi Kapoor, Shabani Azmi, Jennifer Kendall, Naseerudin Shah, Khulbhushan Kharbanda, Tom Alter, Pearl Padamsee, Benjamin Gilani, Nafisa Ali, Ismat Chughtai, Deepti Naval. 1978.

Mirza Ghalib. Dir. Sohrab Modi. Prod. Minerva Movietone, St. Sadat Hasan Manto. Dia. Rajinder Singh Bedi. Perf. Suraiya, Bharat Bhushan, Ulhas, Nigar Sultana, Durga Khote, Mukri, Murad. 1954.

Shatranj ke Khiladi. Dir. Satyajit Ray. Prod. Devki Chitra, St. Premchand. Perf. Sanjeev Kumar, Saeed Jaffrey, Amjad Khan, Richard Attenborough, Shabana Azmi, Farida Jalal, David Abraham, Victor Bannerjee, Farooq Sheikh, Tom Alter, Lila Mishra. 1977.

Umrao Jaan. Dir. Muzaffar Ali. PC Integrated Film. St. Meer Hadi Hassan Ruswa (1899), Co-Scr. & Dia. Shama Zaidi, Javed Siddiqui. Perf. Rekha, Farooq Sheikh, Naseerudin Shah, Raj Babbar, Prema Narayan, Shaukat Kaify, Dina Pathak, Leela Mishra, Gajanan Jagirdar. 1981.

9

Muslims and the Freedom Struggle

Mobility in Captivity in *Junoon* and *Pinjar*

Charu Mathur

Films made in India between 1940–1960, whether in Hindi or in Urdu, were usually historical or romantic musicals built on the heritage of films made in the wake of the pre-independence movement, which showcased Hindu epics and myths, martial exploits of the Rajputs, the struggle of the Maratha kings, Shivaji against the Mughals, or yet in contrast, the glory of India under the Mughals before the arrival of the British. It was an affirmation of national glory. Mughal grandeur was a platform for super productions bringing together all the performing arts. This enabled directors to show a national and cultural symbiosis and demonstrate the deep 'Indianness' of Muslims and their role in the cultural formations. Independence in 1947 marked an urgent need to reaffirm this national consciousness and sensitive filmmakers contributed greatly in diffusing tensions arising from the tragic rupture between Hindus and Muslims that had caused the outbreak of communal riots and culminated in the partition of the country. Indian cinema gave adequate representation to the country's second largest community and created conditions for a genuine nationwide Muslim sensibility in India. However, these films are generally not 'scientific' reconstitutions of the past but rather freewheeling evocations through personal narratives embedded in the backdrop of history (Thoroval 87–89). As the question of Muslim presence continues to be equally or perhaps more crucial to the current nationalistic and worldwide debate, films dealing with inter-religious relationships continue to be relevant in the present times. There is a need to create an aesthetics that enables the viewer to develop a relationship with his own physical, cultural and historic reality.

Since colonisation and the struggle for independence was the most sweeping reality India faced in the 19th and 20th century, a number of films were inspired by this phase of history. Muslims being integral players in the freedom movement, two films, *Junoon* (1978) and *Pinjar* (2003), made a quarter of a century apart engage in the depiction of the Muslim position with its cultural and ideological moorings to arrive at a realistic portrayal of the turbulent times. Both are adaptations of novels and look at two different tragic, though not hopeless stages of India's journey towards independence. The path breaking director Shyam Benegal's film *Junoon*, set among the rural Muslim elite chronicles the period 1857 to 1858 when the soldiers of the East India Company mutinied against the British colonial regime, a rebellion which is perceived to be the first concerted effort towards freedom, and hence the First War of Independence. The second movie *Pinjar* directed by Chandra Prakash Dwivedi is set in pre-partition India and details the rivalry between the Sheikhs and the Shahs. The tragic development of this rivalry gets sucked into the larger holocaust of partition. Set against the background of violence, both the films depict situations where non-Muslim women are held captive in a Muslim household. The extent to which these inter-religious captivities result in transformation in inter-religious relationships is a reflection of the role of humanitarian intervention in politically charged situations.

Benegal's screenplay *Junoon* is an adaptation of Ruskin Bond's novel *A Flight of Pigeons* (1980). Though the novel shows the escape of eight members, the film traces the predicament of three English women of the Labadoor family that escape being massacred in the blood thirsty carnage during the 'Sepoy Mutiny'. An old time associate, Lala Ramjimal helps Ruth Labadoor (played by Nafisa Ali) along with her mother Mariam (played by Jennifer Kendal Kapoor) and her grandmother and hides them in his home, risking the safety of his own family members. But they are ultimately located and brought and kept in his home by the affluent Pathan, Javed (played by Shashi Kapoor). The captor Javed is himself captive of his obsession (*junoon*) for the young Ruth. Ruth, in turn, is haunted by a paranoid fear and revulsion for Javed. His wife Firdaus (played by Shabana Azmi) is gripped by her resentment for the English women. Firdaus's brother Sarfroz (played by Naseeruddin Shah) is possessed by a fierce passion to overthrow the British. Their atrocities have driven him to the sword and we get a glimpse of his obsessive hatred in the bloodbath in the church in which Mr Labadoor is killed.

The Muslim cultural ambience is evoked right in the beginning when the title song sings of the famous Sufi saint Nizamuddin Auliya while the fakir as ministerial soothsayer sways and is transported by the music. The camera slowly traces the arches and domes of the ruins of Rohelkhand, a small British cantonment town in the North Indian plains, while the singing gains momentum and intensity. The captivity of the spell grants the fakir a mobility—the ability to look beyond and foresee the future and he predicts the flight of the British: *Kabutaro ki tarah ud jayengae woh*—They will fly away like pigeons. This forms a more powerful exposition to the events to follow than that of the novel that begins with the massacre in the church. The *fakir* in his crazy manner, all along the movie, sounds any change destined to occur on the political scenario and is a prominent thread that weaves the narrative. In the novel, however, the *fakir's* predictions are simply reported and appear to be supportive of action rather than prophetic.

As the story unfolds, Ruth, her mother and grandmother are forced to move rapidly between three different worlds as represented by three different households: European—their own; Hindu—Ramjimal's as their saviour and the Muslim one that of the Pathan Javed who held them captive. Though the Labadoor women belonged to the enemy camp, they enlist the sympathy of both the Hindus and the Muslims they stayed with. Besides, the double inheritance of their mixed blood enables them to survive as Mariam's mother came from a well-known Muslim family of Rampur while her father had been a French adventurer who had served in the Maratha army.

The situational developments are such that they bring about mobility in the positioning of both the colonisers and the colonised. The British who were in a controlling position suddenly find themselves at the mercy of their 'subjects' during the revolt, while the Indians who had been at the receiving end of the colonial atrocities become the ones in command. This is quite apparent in the movie by juxtaposing the first scene of European grandeur with the ones that follow and show the Englishwomen in pitiable circumstances. The predicament of captivity is such that it humbles the captive and turns the captor arrogant.

This absolute division is not sustained for long though, and sympathetic considerations for fellow human beings act as bridges to tone down barriers. The sense of empathy for the Labadoor women is greater in the women of the households. In Ramjimal's as well as the Pathan Javed's houses, their presence was initially strongly resented by the women of the family but this resentment gradually transforms into a humanitarian concern for the enemy. Ramjimal's relative, Ratna volunteers to wash the clothes of the Englishwomen to save them the trouble and even tries to protect them when Javed comes to take them into custody in Lalaji's absence. Javed's wife Firdaus too gradually begins to develop an understanding of their position in spite of feeling threatened by Ruth whom Javed desires to marry. Chachi jaan and her family are quite friendly towards them and even invite them over to their haveli to stay. Proximity with the 'enemy' brings about a visible change in the manner of the Englishwomen too. Though Mariam is firm in her convictions, she is not without flexibility. Her softening stance towards her Muslim captors takes a tangible form in the act of stitching a dress for chachi jaan's grandchild, who is yet to be born. The song sequence, in the film, where chachi's daughter-in-law (played by Deepti Nawal) and Ruth along with Mariam sing while swinging in the peaceful green surroundings, hints at a certain diffusion of inter-communal tension.

A similar change can be observed in Ruth as well. Earlier, she had dreaded the 'pathan' even in the safety of her own home but later she gradually starts caring for him though he is now her captor. The love interest is, however, more pronounced in the cinematic adaptation than in the novel. The shots that show Javed silently yet compulsively observing Ruth in the darkness of the night draw attention to the fear that she harbours against him and the obsession for her that grips him. While Javed's obsession continues to possess him, Ruth's fear undergoes a transformation. Her earlier exclamations of panic later mellow down to gestures of calm acceptance. Her initial desperate rejection when she tells her mother, 'I don't want to marry him' becomes a point of contrast at a later stage when worried for Javed's well being she questions her mother, 'Do you think Javed would return safely?' (*Junoon*). The novel ends with Ruth's admiration for Javed that smacks of self-love rather than love for him when she says, 'I really admire him, because he thought I was beautiful' (*A Flight of Pigeons* 160). But the movie hints at a deeper emotional involvement as we are informed towards the end that Ruth stays unmarried all her life.

The cultural marker of 'dress' is effectively used in the movie to trace this emotional graph. Ruth's change of heart towards Javed can be seen through her gradual acceptance of the Muslim way of dressing. When Javed brings clothes for the Englishwomen and orders them to dress like the women of his family, he is imposing upon them and simultaneously attempting assimilation which is reflective of his intentions so far as Ruth is concerned. Their acceptance of this dress code is at that point of time a strategy for survival. Both Ruth and Mariam are now seen dressed in the traditional *salwar-kameez* in an attempt to establish an equation of harmony with the enemy. It also emphasises their cultural dislocation in addition to the spatial and political one. Ruth's emotional mobility is however highlighted when in a scene she is shown happily displaying herself to her mother dressed in a Muslim outfit complete with jewellery. Mariam's resistance to the assimilation is clearly evident in her degrading reference to Ruth as resembling a 'nautch girl' (*Junoon*). There is no such sequence in the novel which refrains from projecting any sweeping emotional development in Ruth.

The movie also employs a number of cinematic devices not only to create a specific mood and setting but also as signifiers to communicate meaning. Domesticating pigeons is a popular practice among Indians including the Muslims. In the movie, they have a specific symbolic function of representing the coloniser. Domesticated pigeons in Javed's home reveal his desire to subdue them. His fond care for them speaks of his passion for the English girl, Ruth. Even Firdaus refers to the birds as her *saut*, her rival. Later she also expresses her resentment by not feeding the pigeons. The exercise with the pigeons on the terrace that allows them a controlled mobility gives Javed the satisfaction of being in charge. The flight of pigeons in the first scene connotes the hope that the British would leave the country. The shot that shows Ruth happily watching the kites flying in the sky is suggestive of a change in their favour. In a subsequent visual, the harmless pigeons in the sky are replaced by the aggressive kites dotting the horizon indicative of the return of the British, preying on the Indians. The movie also employs the hookah as an indicator of mood. When Javed is successful in locating and bringing the

English women to his house, he inhales from the hookah in satisfaction. When he is unable to have his way with Ruth he is repeatedly shown blowing his frustration into the hookah while his wife's refusal to prepare the *hookah* for him, speaks of her stand of non-cooperation. Also, the pan offered from the pan-dan is a cultural way of showing hospitality. In the movie, Firdaus offers pan to chachi jaan and her family but never to the English women, an act symptomatic of the huge gap between the two communities which may tone down for a while but remains unbridgeable.

When India's First War of Independence failed, passionate anger was replaced by unbearable anguish in the Muslims and Hindus alike. All through the struggle they had been united in their mission and showed no signs of mutual differences. As shown in the movie no action is taken against the Hindu Lala Ramjimal by the influential Muslim Javed for assisting and hiding family members of the 'enemy'. In fact, by locating and taking the Englishwomen away at a time when Lalaji was not at home, he purposely avoids any direct confrontation. The two dominant religious communities were united in their efforts towards freedom and united in their sense of loss when they did not succeed. The mutual blame game had not yet begun.

The movie, like the novel, works from an Indian perspective where the events of 1857 are concerned. Ruskin Bond in the introduction to the novel points out that most accounts were written by Englishmen who saw events from their own particular point of view so that their people appeared to be more human and deserving of sympathy than their 'mutinous subjects'(7). When the native resorts to revolutionary violence, Fanon points out: 'The native is declared insensible to ethics; he represents not only the absence of values, but also the negation of values' (32). The multiplicity of thematic thrust of *Junoon* is evident in the manner in which the movie simultaneously makes a statement of justification for the revolt and also draws attention to the incidents of sympathetic concern by Indians for the very enemy they were fighting against because under the umbrella of humanity no clear cut division is possible and in such a situation the enemy is looked upon more as an individual and less as a member of the faction he belongs to. The movie also highlights the harmonious coexistence of the two dominant religious groups, the Hindus and the Muslims as both maintain strong religious as well as nationalist moorings. The two, however, do not mutually intersect but rather complement each other to merge with the pan-Indian culture and ideology. Sarfraz, Javed and others never allow there identity as Muslims to interfere with the goal they share with other religious communitiest—he goal of freeing India from the oppressive colonial rule.

Though the First War of Independence failed in its desired objective, it rendered a blow strong enough to shake the complacency of the colonial master. He now, as Fanon observes, changes his tactics: 'At opportune moments he combines his policy of brutal repression with spectacular gestures of friendship, manoeuvres calculated to sow division and "psychological action"' (108). Dwivedi's movie *Pinjar,* traces the changed mood of the freedom struggle wherein the seed of discord between the Hindus and the Muslims had already been strategically sown by the British so that their religious identity supersedes the nationalist one. An adaptation of the novel by Amrita Pritam by the same name, the movie tells the tale of Puro (played by Urmila Matondkar), a young Hindu woman living a happy life with her family in Amritsar in a period circling the time of the partition. In order to look for a suitable groom for her, the family moves to their ancestral village Chattovani that now has fallen under Muslim domination. Soon, she is engaged to a gentle young man named Ramchand (played by Sanjay Suri). Her life takes a somersault just before her wedding when a Muslim youth, Rashid (played by Manoj Vajpai) kidnaps her in order to settle an old score. It is evident that Rashid was rather reluctant to do so but was pressurised by his extended family and made to swear on the holy Quran. The kidnapping is a consequence of strained relations extending backwards by two generations. Puro's grand-uncle had kidnapped Rashid's grand-aunt, kept her in his house for three nights and released her in the streets after defiling her. The foregrounding of religious identity results in a politics of hatred.

Held captive by Rashid in his distant farmhouse, Puro is a victim of an other captivity—the hold that an ancient inter-communal grudge has upon the elderly Muslims. Moreover, the refusal of Puro's parents to take her back is indicative of their imprisonment within a mindset of an archetypal social fabric. The dummy car in which Puro's family is shown to pose for a photograph, in the movie, is a signifier of their attitudinal immobility. Puro's progressive brother Trilok (played by Priyanshu Chatterjee) is the only one who does not figure in the picture. At the time of partition, during a move to shift to Hindustan from the newly formed Pakistan, Ramchand's sister who is also Puro's sister-in-law Lajo (played by Sandali Sinha) is carried away by the attacking Muslim youth and kept in confinement as a kafir girl, ironically in her own house. These multiple states of captivities are not static but rather create a dynamics within, affording religious, personal or attitudinal mobility.

As seen in the film *Junoon,* the female protagonist's attitude towards her captor, in the film *Pinjar* also undergoes a transformation. The novel begins at a point when Puro is already married to her abductor Rashid and the preceding events are revealed by way of reminiscent broodings while she is engaged in the mundane activity of shelling peas. She finds her situation so disgusting that she cannot help comparing Rashid's child in her womb with the worm in the pea. The cinematic adaptation adopts a more chronological pattern and begins by showing Puro as a happy young girl looking forward to her marriage to her fiancé Ramchand. Both the novel and the movie effectively bring out the acute sense of personal and cultural dislocation experienced by the victimised Puro, which is compounded by a painful rejection by her own parents. Though this rejection causes her to grudgingly resign to her fate, she is unable to forgive Rashid whom she holds responsible for her plight. Her marriage to him brings their life closer and Rashid's loving concern for her softens Puro's feelings towards her captor-husband. The novel reveals a precipitation of her feelings at a time when Rashid is down with high fever for almost ten days and Puro unswervingly takes care, to see him recover. In the movie, the change of heart is more gradual and reaches a climax in the last scene when she chooses to stay with Rashid rather than go to India with her family and marry Ramchand. The developments in the novel do not leave that option as Puro is shown mothering two boys, her own and also that of the mad woman. Besides in the novel, Ramchand is now shown already married to Puro's younger sister. The cinematic adaptation does not show her in any way bound by motherly responsibilities and also shows Ramchand as a bachelor, still willing to marry her. The film emphasises Puro's conscious choice and also accentuates her developing attachment to Rashid. The scene, towards the end of the movie, that shows her desperately looking around for him highlights the progressive dismantling of walls of animosity paving way for humanist concern and even affection. However, the building of new ties cannot shrug off the persistent sense of dislocation. This is clearly expressed in Puro's voice-over towards the end of the movie: *Koi ladki Hindu ho ya Musalman, jo bhi ladki lautkar apne thikane pahunchti hai, samjho usi ke sath meri aatma bhi thikane pahunch gai*—When any girl Hindu or Muslim returns to her place of belonging, it is as if my soul has also reached where it belongs (*Pinjar*).

The shifting of religious identity especially under coercive conditions is wrought with mutually conflicting diverse pulls that can be very traumatic. Puro's disturbing experience of relocation from one religious community into another is sensitively negotiated in the movie. Her resignation to the forced assimilation into the Muslim fold through her nikah with Rashid was a way of surviving the painful predicament she finds herself in. From now onwards, she is constantly seen pendulating between and struggling with her dual identity—the Hindu identity of her birth and the Muslim one that is forced upon her. Dressed as a Muslim woman in a sharara, or a burkha she continues to be a Hindu by faith and offers fleeting prayers whenever she comes across a temple. We can witness her gradual shift into the Muslim cultural ethos when in an attempt to locate and rescue Lajo, she disguises as a typical pan-chewing Muslim woman doing the rounds to sell *khes* (woven bedspreads), in Rattoval. When under suspicion she proves her Muslim identity by showing her name—Hamida—tattooed on her arm and is grateful for the very name she had fiercely resented earlier. In a spontaneous utterance of thankfulness to God, she utters *Yah Khuda, Hey Bhagwan!*, with Allah preceding the Hindu God. Though under situational compulsion, this is indicative of her steady embracing of the Muslim identity as her own. Yet, linked with it, at this point of history, is another dislocation—the renunciation of India, the nation she had always belonged to, and adoption of the newly formed nation, Pakistan.

However, it has been observed that in times of adversity women not only adapt to the changed situation but also learn to surmount their individual anguish to bond with and support each other. Amrita Pritam's novel narrates a number of incidents that show how Puro surpasses personal grief to extend a friendly hand to Kammo who is at the mercy of her aunt after her mother' death and her father's desertion. She is also in sympathy with Taro who refuses to reconcile to her married status and is a nervous wreck because her husband continues to live with another woman. The cinematic adaptation, however, maintains its focus on women victimised by the brutality of the partition. Puro is shown helping a Hindu girl, whom she finds hiding in the fields to escape further exploitation by men in the rescue camp, by bringing her home and later sending her back to her people in the care of Ramchand. The clever yet risky manner in which she locates and rescues her sister-in-law Laajo and ensures that, unlike her own self, she is honourably accepted back into the family, is indicative of her ability to look beyond her own misery for the sake of humanity and justice.

Imprisoned in his guilt for abducting Puro, all along Rashid tries to make up for his initial unlawful conduct. That act was committed to appease his community but later, to save Lajo, he works against the interests of his community and risks his own life to rescue her and restore her to her family. The sin of abducting Puro on his horseback seeks redemption through the act, carrying Laajo to safety on the horseback. It is only when Puro finally chooses to stay back with Rashid and accepts him as her husband that he achieves some measure of peace.

Social attitudes also underwent a transformation during the insanity of the partition. Religious fanaticism had led to the division of the country. The traumatic experiences that led to and followed the partition mellowed down the stance of both the Hindus and Muslims. This change is evident in the families of both Rashid and Puro. In the course of the developing action, the grudge of the elders in Rashid's family tones down as they decide not to file a police complaint against Puro's brother whom they suspect of having set fire to Rashid's field. Mobility in social attitudes is also seen when Laajo who suffered a similar fate as Puro is welcomed back in her family.

The madness of violence during the partition set in motion by the Hindu–Muslim religious divide is symbolically represented through the plight of the mad woman and the unreasonable claim over her child by the Hindus highlights the separatist cultural philosophy of the times. Religion had lost its moral redemptive role and was reduced to a 'pinjar', a skeleton, a body without a soul. But, the subordination of the religious identities allows the humanistic ones to surface and allow bridges of faith to develop dismantling walls of hatred. Ramchand, a Hindu, embraces Rashid, a Muslim and the man who abducted his fiancée but also risked his life to bring his sister back. Rooted in their religious faith they learn to value the other as a fellow human being.

There is a gap of a quarter century between the making of the two films *Pinjar* and *Junoon*; and a difference of 90 years in the phases of the freedom struggle that they project. During this intervening period the nation had undergone a major communal transformation under the divisive tactics of the colonial rule. Together the movies make a significant contribution in bringing out the nuances of this change. The religious identity of the Muslims portrayed in *Junoon* is subordinate to their identity as Indians fighting alongside the Hindus and other religious communities to overthrow the British. The focal context of *Pinjar*, on the other hand, is the communal tensions between Muslims and Hindus, Sikhs and other non-Muslim communities where the religious identity overpowers the nationalist one. This relational change points toward a mobility in inter-religious positioning under the controlling tactics of the colonial power.

Religious culture is supposed to have a personal and private frame of reference. When religion addresses the public domain, it attempts to subdue secular engagements and prioritise personal faith in negotiation of relationships. When India launched its First Indian War of Independence in 1857, its two major communities the Hindus and the Muslims participated in the mutiny with equal fervour. It was a struggle that accommodated all pluralities. The achievement of independence was the primary target. But ironically, the moment of independence, when it came, was devoid of jubilation for it involved what Aijaz Ahmad terms as the 'nationalism of mourning, a form of valediction' because what we witnessed was not just the British policy of divide and rule but our own willingness to essentialise religion in the construction of nationhood (119). The role of both Hindus and Muslims followed a similar trajectory in the freedom struggle. The equation between the two communities underwent a change under the colonial power. The nationalist culture of

India split into Hindu and Muslim culture each captive in the culture of communal hatred and could be conquered only by mobilising humanist considerations and mutual tolerance.

Works Cited

Ahmad, Aijaz. *In Theory: Classes Nations Literatures*. New York: Oxford University Press, 1992.

Bond, Ruskin. *A Flight of Pigeons*. Bombay: IBH Publishing Company, 1980.

Fanon, Frantz. *The Wretched of the Earth*. Trans. Constance Farrington. England: Penguin Books, 1967.

Pritam, Amrita. *Pinjar*. New Delhi: Hind Pocket Books, 2003.

Thoroval, Yves. *The Cinemas of India: 1896–2000*. Delhi: Macmillan, 2000.

Filmography

Junoon. Dir. Shyam Benegal. Prod. Shashi Kapoor. Perf. Shashi Kapoor, Nafisa Ali, Jennifer Kendall. 1978.

Pinjar. Dir. Chandra Prakash Dwivedi. Prod. Lucky Star's Entertainment. Perf. Manoj Vajpai, Urmila Matondkar. 2003.

10

Celebrating the Courtesan in Hindi Films

Umrao Jaan and *Pakeezah*

Bandana Chakrabarty

Muslim culture has long occupied a significant place in Indian cinema. Muslim culture would mean the culture developed by beliefs, faith, religious or other practices, customs, way of living, art, language, food habits, economy and all other products of work or thought of the Muslims. Ira Bhaskar and Richard Allen in their book entitled *Islamicate Culture and Indian Cinema* (2009) have classified films recording Muslim history and culture in Indian cinema into four categories and one category is devoted to Muslim courtesan films. The present paper explores the tradition of courtesans in Indian history and the portrayal of their tradition in popular Hindi films. Most of the courtesan or tawaif films were released between 1970 and 1986 that is nearly a quarter century after 1947.

Lucknow, Kanpur and Delhi were once great centres of courtly Muslim culture. Going back to history, in Lucknow, courtesans were celebrated as preeminent exponents of fine arts and as custodians of culture. They were respected and revered not only for their talent but also for their polished etiquette and genteel conversation. They were skilled singers, excelling in North Indian classical music; dancers, excelling in Kathak[1] and poets, excelling in Urdu poetry. They were generally highly refined high-class tawaifs who could pick and choose between the best of suitors. Commenting upon their status of independence, Qureshi observes, 'These women could exercise control over proceedings and also over who should be admitted to the performance' (312). The most accomplished courtesans were said to belong to Lucknow, the capital of Awadh. They were either born into this trade or sold into it as young girls. A tawaif or courtesan had to be adept at *mujra*[2] a non-erotic dance where she paid obeisance to the people in the gathering, the *mehfil* as it were. Skilled male musicians were part of these households (the *kothas*).

Lucknow attained fame as a centre of art as it received patronage from the nawabs of Awadh. Wajid Ali Shah, the last Nawab of Awadh, was a great patron of art and music, gave great impetus to the Lucknow *gharana* of the dance form Kathak. This dance reached its pinnacle during this period as there was great royal patronage and the dancers were amply rewarded for their art. The popularity of Kathak as a dance form was due to the institution of courtesans. They were not only brilliant dancers but also gifted poets. As Sunil Kothari mentions, 'They represented a culture and courtly ambience when poetry, manners and aristocracy were found in a harmonious blend' (30). Some of the famous courtesans of this period were Gulbadan of Benaras, Sukhabadan Benaraswali, Jan Baksha Bandawali, Umrao Jaan, Chandrabai Akbarabadwali. Jaddon, another famous courtesan, had captivated the hearts of people for a long time with her skillful singing and dancing. Wajid Ali Shah also maintained a *Parikhana* of courtesans.

If we peep into Rajasthan history we have the example of the Muslim courtesan Anara Begum who was a very powerful courtesan in the court of the Jodhpur King Raja Gaj Singh, who was a Mansabdar at the time of the Mughal emperor—Shah Jahan. She had a say in the day to day administration as well as the authority to appoint the heir apparent. The elder son, Amar Singh, was forfeited of his heirship and the younger son, Jaswant Singh, was made the heir at Anara Begum's behest.[3] A novel titled *Anna Paswan* written about her and a well named after her, Anara Ki Beri, are proof enough that courtesans had great prestige. Even today Anara Begum's *jootis* are kept in the Mehrangarh Museum.

There were other courtesans who were equally famous in the history of Rajasthan such as Uttamrai, Gulabrai, Jonrai, Kishorebai and several others. The Jaipur *gharana* of Kathak boasts of courtesans who sang and danced in the court for the king and his courtiers. *Dastur Komwar* records a large number of courtesans who were on a regular pay roll and reward list of the state of Jaipur.[4] Gulab Rai wielded great power and had authority to mould the administration according to her wishes during the time of Maharaja Vijay Singh of Jodhpur.[5] During the reign of Maharaja Jagat Singhji of Jaipur, Raskapoor, a talented dancer, was given the title of *Adhrajan*. She had the right to mint coins in her own name. Being an intellectually refined lady she was given the charge of the *pothikhana* (library). She herself gave patronage to eminent scholars—Amrit Rai, being one of them. The Brij Bihari temple in Jaipur was constructed by her.[6] These instances imply that these women exercised authority even beyond the palace where they were given patronage.

Amelia Macizewskhi, an ethno-musicologist, says, 'These were empowered women, the tool of such power being their musical ability. They have given to Hindustani music a cultural treasure which needs to be preserved.' These tawaifs specialised in singing *thumri*[7] and *dadra*[8]—a form of presentation where the singer also used gestures to portray the play upon words. They were custodians of cultural traditions and enjoyed great prestige. Usually the suffix *bai* or *jaan* was appended to the names of these courtesans as markets of their professional status such as Gauhar Jaan or Zohra Bai.

The films under discussion are *Pakeezah* (1971) and *Umrao Jaan* (1982) which have courtesans in a major role. Commenting on Muslim courtesan films such as Kamal Amrohi's *Pakeezah* and Muzaffar Ali's *Umrao Jaan*, Ira Bhaskar is of the view, 'The tawaif or the courtesan has been an important part of these films. The dance and music culture of Lucknow has been portrayed in both these films through the tawaif.' To give a brief recap of the films—*Umrao Jaan* is based on the Urdu novel *Umrao Jaan Ada* (1899) written by Mirza Hadi Ruswa based on the life of the famous Lucknow courtesan. Sumita Chakravarty calls Umrao Jaan as 'the quintessential courtesan film of the Bombay cinema.' In the film, a young girl named Ameeran is kidnapped and sold to Khanum played by Shaukat Kaifi who trains courtesans or tawaifs. The first change that occurs in Ameeran's life is that she has to shed her name—her identity—and take on a new name, that is Umrao. She is taught to read, write, sing, dance and charm rich men. The young Umrao grows up to become the vivacious Rekha who catches the eye of Nawab Sultan played by Farooque Shaikh. The two fall in love, but marriage is not meant for Umrao because the Nawab has to marry the girl of his mother's choice. Later, she flees with a dacoit played by Raj Babbar but he is killed by the police and once again Umrao Jaan is left alone only to return to her old life. When the Britishers attack Lucknow Umrao along with others is forced to flee and she reaches Faizabad—the place where she had spent her childhood and sings the mournful ghazal *Yeh kya jagah hai doston* (what place is this, friends).

In *Pakeezah*, Sahibjaan, played by Meena Kumari, is brought up in a kotha or a brothel by Nawabjaan. She grows up to be a beautiful dancer cum singer. Enraptured by her beauty Salim Ahmad, played by Raaj Kumar, convinces her to elope with him. But she is met with difficulties everywhere. She is recognised everywhere she goes as one belonging to the kotha. Eventually Salim renames her as 'Pakeezah' and takes her to a priest to be legally married but she flees from there only to return to the kotha. Meena Kumari retains her purity despite residing in a kotha and entertaining the debauch at night. Courtesan films depict the heroine as a victim where her story is a story of acceptance of fate, of love, rejection and abandonment. Thus, she has been depicted as a tragic character. Hindi cinema treats these courtesans as sacred goddesses. Though they live in the kotha yet they are considered *pak* or pure. Pakeezah means 'of pure heart'.

The 'kotha' as Madhur Bhandarkar has said (quoted in an article by Kazmi) 'is the most secular place where there is no divide whatsoever. There is a strong camaraderie and emotional bonding here that stands out in stark contrast with the rest of society.' The kotha is portrayed as extremely women-friendly. Here, the most powerful person is the chief courtesan. In *Umrao Jaan* it is Khanum who rules over the household. Even the wealthy patrons accepted the authority of these women. Here men occupied subservient roles as doormen, instructors and musicians. With the advent of the British rule in India aristocratic patronage was less available and these tawaifs lost their homes, their kothas and their ability to live independently.

In Hindi films, the 'courtesan' has been portrayed as a victim of men's lust and as an object of the viewer's pity. Being an entertainer she is also the object of the male gaze. Laura Mulvey in her article 'Visual Pleasure and Narrative Cinema' says' that in a patriarchal society, the pleasure of looking is split between the active/male and the passive/female. In films, the male gaze determines the action. She also states that the female images in films can be analysed as objects to be viewed in relation to three gazes: that of the camera, that of the film's spectators and that of the male characters within the narrative frame. In most courtesan or tawaif films, these women are shown dancing for the pleasure of the male onlookers. In *Umrao Jaan* and *Pakeezah*, the combination of the beauty of the heroines and the accompaniment of music and dance are beautifully interwoven into the narrative. It has been argued that courtesan films fetishises the woman's body especially her feet. In *Pakeezah* Raaj Kumar leaves a note ensconced in Pakeezah's toes when she is in the train which says, '*Aapke paon bahut haseen hai. Inhen zameen par mat utariyega. Maile ho jayengey.*' (Beautiful are your feet. Do not step on the ground. They will be soiled.) It is this beauty, which is the object of male gaze, not any exposure of the body.

The courtesan in both the films is not immodestly dressed. As Rachel Dwyer states, 'One of the pleasures of the courtesan film lies in its elaborate use of clothing and make-up' (42). Both Rekha and Meena Kumari look gorgeous in the films. Stella Bruzzi believes that clothing is an important component of eroticism. In both these films, the heroine's clothes 'heighten sexuality by their opulence and rich color and texture' (472).

If we are to consider what is common between the two films we could say that both have nostalgia—nostalgia largely for the lost Nawabi culture. The pain and loss are depicted by the ghazals about the great era that has faded. Lucknow was the centre for Urdu language and culture. Both Kamal Amrohi and Muzaffar Ali have mourned the loss of the culture of Lucknow. Both films abound in symbols of that era—Persian carpets, courtyards, beautiful chandeliers, fountains, pools and the flowery flow of the Urdu language and the melodious ghazals. Both films are romanticised versions of the tawaif. Both are women who are renamed in the film. Ameeran in *Umrao Jaan* becomes Umrao and Sahibjaan in *Pakeezah* becomes Pakeezah. 'As women who are re-named and thereby take on the identity of a radically social other, the move can only be in one direction' (Chakravarty 276). Both the women live life through a series of lovers/patrons, hoping that one of them may bail her out of the degradation of the *kotha* but freedom is not their lot. In *Umrao Jaan*, the events of 1857 become dislocatory factors. Both are victims of circumstances. What is not common between the two films is perhaps the end where Umrao Jaan remains alone, battered and broken in while Pakeezah gets married. Her marriage, she feels, would grant her respectability. Umrao, however, has discovered her own voice and space as she is now a 'heard' poet. The courtesan films, says Booth, are almost certainly not about the social transformation of actual tawaifs—a tradition that existed long ago but on a less explicit level, they are about 'gender, gender identities, and gender anxieties' (4).

The tawaifs had education, independence, money, power and self-determination in a period when many women were treated worse than cattle or were considered insignificant beings. But they were excluded from domesticity and society. Today, the tawaifs have virtually disappeared but through *Umrao Jaan* and *Pakeezah* the producers of these films have presented the narrative of the courtesan tradition, custom, space and the Muslim ethos.

Notes

1. Kathak is a form of Indian classical dance which originated in northern India. It acquired its distinctive shape and features when it reached the courts of the Mughal rulers in the 16th century. There are three major *gharanas* (schools) of Kathak Jaipur, Lucknow and Banaras (born in the courts of the Kachwaha rulers, the Nawab of Awadh and Varanasi, respectively).
2. Mujra is a form of dance originated by the North Indian courtesans or tawaifs during the Mughal period. It incorporates elements of the Kathak dance and is based on thumris and ghazals. It was traditionally performed at *Mehfils* and in houses called *kothas*.
3. Raghuvir Singh (ed.) *Rajasthan Ke Rajgharano Ka Sanskritik Adhyayan* (Jaipur: Panchsheel Prakashan, 1991) 182–183.
4. *Dastur Komwar*. Vol. 26 Folio 335, 1717 A.D. ff 937, 971, 983; 1806 A.D. in Rajasthan Archives, Bikaner.
5. Padmaja Sharma, *Jodhpur Ke Maharaja Mansingh Aur Unka Kaal*, Thesis, 3.
6. Jagdish Singh Gehlot, *Kachhawahon ka Itihaas* (Hindi). Jodhpur: Rajasthani Granthagar, 136–137.
7. Thumri is a form of semi-classical Hindustani music. The text is romantic or devotional in nature. The lyrics are usually in the Uttar Pradesh dialects of Hindi such as Poorbi and Brijbhasha.
8. Dadra, like thumri, is also a genre of semi-classical (vocal form) Hindustani music mostly performed in Agra and the Bundelkhand region.

Work Cited

Bhaskar, Ira and Richard Allen, eds. *Islamicate Culture of Bombay Cinema*. New Delhi: Tulika Books, 2009.

Booth, Gregory. 'Making a Woman from a Tawaif: Courtesan as Heroes in Hindi Cinema'. *New Zealand Journal of Asian Studies*, December, 2007. 1–26.

Bruzzi, Stella. *Undressing Cinema: Clothing and Identity in the Movies*. London: Routledge, 1997. Online version screen (1999) 40 (4): 472. Viewed on 22 August 2011.

Chakravarty, Sumita. *National Identity in Indian Popular Cinema: 1947–87*. Austin: University of Texas Press, 1993.

Courtney, David. 'The Tawaif'. The Anti-Nautch Movement and the Development of North Indian Classical Music. http://chandrakantha.com/articles/tawaif/2 tawaifs.html. Viewed on 20 August 2010.

Dwyer, Rachel. *Cinema India: The Visual Culture of Hindi Film*. New Brunswick: Rutgers University Press, 2002.

Kazmi, Nikhat. 'Tart with a Heart.' *The Times of India*. 16 January 2010.

Kothari, Sunil. *Kathak: Indian Classical Dance Art*. New Delhi: Abhinav Publications, 1989.

Maciszewshki, Amelia. 'Musicians from Another Era'. *The Hindu*, 27 April 2003.

Mulvey, Laura. 'Visual Pleasure and Narrative Cinema'. *Screen* 16 (3) Autumn 1975. 6–18. Online version viewed on 21 August 2010.

Qureshi, Regula Burckhardt. 'Female Agency and Patrilineal Constraints: Situating Courtesans in Twentieth Century India'. *The Courtesan's Arts*. Martha Feldman and Bonnie Gordon (eds.). Oxford: Oxford University Press, 2006.

Filmography

Pakeezah. Dir. and Prod. Kamal Amrohi. Perf. Meena Kumari, Ashok Kumar, Raaj Kumar. 1971.

Umrao Jaan. Dir. and Prod. Muzaffar Ali. Perf. Rekha, Farooque Shaikh, Naseeruddin Shah. 1982.

11

Women at Crossroads

Bazaar and *Nikaah*

S. Asha

Films both project and critique the society, its politics and its shortcomings. Often they also move ahead and suggest the need to move out of the grooves that hold us back. The representation of Muslim culture has been a subject of cinematic interest for a number of reasons. A sizeable minority, Muslims form the second largest community and are an integral part of the Indian society. From the early historical extravaganzas showcasing the splendour of the Mughal period, with characters as royals, a gradual shift can be discerned in the portrayal of Muslim characters. As the subjects gradually shifted to economic degradation leading to survival in difficult conditions, the Muslim characters came to be presented as being marginalised on all fronts or in perpetual clash with people of other communities.

Muslim women characters have found a dominant representation in films as nautch girls such as *Pakeezah* (1972) and *Umrao Jaan* (1981). They represent the desire and struggle of a woman to find a place in the respectable society. However, during the last decade, there has been some conscious effort at probing into the female psyche more intently, with films such as *Fiza, Sardari Begum* and several others. Filmmakers have always shown interest in questioning social issues concerning women. The most prominent among these is the issue of marginalisation of women, socially and economically. Muslim women have often been presented as prostitutes, helpless, penniless, uneducated, dependent and even physically exploited. As such they stand, 'Triply disadvantaged as members of the minority community, as women and most of all as poor women' (Hasan 64). Women are considered as 'objects' available at the market and where they are traded. This paper seeks to explore certain issues related to the rights of the female to her body in *Bazaar* and *Nikaah* both 1982 films. The two films in consideration deal with certain social evils related to economic and sexual inequality. The two issues are marriage and divorce which have a distinct bearing on the identity of every woman. These issues transcend the confines of Muslim culture thereby need better understanding for granting women more respectability in the society. Both the films under discussion question patriarchal domination and distortions of law which affect women's status. In India, however, as the Personal law is based on religious affiliation it carries with it the inbuilt disadvantages and advantages whatever these may be. Several films have been made on women's issues critiquing their struggle against societal pressures. *Mandi* (1981) and *Saudagar* (1973) are films which take up issues similar to *Bazaar* and *Nikaah* and form a parallel discourse while *Arth* (1982) and *Sardari Begum* (1996) focus on women's agencies and choices, the socially oriented films focus on issues rather than on individuals.

Sagar Sarhadi's film *Bazaar* takes up the social issue of the sale of girls through fake marriages which was prevalent in many parts of India. The setting is Hyderabad wherein a poor family is compelled to sell a minor daughter to a rich man settled in Dubai. The director uses a Muslim background to talk of the institution of marriage by placing the woman in a situation which reduces her to a commodity. Smita Patil plays a conflict-ridden Muslim woman Najma, who becomes instrumental in marrying off an adolescent girl to a debauched old man. She ends up tormented, guilt stricken, wounded but wiser than before and begins a search for her own identity as she begins to critically examine her own position. The trauma of the marginalised both in terms of gender and economy, has been effectively incorporated through the self-reflection forced on her. *Bazaar* attempts to expose several practices at once: the sale of a young girl, which her family enters into for practical gains; the fake marriage of the young virgin to a man who may be much older or may further dispose off her for a higher sum and the trade in the human flesh which had specifically caught the attention of the media in the 80s. Hyderabad offers a perfect setting where the export to Dubai is involved. Another centre was Dholpur in Rajasthan and Vijay Tendulkar wrote his play *Kamala* (1982) keeping that in focus.

Such marriages (and sales) violate several legal provisions. They often involve the sale of minor girls, the money exchanged is not really a bride price customary in some communities and these exchanges bypass the woman's consent. All the time there are other issues which simultaneously clamour for attention: the notion of respectability, the restraint and docility expected from a young girl and the unacknowledged prostitution. *Bazaar* by drawing attention to these violations also examines the role of the different agencies that facilitate such sales—the buyers who abandon all moral values, the keepers of law who turn a blind eye, the families who part with their daughters and the other agencies that serve as middlemen. In addition, in this particular film Najma's later realisation of what she has abetted brings in a whole new dimension to the issue. Suddenly Najma's own love relationship presents a contrast. It compels her to see the differences as well as the similarities. In both cases, there is love. Najma's own selfish interest has led to Shabnam's (Supriya Pathak) unequal marriage and, in the process destroying all chances of Sarju (Farooque Sheikh) and Shabnam's happiness. How is Najma any better than the man who marries Shabnam?

Two scenes featuring Najma and Akhtar offer contrast—the first is the one in which Akhtar apprises Najma of the villain intention persuading her to connive in the bride trade; the second one occurs immediately after with Najma facing the long array of women. This is her first moment of realisation but she is also reminded that she cannot get out of it. Similarly, in *Mandi* (1981), the newly wed bride Phoolmani (Shreela Majumdar) is sold to a brothel by her husband. Prior to this scene there is the scene of the deal of the premises which lodges the brothel. Both land and woman are 'objects for a deal'. In *Bazaar*, the camera-eye captures every moment of Najma's struggle with herself. The cramped interiors correspond with her state of mind. Her feeling of guilt persists both in words and expressions. In the scene where all the expensive purchase of bridal clothes and jewellery is exhibited, quite symbolic of the market, she convincingly states, *Bazaar mein sabse sasti cheez hai to woh hai aurat* (woman is the cheapest thing in the market).

In many films, women have been shown selling their bodies to survive compelled by the need for shelter and money. Hence the space of brothel becomes very prominent as a place for projecting women's woes. In *Pakeezah* and *Umrao Jaan*, the protagonists are forced by circumstances to take recourse to the life in the brothel which is outside the circle of respectability. The women herein are basically artists working for their living. But the fact that they are exploited by men, have no right over their self is realistically projected. The artistic ambience of the brothel is merely a cover for the sad plight of the inmates, many brought forcibly by contriving men who trade them, thus compelling them to live a doomed existence.

Najma, herself is a victim. A brief journey to her past, captured through a flashback reveals her Hyderabad origins of an affluent past but now fallen upon adversity. The state of economic deprivation is so intense that the mother implores her daughter to trade her body for the family's survival. A sad aspect of the life of the nawabs, where they use their daughters to support their high living. Najma walks out of this and elopes with Akhtar, content to remain his mistress for six years hoping to lead a settled life with him as wife, which again revolves round the issue of money. *Mandi* brings out this theme with more force. That women have to take shelter in the brothel to survive is a fact openly acknowledged by one of the prostitutes when she says *Roti kaun dega* (who will give us food) to the social worker who advocates honour. Strangely, Najma is dissuaded from taking up a job in the name of honour, in the scene where she argues about the means to survive with her mother. This dilemma is not confined only to the Muslim women but is a one faced by women of most marginalised classes. Not all of the prostitutes in Rukmanibai's (Shabana Azmi) brothel are Muslim women. In fact, the maiden Zeenat (Smita Patil), so fondly reared by Rukmanibai, has a Hindu parentage, as is later discovered. The patron of the brothel Mr Agrawal (Syed Jaffery) himself is the father of Zeenat.

Indian films have presented home and family as the best place for women. In the 1972 film of *Saudagar*, Mahjubi is a widow when Moti marries her and is accepted by another man when Moti abandons her. Marital security is necessary and desirable constituent of respectability, but women seldom have a role in shaping their destinies. In *Bazaar*, Najma yearns for that status of wife, which she hopes could be her ultimate destiny if she connives with Akhtar (Bharat Kapur) in arranging the marriage. She tells her friend that she will absolve herself of the sin of trading the poor girl by offering a 'chaadar' at the dargah. Her nostalgia for her lost identity as sister and daughter is revealed beautifully in the shot capturing her erecting a pyramid of the letters received. The journey to Hyderabad by train can be seen as a metaphor of her personal quest for identity. The film ends with a shot capturing her boarding the train with conviction of having realised herself. In *Bazaar,* we get a glimpse of Muslim customs as the camera captures women adhering to purdah though not very strictly, their tying strings at the dargah, the chick curtains at home, and above all the typical dialect of Deccani Urdu spoken by the characters impart it a realistic setting.

Sagar Sarhadi uses this issue of bride trade as a story to weave a series of questions related to marriage in the Muslim community. Salim (Naseeruddin Shah) becomes the spokesperson of the director. Through a monologue, though uttered in a drunken state, with the lake in the background which stands as testimony to the depth of his feelings, he pertinently questions the unlimited rights of man in possession of a woman both in marriage and out of it. There is a slight reference to the woman as a sacrificial goat, in the scene of the train journey. *Bazaar* attempts to bring to light the wide disparity between concepts and practices. The agony of being 'marginalised' on all fronts comes through vividly but several questions posed in the film still remain unanswered. They are related to the validity of personal law. In Muslim marriage, since the woman's consent must be given in the marriage ceremony, then how can innocent girls be forcibly married? Muslim marriage is contractual; consent forms the basis, even if at times, the consent may be obtained through pressure. Its main features are: payment of dower (mehr) to the bride, witnesses and the provision for divorce by either party; in itself, is expected to be lifelong especially in Sunni law. Women too can initiate divorce. In this it differs from the traditionally sacrosanct Hindu marriage.

If consent of both parties is essential why cannot the girl resist if not willing? We find Shabnam helpless as a woman and more so as a poor woman. A grim picture is conjured up in the film showing uncles and mediators engaged openly in the bride trade. The poverty-stricken parents seek to give away Shabnam in marriage to the elderly man as they need money to marry off her elder sister. Parental roles in such transactions are critiqued. In the film, Shabnam's parents are projected in a hapless state. Shabnam faces the crude reality of being placed in an unwelcome situation. The image of captivity, wherein a pearl strand is brought to measure her anklet with her screaming *nahin Amma nahin* (no mother no) is heart rending and re-enforces her consciousness of being compelled by force of circumstance. She is escorted home in a speeding rickshaw after her visit to the dargah effectively shot in medium and long shot. Strangely, all the celebrations related to her wedding take place while she is confined in a room. This is in contrast to the open space she gets when she is with her lover. Her innocent love is thwarted; the word repeatedly goes that the old man is marrying her; not buying her. The lover too pays the price for belonging to the economically and socially marginalised section of society as he is beaten up. This becomes more pronounced with the director capturing through panshot a line-up of needy women pleading with Najma to facilitate the marital alliance she is aiming at. Najma's quest for identity ends with her finally abandoning Akhtar but for Shabnam the only course left is suicide. The movie brings out the issue of human trafficking in bold strokes, forcing the realisation on the viewer of a whole network of people involved—family, agents, buyers and others. But there is an honest attempt to bring to light a social evil which has affected several women's lives and continues to do to date.

Another film which deals with two vital issues in the life of a woman—marriage and divorce—is *Nikaah*. Although titled *Nikaah* (Marriage), it attempts to underline the traumatic implications of divorce on the female psyche, as a result of the break-up of a marriage. It also projects the struggle of a woman to search her identity in the wake of such circumstances. The movie begins with a photographic montage of oil paintings which are portraits of women. With the voice over of the female protagonist reciting a poem on feminine identity, they serve to stress upon the subject matter of the film. The protagonist, Nilofer (Salma Agha) is educated as well as economically secure. She is married to a loving husband. She belongs to a rich nawab household with its traditional heritage, which is presented in most of the scenes. The ego of her husband leads to a serious rift between the couple and in a fit of anger the loving husband pronounces 'Talaaq' thrice in order to divorce her. The short scene focuses on the couple's expressions in close-ups. The director B.R. Chopra has made an attempt to attract the attention of the society to a practice which is open to misuse. The film questions the law by which a man can summarily divorce his wife by merely pronouncing the word 'Talaaq' thrice. The form of 'Talaaq' used in the film is 'Talaaq-ul-biddat' which happens to be an unapproved form of divorce in Muslim law. It was introduced in the second century of Muslim era by the Ommeyad kings who had found the restraints imposed by the prophet as interfering with their facility of divorce. 'By this way they have tried to find an escape from the strictness of law for the indulgence of their caprice' (Qureshi 90). The approved form of divorce 'Talaaq-ul-Sunnat', though arbitrarily exercised by men, compels favourable treatment towards women. Another point to be considered is that polygamy is permitted in Islam, but there are many conditions laid down for this practice including equal treatment of all the wives.

Zeenat Shaukat Ali, Professor of Islamic Studies at St. Xavier's College, Mumbai published an article in the *Indian Express* with title: 'Divorce, Divorce, Divorce' where she attempts to clear up misconceptions by Muslims and others about the triple pronouncement of 'Talaaq'. She makes several significant observations that divorce is strongly condemned within Islam and arbitration is recommended as the first step in incompatible marriage. Talaaq-ul-biddat or triple Talaaq is something the prophet never recommended. It was legitimised by Caliph Umer as an emergency measure.

The confusion persists more so as it finds different representation in various films. In *Saudagar*, Moti first tells the Kazi his intention of divorcing Mahjubi, then, does so in his presence with the false allegation of illicit relationship upon his wife. In fact, no witness is required for the divorce. Nutan playing Mahjubi realises how she has been used, tells Moti the husband played by

Amitabh Bachchan, *tumne nikaah nahin, sauda kiya tha* (you made a deal, you did not marry). In another popular film *Mere Huzoor* (1968), the wife accepts divorce as if she was accepting the marriage vows. She uses the words, *Maine kubool kiya'*(I accept). *Nikaah* uses incompatibility and male domination as the grounds for divorce. But it mixes up the various forms for divorce permissible under Muslim law thereby overlooking the positive aspect that, though the right to divorce wrests with the man, the procedure is a long one and enables opportunity for reconciliation. A Muslim man is allowed three chances, that is, three pronouncements of the word 'Talaaq' in three different occasions. There is a waiting period called 'Iddat', during which the wife cannot be subjected to harassment of any kind or expelled from the house. If there is reconciliation during this period, the man can take his wife back. However, after a third pronouncement, the wife is totally prohibited for him. She can marry anyone but if he desires to remarry the same woman it is possible only if another person marries and divorces her.

The mixed interpretation of the various forms of divorce is continued throughout in *Nikaah*. The relatives of both the parties disappear as against the rule that relatives and friends can intervene to arbitrate reconciliation after the first 'utterance' of the word 'Talaaq'. Nilofer struggles to strive in a hostile world which is ready to exploit her at every front as is shown in the scenes related to her search for a job. She ultimately marries Haider (Raj Babbar) who loves her, respects her and provides her security. The question of a man's right to even take back his wife after the third 'Talaaq', along with its rigorous procedure is explained to Wasim (Deepak Parashar) by the Kazi when he seeks his advice on the matter of getting Nilofer back as his wife. The wall-clock is used as an effective symbol of Nilofer's endless wait. The director uses even close-up shots to focus the viewers' attention on it. It also figures prominently in Wasim's remembrance of the past shown through a flash back. Consecutive wedding anniversaries with uncut cakes lying on the bedroom table convey the impact of the rift. Images, both still and moving juxtapose the past and the present in the scene of the second honeymoon offer effective contrast regarding a woman's space. Haider's offer of the open space to Nilofer to share her woes with him is also suggestive of the space he is providing for her identity. The diary is another recurring symbol, it signifies a private space Nilofer has created for herself. Even this is violated when Haider reads it. This attempt at creating a space for expressing her feelings at least to herself, almost leads her to her doom as the contents are misread by Haider. He then decides to give her back to her ex-husband. This again brings us to the question as to whether a woman is a commodity of exchange, to be tossed at free will by men in the society both within marriage and outside it. The feasibility of the law regarding the procedure of remarrying an ex-wife is effectively questioned by Nilofer in the last scene. The long monologue raises the issues regarding her 'being', thus concretising the opening stills of paintings on the identity of a woman. She too, like Najma (*Bazaar*) ends up wounded but wiser. Both films succeed in provoking the conscience of the sensitive viewer.

Note: *Bazaar* reminds us of a related news event, the 'Ameena case', which received wide media coverage. On 11 August 1992, most of the news papers carried the story of the rescue of a 'child-bride', Ameena who was spotted crying bitterly by passengers on flight from Hyderabad to Delhi en route to Riyadh. The flight attendant comforted her and exacted the information that she had been forcibly married to a 60-year-old Saudi Arabian national Yahya Mohammed al-Sageih, who was taking her to Saudi Arabia. The man was arrested when the plane landed in Delhi. Her parents subsequently were arrested too. Public sympathy was with them largely because of their marginal status. Sunder Rajan, Rajeswari. 'The Ameena Case', *Woman and the Politics of Violence,* review essay, *Contributions to Indian Sociology.* clipping (113kpbs) 1/1/2002,*CSCS archive.org.* viewed 21 August.

Works Cited

Hasan, Zoya, ed., *Forging Identities: Community State and Muslim Women.* Karachi, Oxford University Press, 1991.

Qureshi, M.A. '*Muslim Law*'. Allahabad: Central Law Publications, 1997.

Shaukat Ali, Zeenat. 'Divorce, Divorce, Divorce'. *Indian Express*. 19 November 2004.

Filmography

Bazaar. Dir. Sagar Sarhadi. Prod. Vijay Talwar. Perf. Smita Patil, Naseeruddin Shah, Bharat Kapur, Supriya Pathak, Farukh Sheikh. 1982.

Mandi. Dir. Shyam Benegal. Prod. Freni M. Variava and Lalit M. Bijlani. Perf. Shabana Azmi, Smita Patil, Naseeruddin Shah, Kulbhushan Kharbanda, Syed Jaffery. 1984.

Mere Huzoor. Dir. Vinod Kumar. Prod. M.C. Kochar and Vinod Kumar. Perf. Mala Sinha, Jeetendra, Raaj Kumar. 1968.

Nikaah. Dir. B.R. Chopra. Prod. B.R. Chopra. Perf. Salma Agha, Deepak Parashar, Raj Babbar. 1982.

Saudagar. Dir. Sudhendu Roy. Prod. Tarachand Barjatiya. Perf. Nutan, Amitabh Bachchan, Padma Khanna. 1972.

12

Personal Narratives

Socio-Historical Reflections in *Zubeidaa* and *Mammo*

Mini Nanda

> For God's sake leave the Kaaba's veil alone,
> There too may be hidden a god of stone.
>
> Mirza Ghalib[1]

Khalid Mohammad, film critic and journalist, has written the scripts of *Mammo* (1995) and *Zubeidaa* (2001), two personal life narratives which form a part of the larger design in the national tapestry, its past shadowing its present. Shyam Benegal[2] has directed them; they are part of his trilogy based on Mohammad stories. Benegal's cinematic *oeuvre* is marked by visual precision and a social consciousness and he uses time as a special device. Its movement overlaps the past and the present, and links the story and its characters. Music plays a vital role in all his films. There is continuity in these two films; Khalid Mohammad has written his own life into the character of Riyaz, who is the *sutradhaar* (narrator) in both the film, which unfold his *bildungsroman* as well. It is a unique cinematic serendipity, when a son narrates the life and times of his mother, his own life from infancy to adulthood and the lives of his two grandmothers who are real sisters.

The theme of the seminar, 'Representation of Muslim Culture in Hindi Films', has two sides to it, one it differentiates and frames a community with its way of life, its religious practices, rituals and customs. On the flip side, it frames a very important issue that needs to be studied and analysed to see if it alienates or converges with other cultures, in the *Ganga-Jamuni tehzeeb* (syncretic ethos) of Hindustan. Is one culture different from say another culture? Fundamentalists' interpretation of religion casts a shadow on cultures and leads to tragic human fallout. While all cultures in an ideal situation should aspire to grant dignity and respect to both the genders, promote compassion and mutual co-existence and tolerance, it does not happen in real life. Is Muslim culture 'monolithic' or is its layered and nuanced? Today, we see a 'stiffening' of identities as Tabish Khair has observed, we divide living bodies in defining them there is 'the concrete enactment of abstract boundaries' (268).

Mammo crosses these boundaries from Pakistan to India as she enters into her sister Fayazi's life and flat in Mumbai. The film becomes dialectic of two nations, two sisters and two homes. Riyaz or Rizu stands at the threshold of boyhood, looking aghast at the newcomer, who he is certain will cause his grades to fall, with her garrulity. Farida Jalal essays the eponymous role of a feisty woman very competently, one who buries her personal anguish with an unmatched bravado. Allaying Rizu's unvoiced fears, she is very considerate and reads namaaz in the bathroom so as not to disturb the young lad. Rizu is a child like any other nine-year-old, self-centred at times, extremely sensitive at other, but vulnerable at all times. He reads Khalil Gibran and aspires to be a writer, and maintains an account of his life in his diary. He lives with his *naani* (maternal grandmother)—Fayazi who has single-handedly brought him up. His mother Zubeidaa, whom he never knew, is dead and his father had dumped him at the time of his birth.

Benegal captures the nuances of their routine very sensitively. Fayazi is usually seen bent over the kitchen stove, preparing tea and meals, and carrying trays to the table; she nurtures Rizu in silent ways. In the centre of the living room in a compact Mumbai flat, there is a large aquarium. Riyaz is very fastidious about his fish and angry with his grandmothers for talking loudly and disturbing them; every evening he plays western classical gramophone records for them. The aquarium occupies the same pride of place in both the films covering a span of twenty years.

Mehmooda Begum or Mammo, Fayazi and Anwari are three sisters born and brought up in Panipat located in Punjab before Pakistan came into being. Mammo tells Rizu about their childhood in the haveli and the fact that Panipat is now in Haryana. She has her own memories of the partition and the nightmare of crossing over when multitudes were rendered homeless. It is Mammo who recounts the national past to Rezu and the living horror of the displaced and deranged people, with deep pain she relates the horror of a mother crossing over with one child held close to her and another holding her hand. When the child in her arm dies it is suggested to her to submerge the body into the flowing river. The distraught mother throws the living child while clutching the dead one in her arms. The ghazal is the background. *Yeh faasle teri galiyon ke, hum se tay na hua*, (freely translated as—The distance to your lane, could not be covered by me), sets the tone of alienation and despair. Mammo also introduces the eminent writer Manto to Riyaz and the three of them go together to watch a film on partition.

Fayazi is silent about her life and her past; she lives in the present coping with the quotidian exigencies. The living room acquires vibrancy with Mammo around, she gives lessons to young girls on the Quran, she decides to throw a surprise birthday party for Rizu. Once again the flat lights up with festoons and laughter, the children enjoy Mammo's pampering. In fact it is

Rizu and Fayazi who feel distanced from the gaiety, both sit and sulk in another room. Benegal draws up this contrast sharply when the party ends both Fayazi and Rizu spew up all their pent up frustration on Mammo who seeks refuge in the Sufi shrine of Baba Haji Ali and it is here that she is reunited with her contrite sister and nephew. The two share a relationship which is normal—full of love, tears and anger.

There is bitterness for the third sister Anwari who has cheated them out of their share in the haveli. The haveli could also possibly symbolise the nation in microcosm, where all siblings lived happily, but with adulthood and marriage, it led to division and bitterness. When Mammo is married in Pakistan her connection with her maternal home is only through letters. Later as a childless widow, she is cheated out of her share and humiliated by her in-laws. She implores her sister Fayazi to call her back. Fayazi ducks her responsibility with the excuse of shortage of space—Rizu is the silent witness to the history of this family. It is Mammo who corrects his impression that his father is not dead as his grandmother had told him but alive and on the other side of the border. He is charged with the idea of reconnecting and reuniting with him, but his father cuts him off once more, and insults him by refusing any sort of reconciliation. It is a hard lesson for a little boy to learn, and he hugs his grandmother—the only parent he has ever had.

Between the two nations, there lies the buried past of pain which creates a climate of suspicion and political uncertainty. The powers of the state, police and immigration officers in India combine to tear the family apart yet again. Despite following official procedures and bribing the officers with her gold ring, Mammo is forcibly lifted and deported to Pakistan, a couple of days before the Eid festivities begin. It is yet another train that leaves for Pakistan. The officer tells a weeping Mammo that it is not about two sisters; the issue is about two nations. This is Mammo's second displacement. Music acquires the role of a character in Benegal's films, the ghazal in the background sung by Jagjit Singh creates the mood of hopelessness *Mushquilen itni bardhi ki aasan ho gayi* (as the troubles intensified, they became lighter).

Initially Mammo would tell Rizu to set the fish free, later she realises that they are secure in the aquarium just as she craves for a home and security of a family with her sister and nephew. After a hiatus of twenty years, the call bell rings with a note of *déjà vu*, a wiser and older Mammo returns for good. She carries her death certificate along from Pakistan to beat the corrupt system in India. It is Mammo who offers a closure to the story of her life; it is her intrepid individual agency that negotiates familial and national space. As Nissim Ezekiel has said in his poem 'Enterprise', 'Home is where we gather grace.' The enterprise was long and arduous one, it was a *bildungsroman* for Rizu whose journey from childhood to adulthood, was woven with his nani and masi-nani and his mother, the absent figure, whose presence falls like a fourth shadow on the three of them.

In the film *Zubeidaa*, Riyaz, now a young man, sets out on another enterprise, while his first one was home bound, especially tied to his desk and his dairy, he now moves out into the world of his childhood and his mother's life, as he pieces it together from her diary and the places she had lived in and the people she had known.

The opening scene is in a cemetery where a burial is taking place. There is the haunting song in the background, *So gaye hain, kho gaye hain* (all have slipped, all is lost), is like a dirge, a closure of a young vibrant life. The flaming red dupatta, floating in the sky signifies Zubeidaa's desire to transcend reality, she has had her moments of freedom and joy, then finally the tragic fall/flight to death, as the dupatta blows around and settles on the newly pressed grave.

A quick shift to Zubeidaa's girlhood; the patriarch Sulemaan Seth lords over his family and casts a shadow on the lives of his wife Fayazi who remains a doormat, as he flirts around with Roza Davenport, a lively dancer. His vivacious daughter is subdued by his diktat. There are only two manifestations of religion in the film, one at the time of Zubeidaa's forced marriage and the other at the abrupt snapping of her marriage. Muslim Personal Law[3] and strict patriarchal strictures play a tragic role in her life. At the time of her first marriage she sits stoically unmoving behind the bridal veil, refusing to give her consent by saying, *Qubul hai*, her father lies to the maulvi that she has nodded her consent. Later as a young mother, with an infant in her arms she is abandoned by her husband by the word *Talaaq* pronounced thrice. One cannot ignore the groundswell of the times, the new born child, symbolising the nation at birth, born of a divided legacy, the times ahead seem to be full of hardship and the struggle of coming to terms with a broken and fractured past, haunting the present.

The film begins in the 40s and moves on to the 80s. At the time of Zubeidaa's burial in 1952, her father stays away as he has not forgiven his daughter for marrying for love outside the community. The beginning of a new life with her Rajput husband Vijendra Singh is like a fairy tale, he is literally the prince, who seems to take her into the clouds in his two seater plane, away from the pull of discipline and regimentation. But it is poignantly also a position over which she has little control; it is the men, her father, first husband and now her second husband who are in full control. She manages to breathe, to grow in the interstitial spaces. Moving from one home to another, one culture to another, full of expectations, she is grounded by the Rajput royal traditions yet again. Dancing was denied to her earlier in life when her father himself a producer of B grade films, forbade her from dancing in front of the camera or even at home with her fiancé. Later in life, she is humiliated for an impromptu act of joining the women in their *ghoomar* in the palace during the *Gangaur Pooja*. The camera catches the rhythms and the nuances of the festival, filmed at the heritage hotel, Narain Niwas at Jaipur, where the two wives—Mandira Devi and Zubeidaa sit resplendent in their finery. It is a gilded cage and both have to play the role of marionettes. Since Zubeidaa cannot live a constricted life of rituals and traditions she is assigned a haveli that is detached and here begins her second isolation. There is deep anguish and longing for her son whom she has left behind, she also realises that she is a mere plaything. Both mother and son share one historical context is their diary entries, the partition, that had wrecked their lives, denied them a home, a father and a husband.

Again, Zubeidaa wilfully defies the pull of gravity, the social mores and customs and in chasing her dream of love and companionship; she falls to her tragic end. The diary entries give leads to her son; her hidden life and her aspirations are revealed. Riyaz retraces his steps to the palace in Fatehpur, where he finds that his mother is completely erased from memory; there are no photographs of his mother among those adorning the walls. No one even talks of her; on his inquiry he is told that Zubeidaa was a woman of no consequence; she was a naachne gaane waali[4] (a nautch girl). Through Mandira Devi's generosity he is able to retrieve the lost reel of his mother's dance—*Mein albeli* (I'm happy-go-lucky), which is the quintessential Zubeidaa. He, his old grandmother and the old dance master are the sole viewers of this reel.

In these films, there are representations of both Muslim and Rajput culture, but an intolerant patriarchy dominates in both. for Rosa Davenport or Mandira Devi, the scales are tipped against them, religion and rituals are used as sticks to beat them, and overrule their aspirations of love, dignity and compassion.

It is important to remember that the first representation of Muslim ethos in Hindi cinema was not in a specific Muslim film as Iqbal Masud writes in his essay 'Muslim Ethos in Indian Cinema' (Iqbal Masud.http://www.screindia.com/old) or by a Muslim director, but in the film *Devdas,* directed by P.C. Barua

(1935) based on Sarat Chandra Chatterji's novel (1917), a saga of two small-town lovers torn apart by caste and class. Masud emphasises this point by referring to Sudhir Kachar and John M. Ross (1986) who write about the two traditions of lovers, Radha Krishna and Laila Majnu. While Rạdha and Krishna are the divine lovers in Hindu mythology, Laila and Majnu are passionate but doomed lovers in Arabic and Persian forklore and literature. Both the elements are fused in *Devdas.* These two features are common to both traditions. Love is not just spiritual love, but also sexual love elevated to a spiritual plane. Also, Masud quotes the 13th century Persian mystic poet Rumi who says, 'The house of love has doors and roofs made of music, melody and poetry.' This is first seen in *Devdas* which is the distinctive contribution of Muslim ethos to Hindi cinema, with its beautiful blend of Rumi's three elements. Similarly, as Vinay Lal and Ashis Nandy (36) observe that the meta-narrative of history presents each film with the chance to link its own narrative to a universal theme, and provide a context with reference to which the drama unfolded in the film. The emotions of love and hate are not special to any one community, they reside in all cultures. One can add that in Muslim culture as depicted in Hindi films, there is emphasis on music and poetry which resonates with longing and lyrical expression of unrequited love, especially as this contrasts the intense love for poetry and music with the taboos inflicted by patriarchal authority and religious Puritanism.

It is the individual agency which makes life flow even in the face of grave obstacles. The vibrant character of Zubeida, the unending search for his past by Rizu, the regal dignity of Mandira Devi, the despair of Mammo—all add upto humanity coming together with cultures flowing into each other. For the sake of God, as Ghalib said we have to shed our intolerance as all cultures converge, just like the Kaaba's veil and the god of stone.

Notes

1. Mirza Ghalib wrote these lines in 19th century Delhi, quoted in Tabish Khair's, *Muslim Modernities: Essays on Moderation and Mayhem.* Compiled and Edited by Renu Kaul Verma, 2008. Khair observes that the same spirit of inclusion is there in Jelaluddin Balkhi Rumi, the 13th century Persian-Turkish poet and Sufi saint, who said, 'The way of worshipping are not to be ranked as better or worse. Hindus do Hindu things; Dravidian Muslims of India do what they do. It is all worship, and it is all right' (44).
2. Vinay Lal and Ashis Nandy, (eds.) *Fingerprinting Popular Culture,* write that Shyam Benegal was the pioneer and leading light of the defining movement in 1970s of the new/art/experimental/parallel cinema in Hindi. They also observe that Benegal is the only director in the history of Hindi cinema who has come on so Sanskritically strong consistently with Sanskritic titles such as *Ankur* (1973), *Nishant* (1975), *Manthan* and *Bhumika* (both 1976). They observe that, '...his terse and abstract eponymous gravity caused as much of *frisson* as the engaged seriousness of the new subject-matter of his treatment of it'; and that these titles were indicators of their 'realistic, high serious orientation' (70).
3. Refer *In a Minority: Essays on Muslim Women in India.* eds. Zoya Hasan and Ritu Menon. The editors observe in the introduction that the Muslim Personal Law has become an important symbol of minority identity, consequently the defence of this identity has resulted in a steady erosion of the rights of Muslim Women, who are systematically subordinated to the perceived interest of the community (2). They analyse the role of the State vis-à-vis this extremely disadvantaged and vulnerable group and feel that the state has abdicated its responsibility by allowing the Muslim male religious leaders to strengthen their control over them. The State favours an ungendered identity for Muslim woman (2).
4. Sadat Hassan Manto provides a vivid account of Muslim social context (Lal and Nandy 137) in the Hindi film industry in his essay (1984) on Nargis. He points out that she was the daughter of the singer-actress and filmmaker Jaddanbai and Mohan Babu, and the aura of a courtesan's disreputability, seemed to surround her. It made men such as Kesker and Patel at least implicitly call for purification of the national public culture.

Works Cited

Hasan, Zoya and Ritu Menon, eds. *In a Minority: Essays on Muslim Women in India.* New Delhi: OUP, 2005.

Masud, Iqbal. Internet Sources: 'Muslim Ethos in Indian Cinema'. http://www.screindia.com/old; viewed on 5 April 2010.

Khair, Tabish. 'A Muslim Consciousness: The Space of Definitions'. *Muslim Modernities: Essays on Moderation and Mayhem.* Compiled and edited by Renu Kaul Verma. New Delhi: Vitasta Publishing Pvt. Ltd., 2008. 263–280.

Lal, Vinay and Ashis Nandy. *Fingerprinting Popular Culture: The Mythic and the Iconic in Indian Cinema* (2006). New Delhi: OUP, 2007.

Filmography

Mammo. Dir. Shyam Benegal. Prod. NFDC. Story, Khalid Mohammad. Perf. Farida Jalal, Surekha Sikri and Rajit Kapoor. 1995.

Zubeida. Dir. Shyam Benegal. Prod. FKR Productions. Story. Khalid Mohammad. Perf. Karishma Kapoor, Surekha Sikri, Manoj Vajpai and Rekha. 2001.

13

Hybridity and the Filmic Text

Re-visiting *Chaudhvin ka Chand*

Ameena Kazi Ansari

Filmic texts invariably reflect myriad facets of history and society. They are embedded in a socio-cultural matrix that reflects the creators of the film as well its audiences. While the creators of filmic texts endeavour to imaginatively create/recreate a socio-cultural matrix that captures the imagination of their audience, the audiences judge their creativity in terms of being able to relate to the sensitivities and nuances of the milieu and the situational reality portrayed within the films. The common ground, therefore, between the creator and the receiver of the filmic text is the milieu and the reality portrayed in a film. And it is this common feature that invariably underlines the pivotal role that time and history play in the representations of most filmic texts.

Bombay's film industry traces its beginnings to the late 1890s from where it proceeded to become the major industry that it is today in India. From the early films, which revolved round mythology and epics, Bombay cinema has transited through historicals, socials, song-and-dance romances, masala films, angry-young-man films and art films, to contemporary films that are heavily inclined towards ideologues and ideologies. Even the nomenclature of this film industry has been revised and today it is known as 'Bollywood', a name synonymous with its American counterpart, Hollywood. In this evolution, the country's history, and the civilisational traditions emanating therefrom, have had a major role to play.[1]

A quick run through of the country's history points to distinct landmarks. There were the ancient civilisations of the Indus Valley and Harappa. These were succeeded by the Magadh, the Maurya and the Gupta Empires. Then came Muslim rule, which saw the rise and fall of the Delhi Sultanate and the Mughal Empire. The colonial period of British predominance followed and led to the movement for independence, first as the war of independence in 1857, and then as a concerted struggle for freedom in the first half of the 20th century. The partition of the country and independence came in 1947, the Republic of India was established in 1950, and since then India has marched ahead as a nation enjoying the benefits as well as the vagaries of its pluralistic ethos and milieu. Ever since its birth, Bombay cinema has experimented with portraying personages, periods and dimensions of India's storehouse of mythology or its rich diversity of cultures and history. In doing so, it has brought into the limelight the modes and manners, the faith and philosophy, and the subtleties of language and expression that mark the country's plural ethos.

In the second half of the 20th century, Bombay cinema's special focus was the portrayal of multiple facets of Muslim life. This, perhaps, grew out of the turmoil and fragmentation that partition brought in its wake. Though the country was truncated along religious lines, there chose to remain in India a sizeable population of Muslims. Post-partition, especially in the film world that was concentrated in Bombay, Muslims were a significant and influential presence. They came to symbolise and portray a 'Muslimness' in the cinema of that period as they represented an opposition, as well as an alternative, to the divisive stance taken by Muslim political parties and leaders who were instrumental in the partition of the country. In their creative efforts, they were joined by non-Muslims, who appreciated and empathised with their post-partition sensitivities. As such, the filmic creativity of all these individuals became the markers of the national enterprise undertaken at that point in time to carve out the identity of a new postcolonial nation state. Their filmic expressions foregrounded post-partition realities which, in turn, reflected the unity and diversity that was India. Operating through the medium of celluloid, their portrayals simultaneously underlined the national mainstream as also the richness and variety of cultures and sub-cultures that co-existed within this mainstream. It was thus that Bombay cinema came to portray the culture and manners, language and history that is specifically associated with Muslims.

It is necessary to emphasise some of the essential features of the Muslim world and its Muslimness. It has to be stated in no uncertain terms that the Muslim world is not a monolithic entity. It comprises different regions, states and communities, all of which share a faith but otherwise have their own distinct cultures and ways of life. Firstly, it must be clarified that Muslim existence in India does not embody a pan-Islamic way of life across the country. Life and practice differ from region to region, sometimes even from village to village within the same region. Bombay cinema is specifically North Indian in spirit and milieu, exposing a culture and ethos that is distinctly regional. Secondly, in keeping with this spirit and milieu, Urdu is the language of these films. Thirdly, these films generally focus on the elite, upper-class Muslim gentry. Aamir Mufti posits that these films possess 'an ability to metonymically stand in for the culture of the pre-modern elites of North India' (27). Fourthly, these films are usually rooted in a space or a locale that symbolises 18th and 19th century Awadh/Lucknow whose culture, ethos and language are imaginatively re-created and romanticised in the 20th century filmic renditions.

Lucknow resisted and survived the brutal British assaults of 1857 and 1858.[2] It has been a major urban centre of the Indo-Muslim culture which escaped the rioting and devastation that other Muslim hubs witnessed during the partition of 1947.[3] Taken together, these essential features point to the celebration of a bygone era that marked the modes and manners, the wit and humour, as well as the faith and philosophy of the Muslim elite during an era when they enjoyed social dominance, and were looked up to as the models of refinement and the custodians of culture.

While the 1950s and 60s saw the political and social marginalisation of Muslims in the aftermath of partition, it is a period that also witnessed, interestingly, the emergence of films that exoticised 'Muslimness' and depicted the rich cultural tradition of North Indian Muslims.[4] These films embody intricate forms of Muslim life and history as they set out to re-create and periodise mahals and havelis, kings and nawabs, burqa-clad heroines and polished courtesans along lines that are more romantic than real.

In the 50s and 60s, three broad categories of Muslim life have been portrayed as three distinct genres of cinema. These include films which portray facets of history, such as period pieces such as *Mughal-e-Azam*; then there are the Muslim socials such as *Mere Mehboob*; and, of course, one is familiar with films such as *Pakeezah* that delve into the life and art of the Muslim courtesan. Guru Dutt's 1960 classic, *Chaudhvin ka Chand*, is a film of generic hybridity as it conflates all these three generic identities. It attempts to depict image and idiom that are historically viable, socially realistic, culturally compelling, and aesthetically rich in order to represent the Muslim community of a specific time period.

History is symbolically evoked in the film. This is conveyed through the portrayal of Lucknow as a city steeped in history and Muslim *tehzeeb*, which implies a fusion of culture and ethos. From the historical perspective, Lucknow was one of the last citadels of Muslim rule to fall into the hands of the British.

Though its Muslim rulers and populace had fiercely rebutted the British forces in 1857, they had eventually been defeated. Yet the city's *tehzeeb*, marked by fine poetic traditions and music, the courtly manners of its Muslim elite, their beautiful gardens and exquisite cuisine, lives on till this day. It is this facet that *Chaudhvin ka Chand* weaves into a romantic plot that revolves around Lucknow's upper crust Muslim society of the early 1900s. The opening credits of the film appear against the backdrop of a song that highlights and celebrates Lucknow's *tehzeeb* and evokes its persona. The visual is highlighted by the verbal in this composition—*Yeh Lucknow ki sarzameen.*[5] It is interesting to note that the entire song is in the present tense, underlining the fact that the city and its traditions are immortal and seemingly timeless. When the camera pans Lucknow's splendid monuments, it is once again the city's glorious Muslim past that is evoked. The succession of domes, minarets and arches in the opening song underline the predominant style of Islamic architecture. These visuals of the monuments, however, also underline an air of desolation and emptiness that underscores the mood of the film itself. Many of the shots focus on a solitary, burqa-clad figure who crosses over from one side of the frame to the other, thereby adding to the starkness of the plot and its portrayal. Taken together, all these images do highlight the Muslim milieu, but it is a portrayal that also ironically underlines the collapse of the very world that it seeks to eulogise.

On another level, *Chaudhvin ka Chand* seeks to inform its viewers about the Muslim social structure that existed in the early 19th century but has long since disappeared. The film consciously tries to recapture the milieu of that bygone era by depicting three male protagonists who symbolise three distinct social categories of pre-partition Muslim life. They together represent a confluence of social classes brought together by symbolising the wealthy nawab, the colonial bureaucrat and the thrifty trader. There is Pyare Mian, the nawab descended from Lucknow's erstwhile aristocracy, Shaida, his friend, who represents a bureaucracy dominated by Muslim officers, and Aslam, another friend, whom Pyare Mian had helped to set up in life as a trader. The women in the film also embody three well-defined female spaces within the same milieu. They include the 'respectable-household' daughter, Jamila, the coquettish *tawaif* or dancing girl, Tamizan and the lowly menial, Nasiban. The film makes it only too clear that the men are stereotypes of a social interaction that allows them space outside the threshold; the women, it is equally clear, are circumscribed within the walls of their households. Whenever one impinges upon the space of the other, the seeds of tragedy are sown in the film.

The two major episodes that underline this happen, firstly, when Jamila lifts her veil in the public domain of a shrine and catches Pyare Mian's eye to the extent of obsession, and secondly, when Pyare Mian chances upon Jamila in the private domain of her marital home, and she is driven to distraction and remorse for being seen by a strange male. The former episode initiates the plot; the latter pushes it towards a tragic denouement.

Imbued within the social structure portrayed in the film is the tradition of women donning the purdah or burqa as a cultural practice. It is a world in which marriages in respectable families are arranged by elders and young men have to go by their choices. Pyare Mian, however, is swept off his feet when Jamila lifts her veil for a moment at a mela. The entire plot revolves around a series of errors that are wrought by the momentary unveiling of Jamila and consequently, Pyare Mian falling irrevocably in love with her during that fleeting glimpse of her face. In order to confirm her identity so as to be able to get his mother to propose marriage, Pyare Mian calls upon his friends, Aslam and Shaida, to assist him in his mission. Shaida takes recourse to a metaphoric purdah by disguising himself as a faqir in a mela, hoping to be able to once again spot Jamila and help Pyare Mian in making her his wife.

Besides the literal veiling/unveiling of Jamila, the film also focuses on another kind of purdah. This is a metaphoric purdah that is highlighted through the sensitive handling of the camera within the homes of the protagonists. It is here that *Chaudhvin ka Chand* captures the nuanced dynamics of curtains and screens, or *chilmans*,[6] within household settings that mark the *zenana*—the women's section of exclusivity within a house– and the *mardana*– the men's quarters or the domain of public interaction within homes. The demarcations and traditions of the *zenana* and the *mardana* reiterate the boundaries of the spatial dimension of purdah.

The film also highlights the Mughal architectural feature of the *dalaan-dar-dalaan* which roughly translates as 'hall-ways-within-hallways.' Mughal residential places were usually a single-roofed building with numerous pillars. Curtains, *chilmans* and blinds drawn between these pillars transformed a huge hallway into rooms with varying degrees of accessibility. The more private the space, the more dense the wall of curtains to keep out the unwanted gaze or individual. Homes of the protagonists in *Chaudhvin ka Chand* are shown to have a similar internal arrangement of strategically placed sheer curtains or thick screens which filter both individuals, as also their roving glances, according to the level of familiarity that the household allows its visitors. When Pyare Mian surreptitiously transgresses the unwritten but accepted code of this spatial purdah, he has to suffer silently the sharp stings of Jamila's words as well as her swinging cane.

Besides purdah, *Chaudhvin ka Chand* also focuses on the values and the social mores of the Muslim world that it seeks to foreground. It is a world that puts a premium on *sharafat*, yet another important hallmark of both Indian Muslimness and Lucknow. *Sharafat* is a concept which upholds the highest standards of *adab* (etiquette), *tehzeeb* and *zubaan* (the giving of a gentleman's word of honour), and is associated with the Muslim elite as models of uprightness and refinement. In addition to *sharafat*, this elite class honours not only the practice and precept of faith (as is evident in Pyare Mian's mother, a stereotype of piety, grace, tolerance and patience) but also appreciates and encourages musical traditions such as the *qawwali*, the *mujra* and the wedding songs, all of which are subtly interspersed in the film.

The film adopts a play-within-a play technique to emphasise the invaluable *dosti*, or friendship, which united the three friends and compelled them to resort to affirmative action to assist Pyare Mian in his quest for Jamila. Shaida takes to disguises in order to trace the girl Pyare Mian fell in love with at first sight; Aslam, as a true friend, accepts in all humility, the girl selected by Pyare Mian's mother but rejected by Pyare Mian himself who only saw Jamila as the girl he could marry. As the three friends set about their mission of identifying Jamila, the film relies on songs to highlight the turns and twists of the plot. *Chaudhvin ka Chand* closely approximates the western tradition of musicals as its frequent musical scores and lyrics commentate on the unfolding events. This is a hallmark of Guru Dutt's films which push forward his plots through well-integrated songs.

Another cultural marker is the centrality given to Urdu as the via media of communication. From the aristocratic nawab to the lowly menial, Urdu is the language of all their modes and circumstances of communication. It is this idiom that very strongly locates the film within the 'Muslim culture' framework. Its wit and humour are effectively grounded in this language which borrows liberally from Persian and Arabic sources. The richness and romance of Urdu emerge strongly in the lyrics which elliptically expand upon the events that have preceded the song. One of these songs, *Yeh duniya gol hai …*, even reverberates with shades of Sufi philosophy when Shaida sings of the disparities between the outer world of illusion and base human desires, and the inner core of reality and spiritual being.

In combining these different elements of Muslim heritage and history, *Chaudhvin ka Chand* emerges as a drama of humour and manners which reflects an exoticised and romanticised lifestyle. The film, thereby, brings to the fore a storyline and a cinematic technique that constantly reinforces a 'Muslimness' that is essentially north Indian. By synthesising various facets of this identity, *Chaudhvin ka Chand* becomes a celluloid hybrid which is more exotic than real in its portrayal.

In re-visiting this film fifty years after it was made, one becomes aware of where it exceeds or falls short of the mark. In harking back towards the enchanted past of 'Muslim culture', the film symbolically presages the uncertain future that beckoned that very culture it sought to extol. In its representation of a minority community, there is an overt tendency to exoticise and a covert tendency to patronise. As the times and tastes have changed, the genre of Muslim socials like *Chaudhvin ka Chand* has died out and been replaced by depictions of Muslims either as marginalised individuals or as figures of subversion. If one goes by E.M. Forster's perception in *A Passage to India* that 'Islam is an attitude towards life both exquisite and durable,' then *Chaudhvin ka Chand* is its filmic rendition, integrating the myriad facets of history, life and values of a city and a community into its celluloid fabric.

Notes

1. *Gender, Genre and Power in South Asian Expressive Traditions,* eds. Korom and Mills (Philadelphia: University of Pennsylvania Press, 1991), sheds light on the major role that history and social tradition have played in the development of Hindi cinema.
2. In her book, *The Making of Colonial Lucknow: 1856–1877* (Princeton: Princeton University Press, 1984), Veena Talwar Oldenburg focuses on the history of the Awadh/Lucknow during a turbulent phase of its history. This was the period of the Great Indian Rebellion of 1857 and its being put down with an iron hand by the British. The city symbolised one of the last strongholds of Muslim rule that fell into the hands of the British due to inept rulers. In Hindi cinema, this city has come to symbolise the refinements of North India's Muslim culture and language.
3. In her essay, 'Lifestyle as Resistance: The Case of the Courtesans of Lucknow, India' [*Feminist Studies* 16 (2), 1990], Veena Talwar Oldenburg gives an account of another facet of Lucknow. In it she

foregrounds the courtesan culture of Lucknow who gave sustenance to the traditions of Urdu *sher-o-shairi* or poetry.

4. The issue of 'Muslimness' in Hindi cinema is discussed at length in Kalyani Chadha and Anandam P. Kavoori's 'The Muslim Other in Indian Cinema', *Global Bollywood* (NYU Press, 2008).
5. Shakeel Badayuni, an Urdu poet, composed the lyrics of this film. *Yeh Lucknow ki sarzameen* is the opening song in the film, during which the credits appear. Its lyrics celebrate the past glories, culture and values of Lucknow. This song dwells upon all that the soil of Lucknow has engendered. The city symbolises all that is tasteful and refined, beauteous and literary, vibrant and lively, generous and caring. The final stanza is very significant as it dwells upon the friendship or *dosti* that is imbued in the citizens of Lucknow. This spirit of friendship is one of commitment, loyalty and grace, where death is preferable to letting down a friend. It is this idea of true friendship that the film revolves around, ending on a tragic note when a friend realises he has transgressed the bonds of camaraderie and companionship.
6. *Chilmans* were screens made of thin reeds backed up with very fine cotton cloth. They were usually let down in the *zenana* when any of the *zenana* women had to communicate with men outside the circle of immediate family members.

Works Cited

Aamir Mufti. 'A Greater Story-Writer than God: Genre, Gender, and Minority in Late Colonial India'. *Subaltern Studies XI: Community, Gender, and Violence.* Partha Chatterjee and Pradeep Jeganathan (eds.). New York: Columbia University Press, 2000. 1–36.

Filmography

Chaudhvin ka Chand. Dir. M. Sadiq. Prod. Guru Dutt. Perf. Guru Dutt, Waheeda Rehman, Johnny Walker, Rehman, Minu Mumtaz, Uma Devi, Tuntun. 1960.

14

The Question of Legacy in *Muhafiz*

Urmil Talwar

The Merchant-Ivory film *Muhafiz*, winner of the President of India Gold Medal Award for the best picture in 1994, is subtitled *In Custody* for it is based on Anita Desai's novel of the same title. The language used in the movie is Urdu and the English titles are picked from the novel as Anita Desai has scripted the film with Sharukh Hussain. Both Desai's novel *In Custody* and *Muhafiz,* the Merchant-Ivory film, have raised several issues regarding legacy, inheritance and preservation of the language, literature and culture of the Muslims in India. All cultures and languages have passed through this conflict of tradition and modernity but Urdu, the language of the ruler that flourished during the Mughal period became the language of minority in post-partitioned India and this transformation in the Urdu-speaking community has been very remarkably represented in the film *Muhafiz*. Along with this, the explicit issue raised in the film is the legacy of Urdu poetry by an eminent Urdu poet Nur Shahjehanbadi, but the intrinsic issue is the decadence of language, literature and the traditional culture of the poet and of the Muslim aristocracy that was once in power and patronised the language. Another related concern is the acknowledgement of the poetry written by women. Is woman competent enough to write poetry? Whether she can be an intellectual companion/heir? I wish to explore these issues as taken up in the film *Muhafiz.* Many films have depicted the glory of Urdu language, the sophisticate Muslim culture and its decadence, but none has posed the question of the legacy of language and culture as *Muhafiz.*

There are certain marked differences in adapting the novel into the film. Desai's novel is set in old Delhi as the name 'Shahjehanbadi' indicates. The poet belonged to Shahjehanbad which was the old name of Delhi but the director shifted the locale to Bhopal another centre of Muslim culture in India. This is a major shift as Delhi was the capital of the Muslim rulers and a centre of power. Also the age difference between the poet Nur and Deven, the college lecturer, is a gap of a generation, however, in the film Shashi Kapoor and Om Puri who very sensitively play Nur and Deven, respectively seem contemporaries and the film's casting does in part undermine the novel's vision and looses a dimension as the novel contrasts youth and experience. Another point is that the poetry of Faiz is extensively used in the film whereas Desai has only used couplets very sparingly. Another major difference is that Imtiaz Begum writes a letter to Deven in the novel questioning in detail the patriarchal society and her position as a poetess and an disciple of and heir to Nur's poetry, in the film she invites Deven to her room and he refuses to take the diary to read her poems.

The central thrust of the film is on the implications of the status of language. In the very introductory meeting between Nur and Deven, Nur sums up the grievances of the Urdu speakers, in India, 'Urdu poetry? If Urdu is no more, what significance has Urdu poetry? Its dead, finished. Now you see its corpse. Lying here, waiting to be disposed off!'[1] (42). This decline in use of the language is very vividly brought out in this dialogue. An all pervasive sense of disintegration, decay and loss permeates every scene of the movie as an idealist teacher, Deven, searches for a lost literary tradition. He is groping in the dark just as the poet's mind and ideas are groping for words.

The current perception about Urdu is that it is the language of Muslim community, a sectarian language, marking the separatist tendency of the minority from the national collectivity. At the heart of the film is the communally charged Hindi-Urdu debate, and issue of the preservation of the language of a minority community for posterity. This chapter presents a critique of the essentialist nature of the understanding of the language as related to a particular community. Language provides a sense of belonging to a particular religious and cultural community which is integrated with a definite territory of nation and nationality. In fact, the western political thinker Otto Jespersen defines a nation as 'a linguistic unit, a linguistic community' (qtd. in Sarangi 5); others like Barbour and Carmichael consider nation as 'a marker for ethnic groups' (qtd. in Sarangi 4) but Sarangi believes that a nation is a cultural capital to provide instantly a sense of belonging (4). Nation defines community rights and identities; gives political powers and privileges to their users over others. Bhabha posits that the 'performativity of language' (3) is required by the nation in constructing the narrative of the nation. For a country like India, Norman Brown considers language as both an integrative as well as a 'divisive'[2] force (qtd. in Sarangi 13) as the states here have been reorganised on linguistic basis. This has raised several issues related to the teaching of Indian languages, in educational institutions, publication of textbooks for classroom teaching and also the official use of language for administrative work. After independence, with the formation of the constitution, Urdu was given special status as one of the fourteen languages in the Eighth Schedule. All other languages except Sanskrit and Urdu were official languages of the states. But somehow Hindi and Urdu have become 'distinctive national markers' (qtd. in Sarangi 2) of India and Pakistan, respectively.

Historically speaking, Urdu is a hybrid of Hindi and Persian languages and its origin in India can be traced back to the post-Arab invasion.[3] Then it became 'the language of command' (Sarangi 5), widely spoken in North India by people of all communities especially by Sikhs, Hindus, Bengalis, Kashmiris and Muslims alike but the attitude towards Urdu changed after the partition of India in 1947 when Hindi was declared the national language of the country. With the migration of Muslims across newly drawn borders and the proclamation of Urdu as the national language of Pakistan Urdu came to be associated with 'Muslim interest in India'. This pessimistic view of Urdu's survival in India, according to Aijaz Ahmad, is due to the break-up of Urdu writing community across borders, its marginalised status and now it is considered a migrant's tongue which makes it an outsider in its homeland (201–220). In pre-partition days the contribution of Indian Muslims and Urdu language to Indian language and literatures, was immense. Mohammad Hassan in his article 'Muslim Ethos in Indian Literature', tracing the impact writes:

> The Indian Muslim and Urdu language have always been such an integral part of the nation that it will be nearly impossible to identify their distinct role without considering the whole gamut of cultural heritage. One cannot discuss Bengali without Nazrul Islam, or Punjabi without Waris Shah or Kashmiri without Habba Khatoon or Awadhi without Jaisi or Brij without Rahiman or … Indian literature without Ghalib. (146)

The list is endless. He accentuates that the Indian Muslims and Urdu language are an integral part of India and these are inseparable parts of the whole gamut of cultural heritage as Urdu delineates the quintessential Indian culture. Anima Yaqin in her essay 'The Communalisation and Disintegration of Urdu in Anita Desai's *In Custody*' sums up that the novel's 'portrayal of Urdu marks an elegiac farewell to a lost tradition … symbolism is tinged with the tropes of communally charged present, unable to break out of the fragmentary Hindu-Hindi and Muslim-Urdu divide despite her staging the debates within the "secular" Indian-English novel' (139). Contrary to her belief, I find Anita

Desai breaking away from the traditional Hindu-Hindi and Muslim-Urdu divide as also Intizar Husain has argued that cultural tradition of Urdu lies in its shifting regional locations. According to him, Urdu cannot be associated with one region and one culture because it is by nature hybrid and adaptable to new regions (149). In the post-partition India, Hindi is Sanskritised by purging it of Arabic-Persian words and Urdu is sanitised by employing Persian equivalents of Hindustani words, thus pushing the two languages apart. In Uttar Pradesh, Urdu has been especially marginalised and is perceived as an endangered language by the minority who are literate in it. In an interview with Magda Costa, Anita Desai when asked about the decay of Urdu language and literature in her novel replied:

> I was trying to portray the world of Urdu poets, living in Delhi. I was always surrounded by the sound of Urdu poetry, which is mostly recited. Nobody reads it, but one goes to recitations. It is very much the voice of North India ... most Muslims left India to go to Pakistan meant that most schools and universities of Urdu were closed ... I don't think it is going to survive in India ... To some extent it is still written ....(2)

Urdu was given the status of a second language vide ordinance in 1982 in Uttar Pradesh but the ordinance was not converted into legislation in five years. Later in 1989, the official language Amendment Bill declared Hindi as the official language of the state. Now, the survival of the Urdu language that once was the voice of North India in pre-partition days is the major concern of the film. The title song sets the tone of the film. The poet is writing poetry and his mind, his ideas and thoughts are groping for words. There is a quest for the right words, as the following song from the film expresses:

> *My mind is groping for a word*
> *A word as sweet as seduction and bitter as poison*
> *A word that bewitches but is full of rage*
> *My mind is groping for a word*

A word as brimming with passion as the gaze between two lovers
As soft as a kiss
A word shining like a sea of gold
A tune struck up in a lover's arms
My mind is groping for a word
(song in the film, translated in the English subtitles.)

Why is the poet groping for words? Is this the problem of language, or of communication due to a vanishing voice/tongue? All the poetic pieces in the film whether nazm, ghazal or couplets are taken from Faiz Ahmad Faiz who migrated to Pakistan during partition and was imprisoned for sometime. It was a mere unfortunate coincidence that Faiz died the same year *In Custody* was published (1984) and the film was made a decade later. While the poet is writing poetry, the light and the camera focus on a small tomb on an island, the *Moti Masjid*, the *Akhara*, pigeons, and market of Bhopal. These are significant recurrent markers in the film and have symbolic interpretations.

The film has four important scenes when Deven interacts with Nur. It is significant to note that three of these four conversations take place in dark gloomy rooms that presage not only the darkness, decay and death of the Urdu language but also the mystery, the awe and the growing intimacy that slowly develops between the poet and the teacher. In Bhopal, where the film was shot, Deven walks through narrow alleys sidestepping goats and mud puddles to arrive at the flower filled courtyard of a large shabby house of Nur to realise his dream, to meet his favourite poet. In the first interaction, Deven wakes the poet from his siesta. The poet is resting with his back towards the camera. Initially, Nur belittles Murad whose letter of introduction Deven carries with him; the poet is also skeptical of Deven's capabilities as he despised the idea that a teacher of Hindi should interview him. Deven impresses him by reciting his verse with such clarity and precision and fine pronunciation that Nur gives his consent for the interview. Reflecting on the bleak future of Urdu, Nur points towards himself as he says that the language is dead and lying here to be buried. This scene is interrupted by a flashback when Deven remembers from his treasured times as a child with his father who passionately taught him Urdu and its correct pronunciation thereby hinting that the language needs an atmosphere to grow and it can only be preserved and learnt if parents make the effort. Although Deven's genuine attempts of appreciation are spurned by the poet as he associates language with a cultural group and firmly believes that a teacher of Hindi is incapable of appreciating Urdu poetry. One can see that his admirers or the fawning sycophants that surround Nur are not interested in poetry but in *biryani* and whisky, and when they leave the poet he is soiled in his own vomit in his room and it falls to Deven to place him safely on his bed, restore his dignity while the young wife of the poet scoffs at the admirers and curses them for their behaviour. She even calls them jackals who are draining his life blood, sponging on his time when he should be writing poetry. In his subsequent meetings with Nur to record the interview, he realises that Nur which means light is now flickering and his ailing physique metaphorically represents the decline of the language and culture he stands for.

In the second meeting, Deven is invited by Nur to attend his wife's birthday celebrations and Imtiaz Begum sings one of Nur's ghazals followed by another one which she has appropriated as her own. Deven is vexed as he is well read in Nur's poetry and cannot ignore this and speaks up. Leaving the *mehfil*, Nur shares with Deven his unhappiness with Imtiaz Begum, the manner in which she has made him lonely, bereft of his jewels, house, friends, his secretary and audience. The third meeting is arranged in a rented room in the brothel where the voice recording is to take place. Deven's project to record Nur's poetry in the poet's voice for posterity comes to naught. His inabilities to handle the modern gadgets frustrate his project. Deven is unable to record anything worthwhile during this week-long interaction due to lack of a proper technician. He could only record the English recitation of Shelley's 'Nightingale' and the requests for *biryani* and whisky. Though Nur recited his new poems but he felt the spark missing. However, Nur had lain bare his entire life before Deven in the week that he spends with him but Deven is unable to successfully use Nur's voice. Finally, it does not reach the intended audience. Jasbir Jain in her book *Stairs to the Attic* while discussing the novel *In Custody* suggests that the interview was a success as Nur had laid bare his life before Deven and he had everything up there in his head and could reproduce it (109). The interview could not be recorded; it was a failure of the use of technology. But the intimacy in the relationship of Nur and Deven is a message of hope and harmony. If Urdu is to survive then the dedicated non-Muslim population in India should take it as their heritage and this is the message of the film. Once it gets dissociated from its location in a community bias, it will be better for this language of 'ganga-jamni-tehzeeb' to flourish and prosper in India. Next time when Deven goes to meet Nur, Nur takes Deven on a pilgrimage to the tomb of the Saint who blessed him with this gift of poetry, so as to thank him and also to pass on this torch to Deven to keep the flame of Urdu poetry burning. The same tomb is the first scene, the beginning of the film when Nur was writing his poem. The film comes full circle. After this Deven receives the letter and the poems of Nur and when he comes to Bhopal to give the printed version of his work, he attends the funeral procession of the poet. The poet could not see the poems in print which he had sent Deven.

In *Muhafiz* the tragedy of Urdu is mediated through the life of the poet Nur who treats himself as the custodian of language and by implication of the culture associated with it. He glorifies his aristocratic habits—feeding pigeons, having rich food, providing food and liquor to his admirers as a part of the essentialist culture. The film exposes the shallowness of this false pride and the highly romantic attitude towards life which is not possible in this modern world. Close to the Romantic tradition, the film evokes the cultural memory, nostalgia of the past and idealises the 'folk' and a vital subculture buried deep in its own society (Yakin 122).

The film depicts the miserable plight of all three women—Sufiya, Imtiaz and Sarla—suffering under their insensitive and inconsiderate husbands. Of the three Imtiaz, Nur's younger wife is the most outrageous in her behaviour. She insists on telling her story and is fighting to hold her own in a male dominated society. Her insistence on telling her story is symbolic of the Indian Muslim women writers who tell their own tales but these do not receive proper public attention. To Deven she reveals that Nur married her for her 'gifts and abilities' and it was not she who trapped him. But Deven refuses to heed her points as it would have upset his soul. She attempts to assert her independence and self-sufficiency but her quest for identity is thwarted. She is bold enough to call Deven a jackal who has come to relish the blood of Nur's body. Her bold dialogue and discussion presents her as an icon of the New Woman who asserts her rights and abilities. Imtiaz wants to assert her individuality and identity as a poetess and wishes to be taken seriously, but Deven dismisses her as a shrewd and calculating woman, selling Nur's poetry as her own. He does not read her poetry and just rejects her manuscript as a false one. She faces, single-handedly, the ferocious assaults of existence and challenges him to read her Urdu poems:

> ... you feared that I might eclipse the verse of Nur Sahib and other male poets you revere? Was it not intolerable to you that a woman should match their gifts and outstrip them? Are you not guilty of assuming that because you are a male, you have a right to brains, talent, reputation, and achievement, while I, because I was born a female, an condemned to find what satisfaction I can in being maligned, mocked, ignored and neglected?[4] (196)

He refuses to take her diary of poems. This subverts the audience's unsympathetic attitude towards Imtiaz Begum and one begins to question the validity of Deven's attitude towards her, his own wife and women in general. Deven cannot face the truth represented in her statement. Had Deven chosen to read her poetry, he would have been forced to admit the power of articulation and art which women can wield. Thus, Deven never reads it and the audience does not get a whiff of her poetry. Solanki rightly posits that the growth of female characters in Desai's fiction 'is stunted and obstructed. The wholeness which they desire to achieve, at any cost, still eludes them …' (175). In the film, the female characters feel frustrated in the patriarchal system. Sarla shrivels but does not rebel openly. Nur's first wife Sufia Begam is suffering under patriarchy as she could not beget a male child. Annoyed with both the poet and Deven, Imtiaz Begum releases the pigeons to announce the death of an era. The flight of pigeons to freedom is a release from a way of life. When Deven receives the packet from the poet, his letter announces:

> My pigeons have flown, they will never return, … I am dying, too … For my sinful soul's salvation I must make a pilgrimage to Mecca, … Before I leave, I send you new verses—on death. Look after them, in your custody. I'll be grateful if you have them published. (203)

Another image that the director gives us at the death of Nur is the fall of the Siddiqui's haveli. Siddiqui has an impeccable royal majesty about him. A silent spectator he scrutinises the shifting interests of the society. His dilapidated house, a symbol of past grandeur like that of Nur, is sold off to build modern day Malls, offices and a housing complex. The ancestral house vanishes into the dust of Mirpur, like Nur's fading popularity yields to new technologies. The film is not about Nur and Siddiqui but about the loss of all that the Muslim culture and literature have meant to India. It comes to a full circle and ends with the song:

> *Don't grieve. The season will change.*
> *The clouds will lift. The night will end*
> *The wound will heal ….*

It ends on a positive note. The poetry recited in the film is quite meaningful and adds to the progression of thought. Nur feels that his writing days are over but he is appreciated by the audience. The film though ends with the death of Nur but his poetry is alive in the hands of Deven. Murad, a friend of Deven and the editor of *Awaaz,* had requested him to interview Nur for his special number of the journal on Urdu poetry. He chooses Deven to interview Nur deliberately as he belongs to the emergent language group, Hindi. Murad is fervently struggling to keep alive his journal and is aware of the fact that 'the Voice' is not being read or heard as he says, 'Where are the readers? Where are the subscriptions? Who reads Urdu anymore?' *Awaaz* paradoxically divulges that nobody is interested in listening to 'the voice' of Urdu. Murad's pock-marked face serves as a metaphor for an urban Urdu speaker who is tainted by his contempt for Hindi but he accuses Deven of being a traitor to Urdu for he teaches Hindi at Ram Lal College in Mirpur. Murad belittles Deven:

> ... the vegetarian monster Hindi ... that language of peasants ... like these vegetables it flourishes, while Urdu—language of the court in the days of royalty—now languishes in the back lanes and gutters of the city. No place for it to live in the style to which it is accustomed, no emperors, and nawabs to act as its patrons. Only poor I, in a dingy office, trying to bring out a magazine, where it may be kept alive. (15)

Even Nur accuses Deven of disloyalty and is perplexed at his request for an interview. Jaidev, his colleague, calls him 'the man with a double life' who teaches Hindi but contributes Urdu poetry to Murad's journal. On the contrary, whenever Deven interacts with the Urdu-speaking world, he feels like an alien. His sincerity of purpose, his zest and his hero worship of Nur do not help him to realise his dreams. The sordid reality of the day-to-day life clashes with his fragile world of dreams. This collision smashes his hopes and he is caught in middle of a linguistic politics at college. Another important issue is the use of language—its teaching and learning—is related to one's vocation. It is not always a matter of communal responsibility. Murad, Nur and Trivedi all make him feel guilty of his profession as if teaching Hindi while writing Urdu poetry was a grave crime. When Deven applies for a week's leave to conduct an interview with the legendary poet Nur, Trivedi calls him a traitor and threatens him with a transfer and a possible complain to the Principal and the RSS (145). Trivedi's violent reaction reveals how language becomes a signifier of religious identity and national loyalty. The discourse here gains greater relevance in terms of contemporary language based politics. The division of India on the basis of language is the crux of the statement made in the movie as well as in the novel. The Hindi/Urdu controversy that involves communal implications does not allow the languages to become objective mediums of communication. This bitter controversy demonstrates how little the objective similarities between language groups matter when people attach subjective significance to their languages. The political meanings attached to these cultural activities resulting in communal divide rind no reference in the film. With reference to RSS one can gauge the Hindu imperialism, the fundamentalism, and the power politics of the Hindi-speaking belt.

The problematics of the language-culture divide also mark a rejection of the view that considers 'langue' as the real custodian of any language. In the process, it marks preference for Bakhtinian view of language that treats the 'parole' or the language in use as the real language. Language in such a view instead of being related to any community in particular, is related to people who use it irrespective of the community they belong to. In keeping with the Bakhtinian view, Nur brings about the required change, i.e., the custodian of Nur's poetry, his life, his spirit and his soul is not Murad but Deven, thereby releasing Urdu of its Muslim-Urdu communal bias. Language is in the custody of its users. Deven's college has an Urdu department headed by Siddiqui who is interested neither in preserving the language nor in Nur's poetry nor his own heritage, haveli. Though, at Deven's instigation, he does persuade the Registrar to sanction a grant for the tape recorder. But he has no interest in meeting Nur. The old aristocracy has washed their hands off the use of Urdu language, they are giving their children English education. *Muhafiz* is an example of what Rushdie in his essay 'Imaginary Homelands' defines as 'the linguistic struggle' which is but 'a reflection of other struggles taking place in the real world' (17), struggles between cultures within themselves and the influences at work upon our societies.

The film, in part, is a lament for the decay/disuse of Urdu language. The British put the noose round its neck and independence tightened it. Now it survives in the alleys and bylanes of Muslim localities. However, it is important to accept that the richness and variety of its literary and cultural traditions have added to the evolution of literatures and cultures of India.[5] The beauty of the film is that what seems to be a story of the Merchant inevitable tragedies ends on a positive note of rejuvenation. The film, like the narrative, seeks to promote cultural integration and syncretic values and strengthen intercommunity ties, as suggested by Salman Rushdie in his Foreword to this novel. He writes:

> *In Custody* was, therefore, a novel of transformation for its author, a doubly remarkable piece of work, because in this magnificent book Anita Desai chose to write not of solitude but of friendship, of the perils and responsibilities of joining oneself to others rather than holding oneself apart. (2)

The Merchant-Ivory film seeks to demystify the idea of a religio-linguistic collectivity and looks towards art and the way of life of individuals as distinctive cultural representations.

Notes

1. This is a quote from the dialogue of the film. The quote in the book is a long one. Refer Anita Desai's *In Custody,* 42.

2. Norman Brown, 'Religion and Language as Forces Affecting Unity in Asia', in *Annals of the American Academy of Political and Social Sciences*, 318, July 1958, 8–17. He considers language as a disruptive force both in India and Pak.
3. See M.S. Jain. *Muslim Ethos as Reflected in Urdu Literature* for details of the origin of Urdu and how from vernacular it developed into a literary language and brought about community awareness through Urdu literature
4. This passage is a direct quote from the film. The same dialogue is much more detailed in the book. The page reference is to the book for further details. The same is applicable to other quotes from this text.
5. The Hindi/Urdu debate seems unnecessary to me as they are not rival languages. The language of Mir and Ghalib was spoken by millions of people of all religious creeds. In fact, all languages are necessary to promote multiculturalism, the creative potential must be encouraged in the interest of nationwide literary and cultural Renaissance. The Indian Government is taking tangible steps to promote 'langues' by establishing Academies, Translation Bureaus with funds, instituting awards and scholarships and fellowships for literary figures.

Work Cited

Ahmad, Aijaz. *Lineages of the Present: Political Essays*. New Delhi: Tulika, 1996.

Barbour and Carmichael, eds. *Language and Nationalism in Europe*. New York: OUP, 2001.

Bhabha, Homi, ed. *Nation and Narration*. London: Routledge, 1990.

Brown, Norman. 'Religion and Language as Forces Affecting Unity in Asia'. *Annals of the American Academy of Political and Social Sciences*, 318, July 1958. 8–17.

Costa, M. 'Interview with Anita Desai' Barcelona on 30 January 2001. http://www.umiacs.umd.edu\users\sawweb\sawnet\books\desai-interview.html. Originally published in Spanish Magazine *Lateral*. Site visited 22 March 2001.

Desai, Anita. *In Custody*. London: Heinemann, 1984; Edition used New York: Random House, 2007.

Hussain, Imtiaz. 'The Cultural Disposition of Urdu'. *The Annual of Urdu Studies*. Department of Language and Cultures of Asia. USA: University of Wisconsin. Vol. 15. II 2000. 372–6.

Jain, Jasbir. *Stairs to the Attic*: The *Novels of Anita Desai* (1987). Jaipur: Printwell Publishers. 2nd edition. 1999.

Jain, M.S. *Muslim Ethos: As Reflected in Urdu Literature*. Jaipur and New Delhi: Rawat Publications, 2000.

Jaspersen, Otto. *Mankind, Nation and Individual From A Linguistic Point of View*. London: George Allen & Unwin Ltd., 1954.

James, Caryn. 'Ismail Merchant Directs First Feature'. Review, *The New York Times*, 15 April 1994.

Jussawalla, Feroza and Reedway Dassenbrock., eds. *Interviews with Writers of the Post-Colonial World*. Jackson: University Press of Mississippi, 1992.

Metcalf, Barbara D. *Islamic Contestations. Essays on Muslims in India and Pakistan*. New Delhi: Oxford University Press, 2006.

Pollock, Sheldon, ed. *Literary Cultures in History: Reconstruction from South Asia*. New Delhi: Oxford University Press, 2003.

Rushdie, Salman. 'Imaginary Homelands' *Imaginary Homelands*. London: Granta Books, 1992.

Sarangi, Asha, ed. *Themes in Politics: Language and Politics in India*. New Delhi: Oxford University Press, 2009.

Solanki, Mrilanini. Anita Desai's Fiction: Patterns of Survival Strategies. Delhi: Kanishka, 1992.

Yaqin, Anima. 'The Communalisation and Disintegration of Urdu' in Anita Desai's *In Custody*. *Annual of Urdu Studies*. No. 19, 2004. 120–141.

Filmography

Muhafiz. Dir. Ismail Merchant. Prod. Wahid Chowhan. Perf. Shashi Kapoor, Shabana Azmi, Om Puri, Sushma Seth, Parikshat Sahni. 1992.

15

Conflicting Claims on Culture

Train to Pakistan

Indubala Singh

All films are particular ways of seeing the world and have a relation to that dominant trend which is enshrined in the ideology of an age. They represent the very moods of an evolving society and its cultural atmosphere. Culture of any place or region, however, is closely tied to its history, geographical location and the moment in time when culture is being studied. The heart of a culture involves languages, religions, traditions, values and customs. According to Susan Hayward, 'film functions as a cultural articulation of nation and there is reverberation around two fundamental concepts identity and difference' (187).

The spirit of nationalism in India led to the independence of the country on 15 August 1947. Sadly, the partition of India and independence arrived together, one at the price of the other. The traditional communal harmony in India before 1947 enabled the peaceful co-existence of Hindus, Muslims and Sikhs, mutual respect for their places of worship, and a synthesis of cultural practices of inclusiveness. Their common civilisation and outlook on life held them together. Hence, when a separate sovereign state was carved out on religious lines, a new nation Pakistan came into being. Nobody had imagined that the nationhood absolutely vital to the struggle against colonialism will swiftly degenerate and articulate the contradictions of its times leading to conflicting allegiances. It was a losing battle against mass psychoses. Unforeseen migrations of Muslims to Pakistan and of Sikhs and Hindus to India in and around Punjab (and Bengal) took place. There was an exodus of refugees on both sides of the border moving in trains and convoys leading to chaos and disorder. The severance of the umbilical cord pointed towards the dark side of the birth of a nation. The demonic dimensions that the 'others' on both the sides acquired, resulted in destructive fragments and was opposed to reason and culture.

Any recollection of the partition is a painful reminder of the mad frenzy and its horrific repercussions. One gets to know about partition through literary fiction, memoirs and personal testimonies or through memories individual and collective. The film *Train to Pakistan* made in a mixture of Hindi and Punjabi is adapted from a novel by the same name by Khushwant Singh written in English in 1953. Pamela Rooks made the novel into a film in 1997 in observance of the 50th anniversary of the partition, as a partition memorabilia in that sense. It speaks of a historical past which encompasses the reality of the partition and portrays collective memories about the homogeneity vis-à-vis divisive factionalism of a community in the face of disaster. The film evokes a moving portrayal of the partition as a result of which peace and harmony is disrupted along with brotherhood in a mixed Sikh-Hindu-Muslim village called Mano Majra in the rich rural hinterland of Punjab in India. The village of Mano Majra is shown to have only three main buildings, one of them, the local Gurdwara, the other a Mosque and the third, the home of the moneylender Lala Ram Lal, the only Hindu family in the village. However, there are about 70 families in Mano Majra with Sikh and Muslims almost equal in number. The Sikhs are landlords and the Muslims their tenants, who share the tilling of land with their owners, are a reflection on the economics of the partition.

Juggat Singh called Jugga, the main protagonist in the film, is a Jat Sikh and son of a dacoit. He is in love with Nooran, the pretty Muslim damsel, daughter of the blind Iman Baksh, the Mullah. As the film unfolds, he is shown having an affair with Nooran. Meanwhile, Mali another dacoit and his companions, belonging to another village, loot and kill Ram Lal, the Hindu moneylender of the village. But the local magistrate Hukum Chand orders the arrest of Jugga as a suspect in the crime against Ram Lal's murder. Jugga refutes the charge saying that he could not kill a Hindu of his own village as he was like a *Chacha* of his. This bespeaks of the composite cultural connectivity of the village. In fact, the film opens as a flashback with the local magistrate Hukum Chand unravelling the facts of the real incidents that took place in that eventful summer of 1947. Flashbacks as Hayward has observed, 'are a cinematic representation of memory and of history and ultimately of subjective truth' (Hayward 133). Hukum Chand, however, is portrayed as an evolving character, balanced and sober in spite of his hedonistic taste. Pamela Rooks highlights the effect of a young sixteen-year-old Muslim girl called Hasina who is brought to entertain Hukum Chand in the guest house. Hasina sings film songs popular in those times, contributing towards creating an atmosphere.

Mano Majra has a railway station around which the film gets centred. Though it is a small railway station there is constant activity around it though not many trains stop at Mano Majra and the arrival and departure of trains functions like a time keeper. In the modern era, trains had become new rivers, a link with the other side, connecting people. The train in motion was shown in one of the earliest pioneering films and was shot by Freres Lumiere in the film *L' Arrivee d'un train en gare de la Ciotat*. Trains, on account of motion attributed to them like cinema, were a favourite with filmmakers for filming. The train in *Train to Pakistan* which carries passengers from Lahore to Delhi and vice versa, acquires a great significance and brings about symbolically a kind of dynamism in the static, dull, drab village of Mano Majra which is effectively evoked through a strong sound design device used by the music director Kuldip Singh in the cinematic representation of the film. Mano Majra, was one of the little villages which continued to be an oasis of peace, amidst the surrounding chaos. It had always been so until the summer of 1947 till one day a train arrives, like a silent incredible funeral train loaded with dead bodies of thousand of refugees thus changing the very texture of the Mano Majra village.

Once the ghost train arrives Hukum Chand, along with the sub-inspector of Mano Majra, is at his tether's edge and plans to pacify the chaos which otherwise could envision communal disharmony. Subsequently Iqbal, a communist who is actually a Sikh and who had earlier come from Delhi to Mano Majra to bring about communal harmony, is arrested. He is declared to be one of the members of the Muslim League masquerading under a false label. Khushwant Singh in the novel says, 'Iqbal could be Iqbal Singh, Iqbal Chand, Iqbal Mohammed. Iqbal was one of the few names common to the three communities, the Sikhs, the Hindus and the Muslims' (35). Both in the novel and in the film, it has a great significance to the question whether he is a Muslim, Hindu or a Sikh, a fact to be ascertained from a physical examination. In the film, there are two shots of the naked male bottom of Iqbal (enacted by Rajat Kapoor) when he is asked to strip by the police who wanted to check whether he is a Hindu or a Muslim. He is made to strip to find out whether or not he was circumcised. It is however confirmed that he was and he clarifies it by telling them about a surgery he had undergone in England. But he is labelled Muslim; Iqbal protests and feels deeply humiliated. This is a scene which had great difficulty in getting through the censors as his posterior is shown naked. In fact, Pamela Rooks objected to the censor cut demanded for this particular scene, and could see no logic in their stand (Bhatty 15). It rather highlights the fact that when a separate sovereign state was carved out on religious lines, it was ironical that to establish identities as Sikhs, Hindus or Muslims, who had all equally struggled against the British rule until 1947, it was the body which became the testing ground. Jugga, earlier arrested on suspicion of murdering Ram Lal, is still behind bars, and Iqbal and Jugga meet in the closeted claustrophobic space of the jail, which is a visual cinematic contrast to the open green fields of the village denoting freedom.

Meanwhile, Hukum Chand learns that Mali and other dacoits were out to create communal disharmony and the simple Sikh villagers of Mano Majra are being provoked regarding their masculine virility and questioned whether they are potent or impotent. Mali instigates them further by informing them about the trainloads of dead Sikhs and Hindus coming from Lahore and about the rape of Sikh and Hindu womenfolk. A clever game plan is hatched up in order to maintain law and order. Hukum Chand decides to send the Muslims across the border for a safe passage to Pakistan. According to the plan, they are to be sent to the refugee camps at Chandernagore for their safety and from there on they would be sent to Pakistan by train. The pain and pathos, the police brutality, the helplessness of the Muslim population, unhoused and turned into refugees, is very powerfully evoked in this scene when they are pushed into the trucks much against their will. When Nooran's father Imam Baksh breaks the news to Nooran sleeping in her bed oblivious of the happenings, she is shocked and refuses to go to Pakistan. She is with Jugga's child. She walks in the rain towards Jugga's house with the intention to meet him. The entire sequence of shots is cinematically evocative. Rain has been falling incessantly. It symbolises regeneration and arouses in her a feeling of renewed union with him. She hopes that perhaps Jugga had been released from the jail. She waits for Jugga's mother hoping that Jugga might walk in. When Jugga's mother arrives after visiting her Muslim friends, she is shocked to see her sitting in the dark at such a late hour. Nooran musters up courage, addresses her as *Beybey* and tells her that she could not leave for Pakistan since Jugga had promised to marry her. The idea of marriage between her son, a Jat Sikh peasant, and a Muslim Mullah's daughter sends the mother into a frenzy. Nooran goes down on her knees and clasps her legs and tells her that she was with Jugga's child. Jugga's mother's callous indifference towards Nooran softens once she hears that she is with Jugga's child. *Beybey* tells Nooran that she cannot keep her as it would spell trouble for her, but assures her that Jugga would fetch her once he is freed from jail.

As for Hasina, who wants to stay back with Hukum Chand, he dissuades her from doing this since she is a Muslim. Rooks poignantly captures the sensitive bond between the two. Hukum Chand admonishes her caringly that she might marry a refugee and be his wife once she is in Pakistan. In a close up frame, Hasina looks fetchingly innocent as she persists and tells him that singers were neither Hindu nor Muslim as all communities came to hear them. Both Nooran and Hasina face displacements on account of partition, displacements which are both personal and conceptual and hence painful. The Muslims likewise feel uprooted through this forced exodus. Feeling beleaguered, they gather after the *namaz* near the mosque and discuss the change in the atmosphere in the village and whether there was a real or imagined reason for disaffection for the Muslim community. The prominent shot of the mosque where there is a gathering of Muslims is however juxtaposed with the mise en scene in the Gurudwara where there is an inflow of refugees from Pakistan alongwith another shot of dead corpses found floating in the river. Nooran becomes the sight of her blind father Imam Baksh as she sees the long stream of refugees from the higher vantage point of their house. All these shots in the film in quick succession convey the build-up of immediate tension which occurs when religious identities come to the forefront. The viewpoint of the shot is to convey the stark reality which has engulfed the entire village as to how it is going to affect its demography. Most telling of all the stirrings of disquiet are the festering emotions of the bond amongst the villagers who can sense the loaded atmosphere which would lead to the fast impending dislocation of their Muslim brethren and is a perceived threat to their identities. The Muslims feel insecure in their own homes as they see the inflow of refugees across the so called *sarhad*. They realise that dislocation has to be reckoned with most poignantly in the wake of partition. Meet Singh, the Granthi, along with the lambardar of the village and other sensible Sikhs try to pacify them. However, the distraught Muslims of Mano Majra become self-conscious and voice dismay without actually wanting to disrupt ties with their fellow villagers. Apprehensive about the forced dislocation, they experience conflict between rootedness and belongingness towards Mano Majra of which they have been a composite whole. The shabad (hymn) sung by the devotees in the Gurudwara along with the Bhai Sahib, *Awal Allah Noor upaye kudret ke sab bande: Ek noor sai sab jag upgaya: Kaun bhale kaun mandey;* 'It was Allah first and then his light; All human beings are part of his creation; With that one light the entire world came into being; Is there any among them who is good and any who is evil?' This hymn raises the sagging morale of the villagers and it displays their pathetic yet courageous strength with moral resolve of humanism to protect their fellow villagers irrespective of their religion.

Another source of violence is the rampaging of Mali and his hoodlum friends. Even Nooran's father, the blind Imam Baksh, is not spared, as his forehead is scratched by a dagger. The mark on his forehead becomes a religious tilak thus conveying an attack on his religious identity. Nooran who is away to meet Jugga's mother, luckily escapes the ordeal of being raped. Meanwhile a plan is thatched by Mali and his men to kill the Muslims when they leave for Pakistan by train. The plan, to be executed at sunset, is to be effected by stretching a rope across the first span of bridge, which the train would cross. The rope, placed a foot above the height of the funnel of the engine, would sweep all the people sitting on the roof of the train, accounting for the loss of at least four to five hundred lives. Meanwhile Hukum Chand releases Jugga and Iqbal and the sub-inspector informs them that they would find great changes in Mano Majra as the Muslim population had been removed to refugee camps to be deported to Pakistan. On learning this, Jugga ventures out on a mission to save the Muslims put on the train to Pakistan since he wants to save Nooran who is also on the train. Even Hasina, the danseuse, is on the train. The mise en scene of Jugga's bravado has been filmed with great tautness and suspense. Pamela Rooks uses the train as a metaphor and the speed of the train creates a of momentum which seems threateningly menacing almost moving outside the screen.

Pamela Rooks manipulates the look of the viewers in synchronisation with Jugga's anticipation in a tight close-up frame and the innocent passengers sitting in the train oblivious of the fate that awaits them. Nooran is shown sitting pensive, tears flowing down her eyes with no hope for future in her eyes. She's unaware of the fact that Jugga is lurking around somewhere close by to save her life. Jugga with single-minded passion is stretched on the rope and whipping out a small *kirpan* (small dagger worn by the devout Sikhs), slashes at the rope with the *kirpan* and hacks the rope vigorously. Meanwhile the saboteurs realise that there is something amiss and their leader fires at Jugga. He catches the rope under his left armpit and hacks at the rope with his right hand. He is attacked by a volley of shots and finally collapses as a result along with the rope which is snapped at the centre and he falls down. This is a very powerful scene as the train moves over him carrying its passengers safely to the other side. The cutting of the rope and its snapping off is a double symbol: the new creation and metaphorically the birth of a new nation Pakistan and the unborn child given life by its now dead father.

Pamela Rooks highlights this sacrifice pointedly through the acknowledgement of Hukum Chand's salutations to Jugga's bravery and how he holds Jugga in great awe for his brave deed. This is interspersed in a flashback device again as Hukum Chand declares that people like him would do everything to live, but there are people like Jugga who sacrifice their lives and because of this history remembers them. However, in a stirring climax, Pamela Rooks cinematically evokes a search for the deeply hidden human values. Amidst the universal madness and communal frenzy, a sense of humanity pervades through Jugga irrespective of his caste, religion, nationality and his very ordinariness. In the closing frame of the film when the train is shown passing on to Pakistan safely, the Sufiana kalam of the Sufi poet Bulleh Shah is rendered in the background suggesting that fulfillment and joy lies in transcending the ego and experiencing the other human being within one's self. By using the Sufiana Kalam, the cosmic significance of the camaraderie is reflective of the saga of the Sufis who preach peace and love. This shows ability of the composite culture of India to absorb diverse religious, linguistic and ethnic form within the social fabric and the experience of unity in diversity.

In the course of film's viewing, various factors emerge directing the audience's attention towards those elements that signify towards the key moment of cultural conflict throughout the narrative. The partition theme emerges showing conflict on the composite culture of India even if it is initially not foregrounded. However as the film progresses, it evokes the cultural conflict through the articulation of a set of artistic and cultural visions which thwart the construction of cultural nationalism. The film has a tightly constructed narrative, with an intense attention to the details of scenographic design. The opening sequence is already saturated with the kinds of elements capable of establishing the working of the representatives of the 'Raj', the state. However, the film through an intercultural, interwoven approach highlights the thematisation of the nation as an integrated one. It uses contrastive cultural elements showing the Gurdwara and the Mosque to foreground and directs attention towards these specifically symbolic religious and their co-existence as an all encompassing part of composite culture based upon common bonds of culture and heritage of all the communities. However, the conflicting claims of this composite culture come under strain because of the external influence which is instigated by British imperialism manifested through the bureaucracy, the police and the army of the British Raj polarising Hindu, Muslim and Sikh identities for political games. The Muslim brethren who had until then been as much a part of the Mano Majra village alongwith Sikhs and Hindus now feel alienated. Pamela Rooks, daughter of a Punjabi Hindu Sikh couple displays, 'remarkable objectivity with regard to the Muslims of Punjab, who despite being natives of that region for centuries, were uprooted at one fell swoop by Partition of India to which they were not party' (Thorval 198). Through a North Indian ambience she explains as to where and why identities are problematic and where and why they are empowering.

However, only a culture without hope cannot forgive a culture that does not believe in progress or redemption. Nevertheless, the composite culture shared by Hindus, Sikhs and Muslims is shown still alive in the rural areas like Mano Majra is reflected in the film. When the Muslims of Mano Majra are told by the army officer to get onto the trucks as fast as they can in order to be sent to Pakistan, the lambardar of the village who is a Sikh intervenes and seconds the Muslims who say that they belonged to that village and had lived as brothers with Hindus and Sikhs of Mano Majra village. The authority of the lambardar is however undermined and the Muslims are repeatedly warned to hasten the process of leaving the village with their bare essentials. Moving the camera forward on them not only indexes and brackets certain details of their meagre belongings with which they are forced to leave on the army trucks. There is feeling of loss and helplessness on the plight of the Muslims villagers. By zooming in and out at the object, the filmmaker alerts the audience to its importance in an indexical process. It also changes the scale of what the audience was looking at earlier when the train from Pakistan arrives at Mano Majra loaded with mutilated dead bodies. The stark reality has to be confronted with the realisation that both the segments of population had been an integral part of a common cultural heritage, a poignant fact, the Hindus and Sikhs of Mano Majra had not lost sight of. They reached out to their Muslim brethren in their moment of crisis. Both the novel and the film portray a reservoir of authentic human experience which redeem mankind. The long track shots, chiaroscuro lighting and the juxtaposition of extreme long shots evoke richness of her repertoire. What makes the film unique is the double image altering between close ups of main protagonists and the long shots of refugees in the train, moving on tracks surreptitiously. The location of the film is placed in the village Manikpur Sharif of Mullanpur which has an old deserted mosque (behind PGI Hospital, Chandigarh) and creates the realistic ambience of the pre-partition days, further enhanced by the subtle nuances of Dolly Ahluwalia's set designing.

On account of the abusive language used in the film by Jugga and other dacoits in it, the release of the film was delayed because of the censor board clearance. Pamela Rooks however introduced resonances of Amrita Pritam's poem, in Punjabi *Aaj akhaan Waris Shah noon ke uth qabran wichon bol, ik roi si dhi punjab di, tu likh likh maare vaen. aaj lakhaan dhiyan rondian, Waris Shah noon kahen* (I beseech Waris Shah to speak from his grave, one daughter of Punjab, i.e., Heer had cried, you wrote great heart rendering verse. Today lakhs and lakhs daughters of Punjab are crying, I beseech you to write about it from your grave). This poem stirred thousands of Punjabis to the depth of their souls. In fact, Pamela Rooks opens the frame of the film with lyrical music of this poem soulfully rendered by Madan Bala and her accompanists in the background with a zooming long shot of somebody being hanged and Jugga as a young boy very innocently looking on. This loss of innocence gets passed on to the look of experience and knowledge of Hukum Chand inclose-up shot, who narrates the story in a flashback device from his point of view in the film. Pamela Rooks interestingly uses the male eye to see the film, perhaps, since the author of the book is a man.

Both Khushwant Singh as the writer and Pamela Rooks as the director of the film focus on the redemptive vision of Jugga. It is a triumph of love, humanism and faith in the innate goodness of man at a moment of a challenging crisis. In transcending the harsh fact of communal conflict and strife at the time of partition and saving the lives of Nooran and Hasina along with other Muslims, both Jugga and Hukum Chand contribute to the construction of a saner vision of social order. It is this phenomenon that is a pointer to the novel's and film's broader 'ideological agenda', a term borrowed from Madhava Prasad (5). Movies such as these raise a gamut of issues, whether nations have matured enough to face the truth of the past and understand issues with a more objective perspective or whether such issues can also lead to another communal riot. But the redemptive act of Jugga rises above violence and hatred. It signals the possibility of rising above self concerns and narrow divisive hatreds. Capturing a moment in history, Khushwant Singh wrote it some years after the immediate agony of partition had partly been calmed. The film in 1997 came as a reminder to the nation to rise above its resurgent fundamentalisms. It is a call to the human being in us at a time when new hatreds were enveloping us. Religion, identity, nationhood do not always live in harmony, one often conflicts with the other. Jugga rose above it. How many of us are capable of the same?

Works Cited

Bhatty, Nikhat. 'Controversy of Censors and Sensibility'. *The Sunday Times*, 20 September 1997.

Hayward, Susan. *Cinema Studies: The Key Concepts*. New York: Routledge, 2000.

Prasad, Madhava, M. *Ideology of the Hindi Film: A Historical Construction*. Delhi: Oxford University Press, 1998.

Singh, Khushwant. *Train to Pakistan*. New York: Grove Press, 1956. Rpt. New Delhi: Ravi Dayal Publishers, 1988.

Thorval, Yves. *The Cinemas of India (1896–2000)*. New Delhi: Macmillan India Limited, 2000.

Filmography

Train to Pakistan. Dir. Pamela Rooks. Prod. Ravi Gupta, R.V. Pandit and Pamela Rooks, Mus. Kuldip Singh and Taufiq Qureshi, Ly. Isant Kabir, Amrita Pritam and Bulley Shah. Perf. Nirmal Pandey, Mohan Aghase, Rajit Kapoor, Smriti Mishra, Divya Dutta, Mangal Dhillon. 1997.

16

Music as Form of Cultural Representation

With Special Reference to *Sardari Begum*

Divya Walia

'Culture is an extremely complex phenomenon. It has been defined as the sum total of ways of living of a group of human beings, transmitted from one generation to another. It has reference to innumerable relations which exist between individuals, groups, associations and the social whole. It includes their manners, customs and institutions as well as thoughts, sentiments and aspirations expressed or unexpressed, held consciously or felt vaguely, embodied in their systems of philosophy and religion, or expressed through their art, poetry and music' (Tiwari 268). An idea or way of life that we live by is culture, and culture affects us all, no matter where we live or what we do.

Music and dance are the very essence of our culture and thus an indispensable part of the films produced in India. In fact, Indian cinema has come to be known the world over for its musical dimension, for its songs and dances, which lie at the very heart of its cinematic tradition. Swati writes in her article

'Bollywood: Honor Your (and India's) Muslim Heritage': 'Much of the Hindustani music, language, and culture has Muslim roots.' Islamic culture has always been an attraction for Bollywood because of its rich architecture, art and music. According to Ira Bhaskar and Richard Allen in *Islamicate Cultures of Bombay Cinema,* 'this "Islamicate" culture influences the language, poetry, music, ideas, and even the characteristic emotional responses elicited by Bollywood films in general'. Numerous movies with Islamic imagery and culture are a testimony to this. Some of the most popular Indian movies dealing with Muslim culture have evoked this heritage time and again.

When we talk of music in Bollywood one of the first names that comes to our mind is that of *Sardari Begum*. The movie belongs to the category of Muslim courtesan films. The alluring charm of thumri comes alive in this contemporary story of a Muslim singer who falls a victim to both gender discrimination and communal skirmishes. This is the second movie of Shyam Benegal's trilogy of Khalid Mohammed stories (the others are *Mammo* and *Zubeida*). This is probably the best of the trilogy which talks about independent Muslim women who pursued what they wanted to do in life. For Sardari, it was her love of music, the wish to become a great singer. Based on a true story, the movie traces the life of a thumri singer 'Sardari Begum' played by Kirron Kher, through an ambitious *Tribune* reporter, Tehzeeb, who during the course of her investigation on Sardari, discovers that the singer was in fact her aunt, who was disowned by her family for rebelliously learning music from a concubine.

Being a music-based movie, *Sardari Begum* boasts of exceptionally melodious songs in the form of thumris, a diversified form of classical music. Bollywood movies have often used classical and semi-classical forms to represent eras and royal courts. 'Indian film music has a complicated relationship with classical Indian music .... Indian classical music was associated with the royal courts, with religion and with the *Kotha* or houses of courtesans' (Dwyer and Patel 36). The theme of Sardari Begum demanded this kind of musical aura and Shyam Benegal has rendered this genre with almost perfection with Vanraj Bhatia's music and the artful singing of all the singers, especially that of Arati Ankalikar-Tikekar, whose rendering is superb. Though thumri is believed to have its roots in certain early genres of music, it is not until the middle of the 19th century that one notices it becoming enshrined as a form of classical music. The modern thumri is believed to be a 'creation' of Nawab Wajid Ali Shah of Awadh (1822–1887) and his court musician, Sadiq Ali Khan. Wajid Ali Shah himself was a poet, playwright, composer and dancer, under whose lavish patronage the fine arts flourished. It was during his era that several reputed musicians, poets, composers and dancers enhanced their repertoire, along with enriching the light classical form of thumri, the grand revival of the Kathak dance form, and the rise in popularity of Hindustani Theatre. Wajid Ali Shah also composed outstanding thumris under the pen name, 'Akhtar Piya' which are widely sung in repertoires. Thumri originated from the Hindi word 'thumakna' or 'attractive gait' leterally meaning hip-swaying and is one of the most popular genres of semi-classical Indian music in Uttar Pradesh. About thumri, Courtney writes, 'It is a common style of light classical music. The text is romantic and devotional in nature, and usually revolves around a girl's love for Krishna. The language is a dialect of Hindi called *Brij bhasha*. This style is characterised by a greater flexibility with the *raga*. The compositions are usually set to *kaherava* of 8 beats, *addha tal* of 16 beats, or *dipchandi* of 14 beats.'

This form, another critic, points out is one which is, 'distinguished by moderate and suggestive dance movements, equally restrained *abhinaya*, and music which have a gentle and feminine eroticism as its moving spirit. Contemporary thumri has reached its present state through a gradual growth of the musical tendencies and cultural needs of a society which listened to music with more and wider expectations' (Ranade 67).

The setting of the movie *Sardari Begum* in Agra and Delhi is important for its association with this art and the nawabs who introduced and developed this art form in India. 'Parallel with the feudal system of *thikanas* of miniature paintings, the *banis* of *dhrupad-dhamar gayaki* and the *gharanas* of *khayal gayaki, thumri* also had its own *gharanas* like Jaipur and Lucknow, corresponding to *gharanas* of *kathak* dancing' (Purohit 110). This sociomusical phenomenon also bears Islamic impact as 'the gharana bearing so many characteristic features of a caste, was essentially a Muslim creation. Because marriage between close relations was not only permitted but encouraged, in marked contrast to Hindu practice, it allowed the formation of a relatively small circle of specialists' (Neuman 43).

Earlier thumri was associated with the ambience of luxurious kothas and the leisurely courtesan culture prevalent in several parts of North India during the 19th century and the first half of the 20th century. The tags of amatory audacity and the unabashed lifestyles of courtesan-singers and dancers naturally made thumri the object of prudish ire. It was in this courtesan-milieu that this artistic soiree culture musical form grew and developed to its present stature. Once associated with the kothas, and condemned on that account by the fastidious, it is now a popular light form sung at the end of every classical concert by modest and stolid women and men from middle-class homes. The movie reflects on the evolution of this art form from being defamatory to becoming a respectable musical form through the life of *Sardari Begum*.

The movie opens with a scene from the streets of Chandni Chowk area of the walled city of Delhi and the setting itself is Islamic as we come across people and places suggestive of Muslim culture. The males dressed in *jubba*, *kameez* and *kufi*, and the females in *salwar-kameez* with their heads covered and the architectural setting in the background are strikingly Islamic. As we are transported to the house of Sardari, we find her daughter performing the ritual of namaaz. Therefore, the scene at once prepares the ground of its cultural orientation for the viewers.

Once we are in the house of the popular thumri singer, Sardari Begum, the cultural motif is ingeminated through the very first musical notes that are heard. They are in the form of chants from the Quran Sharif in a nearby located mosque. The blend of music and physical setting is remarkable for evoking an association of music with Islamic culture, setting forth an apt representation in the minds of the viewers. Here we are introduced to the first thumri *Chali pi ke nagar* which actually happens to be Sardari's last. She is disturbed by some commotion outside by two political/religious groups who clash outside her house. As she goes to look out from the balcony, a stone hits her on the temple, leading to her death. Henceforth, the movie takes us on a musical journey in bits and pieces through flashbacks from the life and journey of Sardari Begum towards becoming a successful thumri-dadra singer and at the same time establishing the patterns of cultural identity through the various aspects of music in the form of semi-classical genre of thumri.

As we explore the life of Sardari Begum we discern that besides representing the Islamic culture in aesthetic and technical sense, music is also instrumental in bringing before us a picture of the Muslim society prevalent in those days. Music, in this sense, as stated by J.F. Archer, can be interpreted as 'intricately inter-related to societies; as a *commodity sold, purchased and consumed*; as an artifact-probably the most important one in most cases-of a culture, in short, as anything but pure, abstract and self-contained (qtd. in Neuman 42). According to the article 'Music in Islam', music was not a socially acceptable field of art in Islam. Its argumentation was attributed to the references within the context of the Holy Quran along with the Hadith of the Prophet confirming that music is *haraam*. Interpreters of the Quran have defined the term *lahwal hadith* which is mentioned in the Quran as: (i) singing and listening to songs, (ii) purchasing of male and female singers, (iii) purchase of instruments of fun and amusement. One hadith from the Bukhari Shareef, the most authentic Book of Hadith, further confirms unlawfulness of music and singing: 'There will be people of my Ummah who will seek to make lawful: fornication, wine-drinking and the use of ma'aazif (musical instruments).' Closer analysis of the wordings of the Hadith establishes the prohibition of music. Firstly, the words 'seek to make lawful' show that music is not permissible, as logically one can only seek to make lawful that which is not allowed. Secondly, if music was not prohibited, then it would not have been brought within the same context as fornication and wine-drinking ('Music in Islam', www.inter-islam.org).

The social picture presented in the movie too pronounces that music was an art looked down upon and was a forbidden field, especially for females. 'New wave Bollywood saw birth of Muslim social films', a Saudi Gazette report refers to this and writes, 'the two films that Khalid Mohammed wrote for Shyam Benegal, *Mammo* and *Sardari Begum* (1996) are particularly trenchant in their criticism of patriarchal culture.' Thus, in the movie, we find Sardari's father reprimanding her for attending a mehfil. At her insistence on learning music, he scolds her severely and uses the word 'mirasi' derogatively for the singing professionals. Very harshly he remarks, *gaana seekhne ki ijaazat isliye di thi kyunki tune waada kiya tha ki tu mehfilon mein mirasino ki tarah nahin gayegi.* (you were allowed to learn music because you had promised that you will not become a public performer like the mirasis). As a protest and also in order to pursue her art and to realise her ambition of becoming a renowned thumri singer, Sardari runs away from home the same night. Sardari approaches courtesan Idbal bai (Surekha Sikri) to learn thumri singing but before accepting her as a student Idbal bai asks her to sing something. Here again we notice cultural distinctiveness portrayed through music as Sardari opts to sing the kalam of the Urdu Poet Mir Anis.

This journey of hers to becoming an extraordinary thumri singer from an ordinary girl forms the central theme of the movie, though at the same time, it continues to bring before its viewers the various dimensions of the semi-classical form of thumri and its cultural bearings. Music is so much a passion for Sardari that she places it above all else—even education—as she herself says at one point in the movie *Padhai main kya rakha hai...mausiki ek fann hai ... khuda ne achha gala diya hain to gana chahiye* (What is there in education! Music is an art/skill and all those who have been blessed with a melodious voice should pursue it seriously).

The next musical aspect in the movie bearing the stamp of Muslim culture is the depiction of the physical setting in which thumri is performed. Sardari after undergoing a formal training in music starts performing in *mehfils*. The word *mehfil* derives from the Urdu language, which in turn derives from the Arabic word *mehfil* which means 'a gathering to entertain (or praise someone).' To quote from 'About Mehfil' in *History of Hindustani Music: Developments during the 13th and 14th century Hindustani Music*. 'Historically, *mehfil*s were presented in the homes or palaces of Muslim royalty or noblemen, who acted as these artists' patrons. With the Muslim rulers came the mehfil, gatherings of musicians, singers, dancers and poets at the homes of noblemen and royals. These gatherings were for the purpose of patronising artistes and performers in their skills and giving them platforms to display their talents.' The movie captures this aspect of mehfil and presents it with an unquestionable justice to the original form and setting. The use of gestures to greet and to show gratitude in the form of 'adaab' during the performance has also been used by the artists and the audience to denote the culture imprint of Islam.

Another significant aspect of music which renders culture and bears attributes of cultural identity can be distinguished in the form of instruments used and the way the musicians have been presented. In the movie, the instruments that have been used prominently are harmonium, tabla, tanpura and sarangi.

About sarangi, Yves Thoraval writes in *The Cinemas of India* (2000), 'It was cultivated in the courts of Hindu maharajas—whose musicians were usually Muslims—or in the courts of 'nawabs' (Muslim princes) found in the northern, central or eastern part of the country, whose subjects could in large part be Hindus (for example, the State of Hyderabad, which had a largely Hindu population and Muslim rulers)' (55). Similarly, invention of the Indian abla is also traditionally attributed to Amîr Khusrau, 'a Persian-writing poet of medieval India and an iconic figure in the cultural history of the Indian subcontinent. A Sufi mystic and a spiritual disciple of Nizamuddin Auliya of Delhi, Amîr Khusrau was not only a notable poet but also a prolific musician' ('Amir Khusrau', *Book Rags*). Thus we notice an implicit cultural expression in some of the instruments that accompany thumri style of singing.

Though harmonium, tabla, tanpura and sarangi are the instruments that are always associated with thumri singing, yet in the movie they strike us as manifestations of Islamic culture because of their origin or use. The musicians who are playing them give an impression of cultural linkage through their attire while performing. Their outfits are *jubba*, *kameez* and *kufi* for males and the females are wearing *salwar-kameez* with their heads covered throughout. This kind of cultural connotation is significant as expressed by Rachel Dwyer and Divia Patel in *Cinema India: The Visual Culture of Hindi Film*, 'While many Hindu women veil themselves in the presence of older men by covering their heads and sometimes their faces, the veil is largely associated with Islam. This is true in the films also, and it plays important roles in some genres, such as the Muslim social and the courtesan films' (87).

Talking of lyrics as an essential component of any song, it is not without considering it as a reflection of culture that we can talk about music in the context of culture: 'Where music is subject to vague interpretations and may alienate people according to subculture, lyrics are a more concrete form of expression. Lyrics are words that are sung or spoken with musical accompaniment, or sung without accompaniment. Lyrics embody the sentiment the writer is trying to convey in a ridged manner, with less free interpretation and more definitive meaning than in music alone

(Lombardi: web). Though the language of thumri is basically a dialect of Hindi called *Braj Bhasha* and it is only through its setting and ambience that the movie projects Muslim culture, yet in the movie we also come across a ghazal 'Huzoor hum par itna karam karte to achha tha' and we also find a couple of references to ghazal compositions in the musical career of Sardari. Ghazal singing is typically suggestive of Muslim culture but by embracing it with thumri singing, a North Indian genre of music, the filmmaker has again attempted to emphatically manifest Muslim culture. In fact, the type of thumri singing that is popular in Lucknow is 'decorative and more explicit in expressing emotion, it has close ties with dance and shows affinity with the *ghazal* (Ranade 67). Talking of this kind of integration in Indian cinema, Yves Thoraval writes:

> The classical and semi-classical music from the north and northwest Indian Hindu–Muslim cultural symbiosis has found a special place in Hindi film music. Two types of music from this tradition have been especially integrated—mainly consisting of poetry combined with music. One is the qawwali from the Sufi tradition—a kind of spiritual love poetry set to jubilantly melodic music; the other is the ghazal (love poetry in Arabic Persian). The latter had been introduced in India by the elite of the Turkish and Afghan Muslim conquerors whose literary language was Persian, and had been further cultivated in the courts of the Indian Muslim Rulers. (Thoraval 62)

Inclusion of ghazal and use of Urdu terminology to discuss music with words such as *mausiki*, *fann*, *adakara*, *mehfil* are some other exemplifications of giving the movie Islamic cultural expression:

> Besides the characteristics of Persian civilisation which have been passed on to Indian civilisation, mainly music and dance (as well as certain literary or artistic forms, like architecture, decoration or the miniature) and have been integrated into Indo-Persian culture, the Urdu language is one of the legacies

> of Islam in India. Along with Persian, it became the language of the administration and the Muslim courts. One of these courts where the language flourished was Lucknow in the kingdom of Awadh (presently in Uttar Pradesh), especially in the 18th–19th century. (Thoraval 69)

The climax of the movie also is remarkable for illustrating the power of music and its diversity in various cultures. It is the chant of *jai kanhaiya lal ki* that adds fire to the fuel of communal tension and leads to riots among the group of Hindu and Muslim supporters and ultimately results in the death of Sardari begum, who at that time was singing the thumri *'chali pi ke nagar'*. This becomes ironical for a thumri revolves around a girl's love for Lord Krishna and in the above composition Sardari was referring to lord Krishna as her lover and was planning to move to His home. So on one hand, music leads to clashes and separation and on the other, it talks of communion. Music can communicate varied ideas and notions and can lead to varied interpretations by various cultures, as illustrated in this scene of the movie

The movie ends with the same scene from the streets of Delhi and the same thumri '*Chali pi ke nagar*' in the background with which it had started, though this time it is Sakina, Sardari's daughter who is singing that. This could be an attempt by the filmmaker to stress upon the timelessness of art such as music and culture, and to suggest the viewers the invaluable inheritance in the form of art which will now be preserved and carried forward by Sakina as a legacy. Despite Sakina's dislike for her mother who forced her to withdraw from other pleasures of life for the sake of her musical talent, Sakina towards the end indicates that music is what she has received as an inheritance and will continue to live and grow with it without any malignance for the art.

The movie is equally divided between the flashes from past and the scenes from the present. The flashbacks appear at such regular intervals and are so finely woven with the story in the present that they too give a kind of rhythmic pattern and a well-defined structure to the movie and the story by their regularity. The songs of the movie in the form of thumris and ghazals are unparalleled for their melody and rhythm. The thumris that really touched the heart of the audience and became popular are '*Chahe maar daalo raja*' and '*More kanha jo aaye palat ke*' in 'dadra' and 'teen taal' respectively. These are the thumris with which Sardari started her musical career and so are important from the point of view of the story too. The music of the film in the form of thumris and ghazals is almost like a counter theme and evolves with the story. It becomes a carrier of cultural impressions and takes quite a number of aspects into its fold thereby rendering justice to the presentation.

Critics and commentators have drawn attention to the contemporary relevance of the theme and the counter discourse it constructs in a post-Babri Masjid era:

> 'Set in the contemporary post Hindu-nationalist mobilisation period of the 1990s, *Sardari Begum* reworks the main elements of the Courtesan film to confront a new set of socio-political issues, even as it demonstrates the persistent appeal of the genre. At the same time, *Sardari Begum*, like other New Wave Films, also engages and transforms the idioms of the Muslim Social in the manner it addresses the political and social pressures that face the Muslim community in the context of Hindu communalism'. (Source: *Muslim Cultures of Bombay Cinema,* New York University Abu Dhabi)

Through this close study of *Sardari Begum* I have attempted to emphasise the power of expression of art such as Music in bringing out the social and cultural patterns of a community and also establishing its identity. Music can represent culture by bringing out its diverse aspects in a unique and a very powerful manner just as it does in *Sardari Begum*. In the movie, the singing forms thumri-dadra act as both the literal and the symbolic motifs rendering cultural and social manifestations of an art form.

Works Cited

'About Mehful', 'History of Hindustani Music: Developments During the 13th and 14th Century Hindustani Music'. *Rhythm n Raga*. n.d. Web. 22 January 2011. http://rhythmnraga.org/1&3century.html

Amir Khusrau. *BookRags*. n.d. Web 16 June 2011. http://www.bookrags.com/wiki/Amir_Khusro

Bhaskar, Ira and Allen, Richard. *Islamicate Cultures of Bombay Cinema*. New Delhi: Tulika, 2009.

'Book Examines Muslim Portrayal in Bollywood'. Saudi Gazette Report. *Saudi Gazette*, Internet edition. n.d. Web. 11 July 2010. http://www.saudigazette.com.sa/index.cfm?method=home.regcon &contentID= 2010060374211

Courtney, David. 'Thumri (Thumree)—Semiclassical Song'. n.d. Web. 17 December 2011. http://www.chandrakantha.com-Music of India

Dwyer, Rachel and Patel, Divia. 'Film Style: Settings and Costume'. *Cinema India: The Visual Culture of Hindi Film*. New Jersey: Rutgers University Press, 2002.

Lombardi, Victor. 'Music and Censorship'. December 1991. n.d. Web. 30 May 2010 http://www.noisebetweenstations.com/personal/essays/music_censorship.html

Muslim Cultures of Bombay Cinema. New York University. Abu Dhabi: Abu Dhabi. n.d. Web. 18 January 2011. http://nyuad.nyu.edu/pdfs/institute_ events/filmfest_22009.pdf

'Music in Islam' n.d. Web. 15 January 2011. http://www.inter-islam.org/Prohibitions/Mansy_music. htm

Neuman, Daniel M. 'The Social E :ology of Hindustani Music'. *Sociology of Oriental Music: A Reader*. O.P. Joshi (ed.). Jaipur: Illustrated Book Publishers. 1992. 41–66.

Purohit, Vinayak. 'Sociology of Thumri'. *Sociology of Oriental Music: A Reader*. Ed. O.P Joshi. Jaipur: Illustrated Book Publishers, 1992. 105–113.

Ranade, Ashoka Da. 'Forms of Music'. *Hindustani Music*. New Delhi: National Book Trust, 2002.

Swati. 'Bollywood: Honor Your (and India's) Muslim Heritage'. *The Bollywood Observer*. 27 April 2010. n.d. Web. 21 January 2011. http://www.thebollywood observer.com/?p=212

Thoraval, Yves. 'The Supremacy of Indian Cinema'. *The Cinemas of India*. Delhi: Macmillan, 2000.

Tiwari, Kalika Prasad. 'Society and Culture'. *Foundations of Indian Culture*. Jaipur: Pointer Publishers, 2001.

Filmography

Mammo. Dir. Shyam Benegal. Prod. NFDC. Perf. Farida Jalal, Surekha Sikri and Rajit Kapoor. 1994.

Sardari Begum. Dir. Shyam Benegal. Prod. Plus Films. Perf. Kirron Kher, Amrish Puri and Rajit Kapur and Rajeshwari Sachdev. 1996.

Zubeida. Dir. Shyam Benegal. Prod. Yashraj Films. Perf. Karisma Kapoor, Manoj Bajpai and Amrish Puri. 2001.

17

Perspectives on Language, Culture and Identity

A Study of *Umrao Jaan*

Samina Khan

Yeh Kya Jagah hai Dosto
Yeh Konsa Dayar hai
Had-e-Nigah tak Jahan
Ghubar hi Ghubar hai

(What place is this, oh friends
What threshold is this?
Where upto the limits of the gaze
Clouds of dust arise).

This haunting couplet from *Umrao Jaan*, commenting on the post-1857 historical scenario, manifests the friendly sharing that existed between Muslim culture, Urdu language and Hindi cinema since the inception of cinema in India. Urdu language added significant vitalising influence for the popularity of the Hindi films through Urdu scripts with a massive dialogue appeal and lyrical songs with a blend of shayri (ghazal form in Urdu poetry) and other art forms such as kathak, thumri and mujra.

The landmark film *Mughal-e-Azam* marked the public acceptance for the use of even a complex (less colloquial) Urdu diction. The film promoted 'spoken Urdu' to an extent where the knowledge of Urdu language became a necessity for the actors, scripts writers, directors and music composers to achieve any worthwhile success in the field of Hindi cinema.

Umrao Jaan Ada was originally written as a novel in Urdu by Mirza Mohammad Hadi Ruswa in 1899 and translated into English by Khushwant Singh and M.A. Hussaini in 1961. The film *Umrao Jaan* is based on Ruswa's novel of the same name. Muzaffar Ali, Shama Zaidi and Jawed Siddiqui adopted the script for the screen in 1981, casting Rekha as the chief protagonist Umrao Jaan. In a recent remake by J.P. Dutta in 2006, Aishwarya Rai figured as the heroine of the film. The background of the film is colonial Lucknow and Awadh and it deals with the lives of courtesans known as 'tawaifs'. *Umrao Jaan* presents a blend of theatrically, feminist perspective and Islamic values. The character of Umrao Jaan is a presentation of a Muslim woman's quest for a dignified identity and metamorphosis of some such women who are multiply marginalised on account of patriarchy and society.

The present paper proposes to analyse *Umrao Jaan* as a cinematographic version that serves as a model to study reinterpretation of Islamic values, marketable Muslim culture, the status of Urdu in the recent films and the mixed identity of Muslim women with their other counter parts in the Indian context.[1] Creative, passionate and experimental, depiction of Umrao Jaan's character focuses on an approach to reshape democratic apprehension of Muslim culture in India. The journey from *Umrao Jaan* to *My Name is Khan* is an effort to reconstruct public opinion against prevailing misconceptions about core Islamic ideals of humanism, gender equality, social justice and peaceful coexistence. The poetry and other reference are used in the paper are from 1981 version of Muzaffar Ali's *Umrao Jaan* figuring Rekha as the lead character.

Indian history and culture has had a mixed blend of shared past with invaders, settlers, colonisers, travellers, traders, Sufis, tribals and native power groups. This includes the Mughal imperial period's impact, Lakhnawi courtesan culture, Muslim aristocratic architecture and art forms like the mushaira, mujra, ghazal and qawwali.

The representation and delicate handling of 'Islamicate culture' in Indian films is a challenging area for the filmmakers.[2] Indian cinema seems to be more interested in 'marketable' Muslim culture and its aspects rather than the lesser known, fascinating and aesthetically gratifying Muslim 'tehzeeb' or aristocratic civility which was established as a genre for 'Muslim Socials' in Bombay cinema. In the postcolonial democratic and secular fabric of the Indian society, it is difficult to attain a systematic, sane and comprehensive understanding of Muslim culture. Popular misconceptions about Islamic values may lead to misrepresentation of their sensitivity and identity.

Islam is mainly criticised for not having any conception of gender justice. Islamic theological values are widely misunderstood as gender discriminatory and violence supportive. Muslims have infinite faith in the Quran as a revealed text with timeless set of values, hence an average Muslim considers Islam a complete way of life. The age-old Islamic traditions, provisions of purdah (veil), talaaq (divorce) and polygamy (keeping more than one wife) are now perceived as symbols of suppression that deprive women of their democratic rights and free will to choose an authentic mode of existence along with social respect. A widespread assumption is that Muslim women do not consciously want change; their attempt to be creative in any form may cause anarchy or anxiety in the society.

For Akbar S. Ahmad, an Islamic scholar of international repute, the current change in the Islamic world regarding the situation vis-à-vis women comes down to a simple equation, The position of women in the Muslim society mirrors the destiny of Islam, when Islam is secured and confident so are its women;

when Islam is threatened and under pressure so, too, are they (*Encyclopedia of Muslim Women*, I. 2003, 69).

To an extent Hindi films are projecting a reinterpretation of Islamic values and attempt to place Muslim culture as part of a'collective entity'. Qurratul-Ain Haider[3] rightly commented that:

> The various economic and sociological problems of the Muslim community cannot be isolated from the problems of the general backwardness and poverty of Indian masses. Muslim women are as modern and backward as their counterparts in the various income groups in other communities. (Ibid. IV, 74)

Cinema can sensitise the mindsets that all popular misconceptions about Islamic values are political and social convenience of power groups or the choice of the individuals. It has no sanction in the *Quran*. For example, a women under Islam occupies a position of eminence. Islam grants her an equal status with men. Textual Islamic values relating to women are less gender discriminatory as prophet Mohammed was the earliest feminist who said 'Treat your women well and be kind to them' the veil is used as protection, it is a symbol of choice, dignity and defense in Islam similarly, 'Talaq' is not as discriminatory as it is made to seem in popular imagination. Muslim women also can seek divorce and the provision of exercising the right is deliberately made difficult for men as well. Keeping more than one wife is also conditional as men who opt for such a practice, under any circumstances, have to share equal love and means with all wives. Keeping in view the Islamic laws about this practice it has almost fallen into disuse now.

Umrao Jaan's character is not confined to a specific period or a plot. Her identity as a woman, who can seek acknowledgement without assertion or revolt, is timeless.[4] She is capable of turning suffering into insight.

Justju jiski thi usko to na paya ham nein
Is bahane se magar dekhli duniya hum nein

(I did not find the object of my quest
But on this count, I have seen the whole world)

She constructs a notion of human understanding about the reality of the world.

Na jis ka naam hai na shakl na rang hai koi
Ek aisi shey ka kyon hamen azal se intezar hai ...

(An existence we await from eternity has no name, face and colour)

Gardish-e-halaat ka ahsan he bahut?
Ye zamin chand se bahtar nazar ati he hame ...

(Time has done me such a great favour today the earth seems better to me than the moon today)

Umrao Jaan is an average looking Ameeran who has a girlhood of an ordinary girl with ordinary desires and fears. But she is abducted and her attempts to escape are futile.

Umrao Jaan, according to Shahryar, is a planned portrayal by Muzaffar Ali in order to give an expression to a woman's resourcefulness and determination to excel despite her circumstances.[5] She was conscious of her ordinary looks and dusky complexion that is why she worked harder for skill orientations as a singer, poetess and dancer. She is depicted as an emotionally strong, creative woman with intellectual power and a realistic consciousness. She is woman who learns from every loss and turns it to her advantage. Women remain financially insecure in a male-dominated society, but Umrao Jaan consciously guarded her economic side (*shayri se pet nahi bharta*). Umrao Jaan is professionally preoccupied with a sense that a 'tawaif' should not expect any relationship to be the permanent basis of happiness and settlement in life. Kamal Amrohi's 1971 *Pakeezah* was an exception, where rehabilitation was the need of the plot). She serves as a model for all women who experience negative emotions of jealously or revenge in any relationship with a man, where instead of 'knowing' men, women wish to 'possess' men. Umrao leaves a message in disguise that true love's search is endless, perfect man is a difficult accomplishment, no love is sincerer than love for food and life is unpredictable. For her, 'love' is a creative energy, a device to trap high profile Nawabs or a spiritual culture that adds sublimity to the emotional existence.

Tujhko ruswa na kiya khud bhi pasheman na huye
Ishq ki rasm ko is tarah nibhaya hum ne ...

(You were not humiliated I was not embarrassed The tradition of love we maintained with dignity)

The need of spiritual culture of love was felt and a blend of intellectual and aesthetic, sensual and spiritual is manifested through poetic lyricism. The lyrics become the essence of meaning as they evoke romantic depths. 'How to love' and 'be loved' falls into a tradition or cultural orientation and the emotional refinement as a training to be received from life's experiences. She reclaims her identity to be further identified with the culture of Lucknow where 'dignity' is maintained even in ruin, fall and destruction (may be emotional, financial or political).

The film, towards the end reveals another aspect of her identity where she is a witness to the 1857 war of independences when people are fleeing from Faizabad. Her native place makes her nostalgic at which time she is conscious that her identity as a 'tawaif' should not harm her family status. Her brother whom she used to carry on her back refuses to accept here back. She realises that there is no way she can regain what the abduction had taken away.

Zindagi dekhiye kya rang dikhati hai hamen
Jab bhi milti he mujhe ajnabi lagti kyon hai
Zindagi tujh ko to bas khwab me dekha hum ne

(Let's see what life has to reveal to me. Whenever I see life it seems a stranger to me. Life, unfortunately, has only been seen by me in a dream)

In a scene, she is shown removing the dust from a mirror in order to see her own new image and identity as a patron of art and music in Lucknow.

The film *Umrao Jaan* (Muzaffar Ali) makes use of good refined Urdu language, poetry, art forms, ghazals and mujra. The character of a poetess also facilitates the use of an exquisite diction. Rekha worked hard to be convincing in her deliveries and to project intricacies of language and delicacies of the Urdu language and Muslim culture.

Shahryar, a modern Urdu poet returns to classical usage in his language and style. However because of the intensity and freshness of his thought and tone, his poems remain totally compatible with his modernist existentialist current.[6] He is an intellectual poet, a right choice to be the lyricist for the film, whose poetry strongly expresses an ideological non-commitment, whose roots lie in the poet's desire for self-realisation and his attempt to understand modern problems.

Success is an unpredictable formula in the field of cinema. We constantly see experiments with technique in films to create impact with outward devices. It is noteworthy that in films such as *Umrao Jaan* pathos and association with the fictional plot and characters come from within the script, not from any cinematographic devices used from outside. Lyricism and language enhance and supplement it but 'image' 'shot close-up' light and darkening effects are equally important.

What we designate as Muslim culture in films does not authentic validity from Islamic values. Islam in theory is different from practice and dress, language or mannerism is a complex and derived product of culture. The Kotha culture depicted in *Umrao Jaan* is neither Lucknawi Muslim tehzeeb nor pure Islamic representation of Muslim culture. Muzaffar Ali categorically stated after the release of Satyajit Ray's *Shatranj ke Khiladi* (1977) that a more authentic film to popularise Lucknawi culture could be attempted. 'Kotha' was used in the film as a stage and location, a meeting point for various culture representatives from different classes of the society. (From Nawabs to dacoits, jewellers to washerman, housewives to maids, ordinary sex workers to policemen etc.) Kothas were cultural centres in those days. Socially marginalised groups were not economically or politically deprived of power and money. Female establishments and women dominated systems as projected in *Umrao Jaan* could capture a subtle moderated and democratic version of Muslim culture in India. Umrao Jaan's glamorised appeal is juxtaposed with a crude public opinion about her 'Randi', a very derogatory term, is used several times to avoid the glorification of the character. She laments her fate and establishes superiority of marital life over any other less dignified mode of existence for women. She mentions this while talking to her old childhood friend Ramdai.

To conclude, it seems as if cinema is more in touch with reality than literal minded activist/journalist who only informs about off-screen political and subtle associations of the celebrities and their safe playing strategies that may harm the democratic spirit. Theatre can transport people to a fictional, ideal and nameless romantic world where they focus on something very small, very human. It can make us believe that what we need now more than ever is humanity to revitalise hope and glory of a lost culture. *Umrao Jaan* captures the atmosphere of an aspect of culture fast being erased by modernisation, mechanisation and globalisation.

Notes

1. No authority of Islamic laws 'Shariyat' is claimed here. The paper attempts to analyse the impact of social and spiritual values on Indian cinema as acceptable form for an average Muslim.
2. The term 'Islamicate' is used to designate these narrative and expressive forms in order to acknowledge the sense in which they cannot be reduced simply to the influence of Islam defined in purely religious terms nor is their influence reducible to purely Islamic contexts.

3. Qurattul Ain Hyder, an Urdu novelist, short story writer and academician and journalist born in Aligarh Uttar Pradesh (1926–2007). Her important work include *Aag ka Dariya (River of Fire)* and 12 novels and four collections of short stories.
4. In the remake of the film, *Umrao Jaan* opens with a narrative of her life's story to the biographer apparently indicating towards Ruswa. Fictional is made real and the real is made fictional in order to enhance impact and credibility. After the release of the film, says Shahriyar, people searched for Umrao in the streets of Lucknow (an interview was conducted with Shahriyar at his residence Safina Apartment, Aligarh on 20 March 2010).
5. A conversation was conducted with Shahryar while writing this paper on the making of *Umrao Jaan* referred here.
6. Kunwar Akhlaq Mohammad Khan 'Shahryar' is known to his contribution to Urdu Literature include, the editing of literary magazines, compilation of books, participation in radio and television programmes, and serving on national selection committees and juries for literary awards. His poetry has been translated into English, French, German, Bengali and Telegu. He has written the songs and ghazals for *Gaman* and *Umrao Jaan.*

Works Cited

Bhaskar, Ira and Richard Allen. *Islamicate Culture of Bombay Cinema*, New Delhi: Tulika Books. 2009.

Chakravarty, Sunita. 'Women and the Burden of Postcoloniality: The Courtesian Film Genre'. *National Identity in Indian Popular Cinema* (1947–1987). Austin: Austin University Press, 1993. 269–293.

Chaturvedi, Archana., ed. *Encyclopedia of Muslim Women.* 6 volumes. Volume 1. New Delhi: Commonwealth Publishers, 2003.

Christine, Gledhill. 'Recent Developments in Feminist Criticism'. *Film Theory and Criticism.* Leo Braudy and Marshall Cohen (eds.). New York: Oxford University Press. 1974.

Dimitris Eleftheriotis and Galy Needham. eds. *Asian Cinemas: A Reader and Guide.* Needham: Edinburgh University Press. 2006.

Jain, Jasbir and Sudha Rai. eds. *Films and Feminism.* Jaipur: Rawat Publications, 2002.

Kabir, N.M. *Talking Films*, Conversations on Hindi Cinema with Javed Akhtar. New York: Oxford University Press, 1991.

Kazmi, Fareed. 'Muslim Socials and the Female Protagonists: Seeing a Dominant Discourse at 'work' *Forging Identities: Gender Communities and the State*. Zoya Hasan (ed.), New Delhi: Kali for Women, 1994.

Khursheed, Salam. 'Umrao Jaan Ada' in *Tanqeedein* (Critical Appraisals). Lucknow: Sarfaraz Quomi Press. 1957, 101–181.

Pauwels, Heidi R.M., ed. *Indian Literature and Popular Cinema: Recasting Classics*. New York: Routledge. 2007.

Main, C.M. *Urdu Texts and Contexts: The Selected Essays of C.M. Main*. Delhi: Permanent Black, 2004.

Mathew, D. and Shakle, C., eds. *An Anthology of Classical Urdu Love Lyrics*. London: Oxford University Press, 1972.

Ramachalen T.M., ed. *70 Years of Indian Cinema*. Bombay: Cinema India International Pub., 1985.

Ruswa, Mirza Mohd. Hadi, *Umrao Jaan Ada*: *Courtesan of Lucknow*. Trans. Khushwant Singh and M.A. Husaini. Bombay: Orient Longman, 1961.

Ruswa, Mirza Mohd. Hadi *Umrao Jaan Ada* (Hindi), Allahabad: Ram Narayanlal Benimadhav Publication, 1978.

Oldenburg, Veena Talwar. 'Life Style as Resistance: The Case of the Courtesans of Lucknow'. *Contesting Power: Resistance and Everyday Social Relations in South Asia*. Eds. Douglas Haynes and Gyan Prakash, Berkeley: California University Press, 1992. 23–61.

Filmography

Umrao Jaan. Dir. and Prod. Muzaffar Ali. Perf. Rekha, Farooq Shaikh, Naseeruddin Shah, Raj Babbar, Shaukat Azmi. 1981.

Umrao Jaan. Dir. and Prod. J.P. Dutta. Perf. Abhishek Bachchan, Aishwarya Rai, Shabana Azmi, Suniel Shetty, Divya Dutta, Himani Shivpuri, Puru Raaj Kumar, Kulbhushan Kharbanda, Ayesha Jhulka, Parikshat Sahni, Maya Alagh. 2006.

Index